ACCESS 2000
NO EXPERIENCE REQUIRED

ACCESS 2000
NO EXPERIENCE REQUIRED™·

Celeste Robinson

SYBEX®

San Francisco • Paris • Düsseldorf • Soest • London

Associate Publisher: Amy Romanoff
Contracts and Licensing Manager: Kristine O'Callaghan
Acquisitions and Developmental Editor: Melanie Spiller
Editor: Emily K. Wolman
Technical Editor: Tyler Regas
Book Designers: Patrick Dintino, Catalin Dulfu, Maureen Forys
Graphic Illustrator: Tony Jonick
Electronic Publishing Specialists: Tony Jonick, Kate Kaminski
Production Coordinators: Julie Sakaue, Susan Berge
Indexer: Marilyn Smith
Cover Designer: Design Site
Cover Illustrator: Jack D. Myers

Library of Congress Card Number: 98-89346
ISBN: 0-7821-2485-2

Manufactured in the United States of America

10 9 8 7 6 5 4 3 2 1

To organic farmers and their supporters everywhere.

Acknowledgments

I'd first like to thank Melanie Spiller, the acquisitions and developmental editor at Sybex who invited me to write this book. This is exactly the type of project I've been wanting to work on: a book on Access that teaches the reader how to do real life database work without having to invest a huge amount of time learning every detail of the program.

I'd also like to thank my editor at Sybex, Emily Wolman, for her endless enthusiasm and good spirits. Working with Emily has definitely been a pleasure. I also want to thank Contracts and Licensing Manager Kristine O'Callaghan for her ongoing help with the business matters related to working on a Sybex book.

Additional thanks go to the technical editor, Tyler Regas, for his thorough checking of the text and valuable suggestions for improvements, and to Julie Sakaue and Susan Berge, production coordinators; Tony Jonick and Kate Kaminski, desktop publishers; and Marilyn Smith, indexer.

And lastly, thanks to my family, for being patient and helping each other while I was busy working on this book; and to my neighbor and friend, Wendy Smith, for her generous help with the smallest members of my brood.

Contents at a Glance

Table of Contents

Introduction

No experience required. Will train. That's the promise of this book. By the time you're finished reading it, you should be able to create a working database in Access 2000 that pays for itself over and over again in terms of the time it takes to set it up.

Access 2000 is a super powerful program with dozens of features to help you with your information management. Because Microsoft constantly expands the capabilities of Access for both new database users and programmers, it includes an amazing array of tools. For new Access 2000 users, the problem is figuring out where to start and what tools to use for a particular task.

This book is designed to give you the essential knowledge you need to work with Access 2000 effectively without requiring hours of intense study. It includes lots of examples of how to accomplish basics like planning a database, creating tables, designing forms and reports to present your information, and automating tasks such as navigating through a database.

You'll find more than just the basics here, however. Tips on alternative ways to accomplish tasks and to save time are sprinkled throughout the text. One skill is devoted to showing you how to publish your Access data to the World Wide Web using a new feature of Access 2000, data access pages. Another section explains how to capitalize on the way Access 2000 works with other Office 2000 programs. By the time you finish working with this book, you should truly be an expert Access 2000 user and know how to make it work for your own projects.

What You Need

All you need to follow the examples in this book is a computer running Windows 95/98 or Windows NT, and either Office 2000 Premium Edition or Access 2000. You should have at least 32MB of memory on your computer, a Pentium processor, and about 200MB of disk space for a typical Office installation.

How This Book Is Organized

This book is organized in skills that cover the basics of building an Access 2000 database and turning it into an application. Although you can read through the entire book from beginning to end, it is designed to be an easy reference for completing specific types of tasks:

- Understanding what Access does and how it's organized
- Planning a database
- Building and relating database tables
- Entering, viewing, finding, and sorting data
- Using AutoForms and the Form Wizard
- Customizing forms
- Finding data with filters and queries
- Mastering advanced queries
- Creating and customizing reports
- Using charts to summarize data
- Importing, exporting, and sharing data with other programs
- Database housekeeping
- Creating Web pages that show Access data
- Using command buttons and macros to automate a database
- Creating an application
- Customizing Access

The examples in most of the text use a database called Timekeeper, but are written in such a way that you can easily apply them to your own projects. If you'd like to use the Timekeeper database as you go through the text, follow the examples in Skills 2 and 3 that show you how to plan and create database tables.

Conventions in the Text

The intention is, of course, for you to be able to follow the instructions in this book easily. There are just a few conventions to be aware of as you read:

- Menu commands are shown like this: File ➤ Get External Data ➤ Import. This string of commands means choose File from the Access main menu, and then choose Get External Data and Import from the pop-up menus that appear. Some menus in Access 2000 now have More buttons (down arrows) that you can click to show an expanded version of the menu. Or, you can pause after you open a menu and wait for the expanded options to appear. If you don't find a menu choice right away, check the expanded menu to see if it's hidden there.

- New terms that are introduced are shown in italics as in "Access is a *relational database*."

- In the examples, text that you need to enter is shown in boldface: "Enter **My Table** in the dialog box that asks you for a filename."

- The term Windows applies to Windows 95, Windows 98, and Windows NT, unless otherwise noted. None of the material in this book is relevant to Windows 3.*x*.

Notes, Tips, Warnings, and Margin Icons

As you read through the book, you'll find boxes for notes, tips, and warnings.

NOTE NOTE NOTE NOTE NOTE NOTE NOTE NOTE NOTE NOTE NOTE NOTE NOTE NOTE

Notes provide information that may help you understand a topic better.

TIP TIP TIP TIP TIP TIP TIP TIP TIP TIP TIP TIP TIP TIP TIP TIP TIP TIP TIP TIP TIP TIP

Tips usually point out ways to save time doing typical database tasks.

WARNING WARNING WARNING WARNING WARNING WARNING WARNING WARNING

Warnings mark the spots where you should be careful to follow instructions closely so as not to lose or otherwise damage your design work or data.

When the text refers to a button on one of the Access toolbars, an icon for the tool is shown in the margin so you can find it quickly in the Access window. In most cases, margin icons only appear the first time a tool is referenced. You can also refer to the inside back covers of the book for a quick visual guide to some of the commonly used features of the Form and Report Design view window.

Comments Welcome!

Thank you for buying this book. I hope you find it helpful in accomplishing whatever you set out to do with Access 2000. If you have any comments on the book, please send them to:

Celeste Robinson
c/o SYBEX Inc.
1151 Marina Village Parkway
Alameda, CA 94501

Access Basics

Access: A Relational Database

If you're planning to use Access 2000, chances are you already know what a database is. Just in case you're not sure, however, here's a super-brief definition before we get started.

In a nutshell, a *database* is a collection of data. Your phone book is a simple database and so is your checkbook. A history of a company's orders, invoices, and payments is an example of a more complicated database, as is a log of a salesperson's contacts with clients and any related follow-up plans.

Access is a flexible program that works for both simple and complex database projects. It's also a *relational database*, which means it lets you define relationships between different types of information (like customers and their orders) so you can use them together. But before you get buried in lots of database theory, let's get going and learn as we work.

Get Started

To launch Access, click the Microsoft Access 2000 button on the Microsoft Office Shortcut Bar, or click the Start button and choose Programs ➣ Microsoft Access from the menu. When Access starts, you'll see a dialog box like the one in Figure 1.1. The names you see listed in the bottom half of the dialog box will vary depending on the database projects you've already started. At this point, you can:

- Create a database from scratch or with the Database Wizard

- Create a data access page for viewing Access data with Internet Explorer

- Create an Access project

- Open a database or project you've already created

TIP TIP TIP TIP TIP TIP TIP TIP TIP TIP TIP TIP TIP TIP TIP TIP TIP TIP TIP TIP TIP TIP

If you want to bring the Microsoft Office Shortcut Bar into view on the Windows Desktop, click the Start button and choose Programs ➣ Office Tools ➣ Microsoft Office Shortcut Bar from the menus. To hide the Shortcut Bar, double-click the Office icon in the blue section of the Shortcut Bar, or right-click the blue area and choose Exit.

FIGURE 1.1: Access' opening dialog box lets you create a new Access file or open one you've worked with before.

NOTE NOTE NOTE NOTE NOTE NOTE NOTE NOTE NOTE NOTE NOTE NOTE NOTE NOTE NOTE

An Access *project* is similar to an Access database, but it contains no data tables. Instead, it is connected to an SQL server that holds the tables for the project. Though much of the information pertaining to databases in this book is applicable to projects as well, see Appendix B for more information on when to use a project and how to create one.

Later in this chapter, you'll see how to create a new database using the Database Wizard. First, here's an overview of how an Access database is organized.

Elements of an Access Database

The heart of a database is the information it holds. But there are other important elements, usually referred to as *objects*, in an Access database. Here are the kinds of objects you'll be working with:

> **Tables** hold information.
>
> **Queries** let you ask questions about your data or make changes to data.
>
> **Forms** are for viewing and editing information.

Pages are HTML (Hypertext Markup Language) files that let you view Access data with Internet Explorer.

Reports are for summarizing and printing data.

Macros perform one or more database actions automatically.

Modules are another type of Access object that you may or may not work with. A module is a program you write using VB (Visual Basic, the programming language included with Office 2000) to automate and customize database functions. In this book, you'll see how to create a customized database, but it will all be done without programming.

NOTE NOTE NOTE NOTE NOTE NOTE NOTE NOTE NOTE NOTE NOTE NOTE NOTE NOTE NOTE

For more information on creating Access applications with VB, see the forthcoming *Access 2000 VBA Handbook* (Sybex, summer 1999).

Tables

Any information you enter in an Access database gets stored in a *table*. Figure 1.2 shows two tables from a Contact Management database created with the Database Wizard: a table called Contacts and another named Calls. These tables hold information about people and the calls made to them.

As you can see in Figure 1.2, a table consists of rows and columns of values. In database lingo, the rows are called *records*, and the columns are *fields*.

There are lots of different ways to create tables in Access. The various options are explored in Skill 3, "Build Tables."

Queries

Queries are most often used to ask questions about your data. You can formulate simple queries that look for records in a single table, or design complex queries that involve multiple tables and criteria. Here are some examples of the kinds of questions you can ask with a query:

- "Which customers have placed orders in the last three months?"

- "How many new leads did I contact last week?"

- "Show me my total sales for the last six months of 1998 broken down by product and month."

Fields

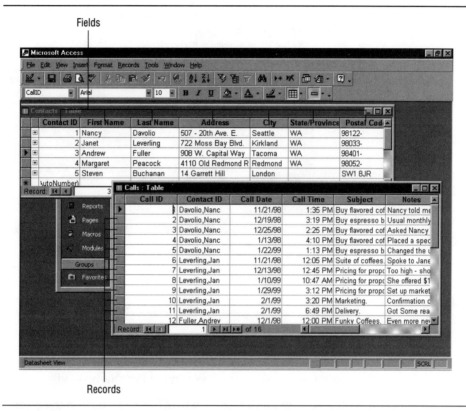

Records

FIGURE 1.2: Contacts and Calls are two of the tables included in the Contact Management database created by the Database Wizard. Each record in the Contacts table describes a person. The records in Calls describe the calls made to people in the Contacts table.

Select Queries

Figure 1.3 shows a fairly simple query that looks for all calls to Nancy in a table named Calls. This type of query is called a *select* query. It finds any records that answer the question posed by the query and displays them when the query is run.

This chapter won't get into a lot of detail about how to formulate a query, but there are a few other things about the query in Figure 1.3 that may be interesting to you:

- The field names in the Field row, along with the check marks in the Show row, tell Access which fields to show when the query is run.

This line tells Access how to link
the two tables involved in the query.

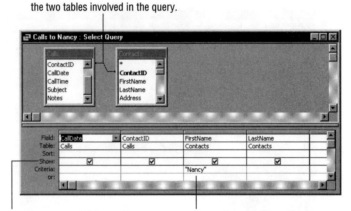

The check marks in the Show row
tell Access what fields to show
when the query is run.

This criteria tells Access to look for
records with "Nancy" in the FirstName field.

FIGURE 1.3:   A query that looks for calls to a person named Nancy

- "Nancy" in the FirstName column of the Criteria row tells Access to look only for records with Nancy in the FirstName field.

- If you check the top part of the Query window in the figure, you can see that the Calls table is linked to the Contacts table on the ContactID field. Access uses this link to gather information from both tables at the same time. (Relationships are discussed further in Skill 2, "Plan a Database," and Skill 3, "Build Tables.")

When you run a query, Access displays the results in *Datasheet view*, a simple arrangement of rows and columns of field values. (See Figure 1.4. Note that the tables in Figure 1.2 are also displayed in Datasheet view.) The query result in the figure includes only the calls made to Nancy and shows only the fields from the Calls and Contacts tables that were checked in Figure 1.3.

In Skill 7, "Find Data with Filters and Queries," we'll look at select queries more closely and go through several examples that show how to use the Query Design window.

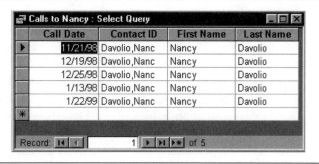

FIGURE 1.4: The result of the query in Figure 1.3 shown in a Datasheet view. Access automatically looks up and displays the names for each ContactID.

Other Types of Queries

Options in the Query Design window don't end with Select queries. Queries can be used to change data as well as look for it. You can use queries to crosstabulate data, create tables, delete records, or even add records to one table from another:

Crosstab Queries   These queries summarize data by categories so you can answer questions like "What were my sales by product for each month last year?" There's a Crosstab Wizard to help you set up these queries.

Make-Table Queries   When you turn a select query into a Make-Table query, it writes the results to a completely new table.

Update Queries   With Update queries, you can make global changes to a table (like changing all of a field's values to uppercase), do find-and-replace edits, or update one table against another.

Append Queries   Use these queries to add information from one table to another.

Delete Queries   Instead of deleting records from a table one by one, you can use a Delete query to do quick deletes of entire groups of records.

In Skill 8, "Master Advanced Queries," you'll find out how to make use of all these special purpose queries.

Forms

When you open a table in Access, it gets presented in Datasheet view. Check the window called "Contacts : Table" in the background of Figure 1.5 to see an example of what Datasheet view looks like.

The same figure shows a record from the Contacts table presented in *Form view* in the window called Contacts. In Form view, you can see all the fields for Nancy Davolio's record at once. In contrast, Datasheet view displays a limited amount of fields at the same time, and you have to scroll sideways through the Table window to view a person's entire record. In most cases, using a form makes it easier to enter, edit, and view data.

Datasheet view displays one record per
line with a limited number of fields visible.

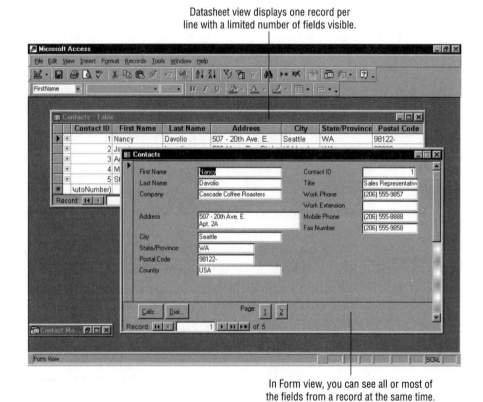

In Form view, you can see all or most of
the fields from a record at the same time.

FIGURE 1.5: Records from the Contacts table shown in both Datasheet view and Form view

The Form Wizard and AutoForms

Putting together a database form from scratch is a tedious task, but thankfully there's plenty of help available. Access 2000 has a *Form Wizard* that will create a form after asking you a bunch of questions about what you want to see. The form that is discussed in the "Multi-table Forms" section was created with the Form Wizard.

If you want to go an even quicker route, you can use the AutoForm feature to create the following types of forms without providing any information other than the name of a table or a query:

Columnar This type of AutoForm creates a form with one record per page and fields arranged in a column like this:

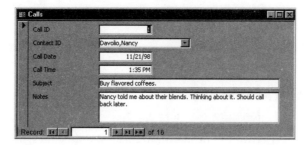

Tabular This AutoForm arranges fields in a tabular format where they line up in rows rather than columns:

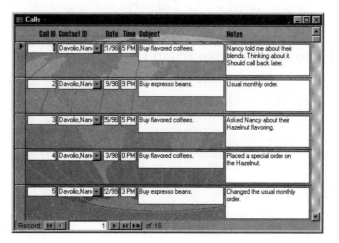

Datasheet   A form created with this AutoForm option shows multiple records in the Form window just like in a Table window:

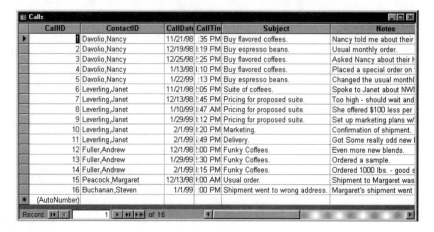

Multi-table Forms

The forms we've looked at so far have included fields from only one table, but Access doesn't limit you to these simple views. You can show information from more than one table at the same time, like in Figure 1.6. The form in the figure shows the record for Nancy Davolio from the Contacts table at the top of the form window. Underneath Nancy's description is another form, called a *subform*, that shows all of Nancy's records in the Calls table. In this example, the call records are in Datasheet view, but they can appear in any of the formats listed in the last section.

Special Purpose Form Objects

Forms can also include graphics, hyperlinks to Web sites or other data, OLE objects (links to other Windows programs), and other special purpose objects. In Skill 5, "Use AutoForms and the Form Wizard," and Skill 6, "Customize Forms," you'll go through several step-by-step examples of how to create forms and jazz them up with the tools in the Form Design window.

Pages

Pages, or *data access pages*, are a new feature of Access in Office 2000. These objects can be used to browse Access data with Internet Explorer, as well as with Access itself. Unlike forms and reports, which are stored as part of an Access database, pages are saved as HTML files that are separate from the database they are associated with.

Fields from Nancy's record in the Contacts table

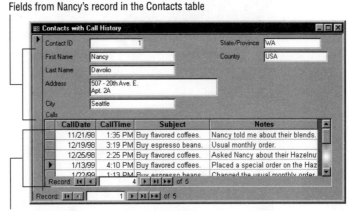

Records for calls to Nancy from the Calls table

FIGURE 1.6: This multi-table form shows related information from the Contacts and Calls tables at the same time.

Figure 1.7 shows a page that displays records from the Contacts tables in the Contact Management1 database. The same page is shown in Figure 1.8 viewed with Internet Explorer.

If you compare the record navigation controls at the bottom of the Contacts page (Figure 1.7) to those on the form in Figure 1.6, you'll see that they are somewhat different from each other. The Navigation toolbar at the bottom of the page in Figure 1.7 includes buttons for deleting records, undoing changes, and working with filters, as well as for moving between records and adding new records.

NOTE NOTE NOTE NOTE NOTE NOTE NOTE NOTE NOTE NOTE NOTE NOTE NOTE NOTE NOTE

Other properties of data access pages also vary from those of forms, as you'll see later. Skill 13, "Create Web Pages with Access," explains how to create pages using the Page Wizard or from scratch. In that skill, you'll also find out more about the differences between simple pages like the ones shown in Figures 1.7 and 1.8 and grouped pages that let you expand or collapse your view of detail data.

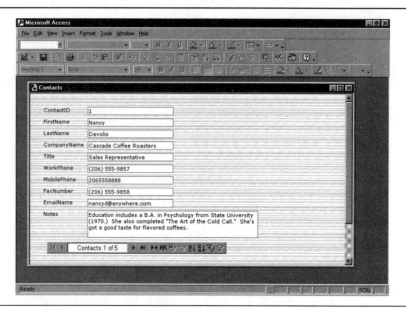

FIGURE 1.7: This data access page shows records from the Contacts table in the Contact Management1 database. The page is being viewed with Access.

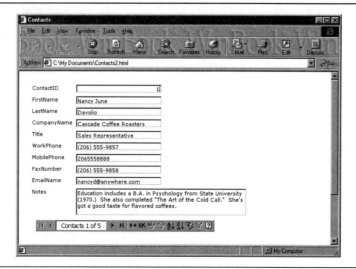

FIGURE 1.8: This is the same data access page shown in Figure 1.7 being viewed from Internet Explorer.

Reports

Reports are another type of object you can use in Access to view or print your data. Figure 1.9 shows a simple alphabetical listing of the people in the Contacts table that was printed using an Access report.

Alphabetical Contact Listing

	Contact Name	Company Name	Title	Work Phone	Ext.	Fax Number
B						
	Buchanan, Steven	Health Food Store	Purchase Manager	(71) 555-2222		
D						
	Davolio, Nancy	Cascade Coffee Roasters	Sales Representative	(206) 555-9857		(206) 555-9858
F						
	Fuller, Andrew	Volcano Coffee Company	Sales Representative	(206) 555-9482		(206) 555-9483
L						
	Leverling, Janet	Northwind Traders	Vice President, New Produc	(206) 555-3412		(206) 555-3413
P						
	Peacock, Margaret	Fourth Coffee	Purchase Manager	(206) 555-8122		(206) 555-8123

FIGURE 1.9: This listing of people in the Contacts table was printed using an Access report.

You can create reports from scratch with Access, but you will probably never need to with all the tools available to help you:

- The *Report Wizard* guides you through every step of designing a report, from selecting fields to choosing a style for the printed page.

- *AutoReport* can create a columnar or tabular report for you with one mouse click.

- The *Chart Wizard* assists you with creating all kinds of graphs from pie charts to 3-D bar graphs that show multiple series of data.

- The *Label Wizard* creates reports to print labels that fit standard formats (like Avery 5161) or layouts you design yourself.

Differences between Forms and Reports

Reports are similar to forms and, in fact, the Report Design window shares many of the features of the Form Design window. Yet there are some important differences between these two types of objects.

One difference is that forms are primarily used to edit or view data on your computer screen. When you move through a form, you usually navigate from one record to another, perhaps displaying related records from other tables as you do so. Reports can be previewed on the screen, as well, but their main purpose is to present information nicely on a printed page.

Another difference between forms and reports is that reports have special features to help you summarize data. For example, a report can group sales records by salesperson and month, and give you a summary of the total sales for each person by month. It's not possible to view this kind of summary information using a form unless you go through some hoops with queries first.

Multi-table Reports

Just as with forms, reports can present data from more than one table at the same time. These are called *multi-table reports*. The report in Figure 1.10 shows a list of the records in Calls for each person in the Contacts table.

NOTE NOTE NOTE NOTE NOTE NOTE NOTE NOTE NOTE NOTE NOTE NOTE NOTE NOTE NOTE

In Skill 9, "Create and Customize Reports," you'll see how to create multi-table reports and summary reports using the Report Wizard. You'll also learn how to customize the designs the wizard produces to get just the output you need for your database or project.

Macros

There's one more type of object you'll be using in the Database window: macros. A *macro* automatically executes one or more database commands when you run it. Macros are great for tasks that you do over and over again. If you spend some time to set up a macro to do this kind of repetitive job, your investment will be paid back many times over.

Here are a few examples of database jobs you could automate with a macro:

- Print a bunch of month-end reports.

- Add a new record to a table, date- and time-stamp it, and fill in your initials.

- Import a data file, run some queries to format the new data, and add the resulting information to another table in your database.

- Print letters for customers and make notes in the customers' records of when the letters were sent.

- Copy data from one form to another.

Contacts with Call Histories

First Name	Last Name	Work Phone	Date	Time	Subject	Notes
Nancy	Davolio	(206) 555-9857				
			12/19/97	3:19 PM	Buy espresso beans.	Usual monthly order.
			12/25/97	2:25 PM	Buy flavored coffees.	Asked Nancy about their Hazelnut flavoring.
			1/13/97	4:10 PM	Buy flavored coffees.	Placed a special order on the Hazelnut.
			1/22/98	1:13 PM	Buy espresso beans.	Changed the usual monthly order.
			11/21/97	1:35 PM	Buy flavored coffees.	Nancy told me about their blends. Thinking about it. Should call back later.
Janet	Leverling	(206) 555-3412				
			1/29/98	3:12 PM	Pricing for proposed suite.	Set up marketing plans w/ Janet.
			11/21/97	12:05 PM	Suite of coffees.	Spoke to Janet about NWIND carrying a coffee collection designed by us.
			1/10/98	10:47 AM	Pricing for proposed suite.	She offered $100 less per order (12 packages / order) - OK.
			2/1/98	3:20 PM	Marketing.	Confirmation of shipment.
			2/1/98	6:49 PM	Delivery.	Got Some really odd new blends.
			12/13/97	12:45 PM	Pricing for proposed suite.	Too high - should wait and see if Janet comes around.
Andrew	Fuller	(206) 555-9482				
			12/1/97	12:00 PM	Funky Coffees.	Even more new blends.
			1/29/98	2:30 PM	Funky Coffees.	Ordered a sample.
			2/1/98	3:15 PM	Funky Coffees.	Ordered 1000 lbs. - good stuff
Margaret	Peacock	(206) 555-8122				
			12/13/97	9:00 AM	Usual order.	Shipment to Margaret was late, oops.
Steven	Buchanan	(71) 555-2222				
			1/1/98	1:00 PM	Shipment went to wrong ac	Margaret's shipment went to Steven, oops.

FIGURE 1.10: This multi-table report shows information from both the Contacts and Calls tables.

After a macro is set up, you can run it from the Database window or attach it to a *command button* on a form. Skill 14, "Bypass Database Drudgery with Command Buttons and Macros," shows you how to set up macros and attach them to command buttons.

As mentioned earlier, a *module* is another type of object that can be part of an Access database. Modules hold programming code that works with objects like tables, queries, and forms.

NOTE NOTE NOTE NOTE NOTE NOTE NOTE NOTE NOTE NOTE NOTE NOTE NOTE NOTE
This book will focus on macros instead of modules since macros are easier to formulate and can be used to automate most database tasks, even if you're not a programmer.

A Database Plan

Even though you won't find a button for "Database Plan" in the Database window, this is probably the most important element of any database. Before you start creating any tables, forms, or reports, the first thing you need to do is figure out exactly *what* you need from your Access database.

Of course, it's impossible to devise a perfect plan when you might not yet have all the experience you need to make optimal choices. (Hopefully you'll have that experience by the time you're done with this book!) But it's still a good idea to devote some time considering these questions before you jump into a creating a database:

- Where is my data going to come from? Will I enter it myself, or can I import it from another source? If the data already exists, can I link to it directly from Access? And do I need to share the data with other people?

- If the data I'm using is on a SQL server, should I use an Access database or a project file? (Check Appendix B for more information on what to consider when making this decision.)

- What kind of standards do I want the data to conform to?

- How do I want to view information on the screen?

- Do I have to do any calculations or run through other kinds of processes with my data?

- What reports or charts do I need to print or send to other people?

- Does any of the data need to be accessed from the Web?

- What kinds of tasks will I need to do over and over again?

- Are other people going to be using my database? If so, what can I do to make it easier for them do their work?

These questions are looked at in more detail in Skill 2, "Plan a Database," with the intention of minimizing the work involved in getting a database up and running.

Create a New Database with the Database Wizard

Now that you are familiar with what a database is and what its components are, you're ready to put that knowledge to use. After you launch Access to begin work on a new application, the next step is to create a database or a project to hold your work. A database is used to illustrate the examples in the rest of this chapter, but many of the basic concepts that will be presented apply to projects as well. If you want to work with the examples on your own computer, follow these steps to create a new database using the Database Wizard:

1. In the opening dialog box shown in Figure 1.1, select Access Database Wizards, Pages, And Projects. Then click OK.

2. Click the Databases tab in the New dialog box.

3. Double-click the icon for Contact Management.

4. In the File New Database dialog box that opens, click Create. (You don't have to change the default name for the new database.)

5. In the first Database Wizard dialog box, click Next.

6. Select a style for the background of the forms in the new database and click Next.

7. Choose a style for your reports and click Next.

8. Enter a title for your database and click Next.

9. Click Finish to create the new database and open it.

After Access finishes its work, you'll see a window called Main Switchboard like the one in Figure 1.11. The Database Wizard includes *switchboards*, special purpose forms that work like menus, in any new databases it creates. These switchboards have buttons you can click to choose tasks or leave the database. You can also add switchboards to databases or projects that you create without the help of the Database Wizard, as you'll see in Skill 15, "Create an Application."

You don't need to use the Main Switchboard now, so click its Close button and open the Database window by clicking the Restore button pointed out in Figure 1.11.

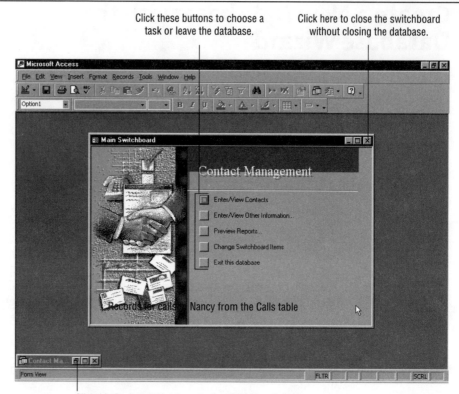

Click these buttons to choose a task or leave the database.

Click here to close the switchboard without closing the database.

Click this Restore button to open the Database window.

FIGURE 1.11: The Database Wizard includes switchboards in all new databases it creates. A switchboard has buttons you can click to easily navigate through a database.

The Database Window

Every Access database has a *Database window*. This window has an Objects bar with buttons for these types of objects: Tables, Queries, Forms, Reports, Pages, Macros, and Modules. It also has its own toolbar with buttons for the following actions:

Open   Use this button to open a database object so you can work with it.

Preview   (Reports only) Click this button to display a report in a Preview window.

Run (Macros and Modules only) Use this button to run a macro or a module.

Design Click this button to change the design of the selected object.

New Use this button to create a new database object.

Figure 1.12 shows the Database window for a Contact Management database created by the Database Wizard.

1. Click the button for the type of object you want to work with.

3. Click Open, Preview, Run, Design, or New, depending on what you need to do.

Click here to close the database.

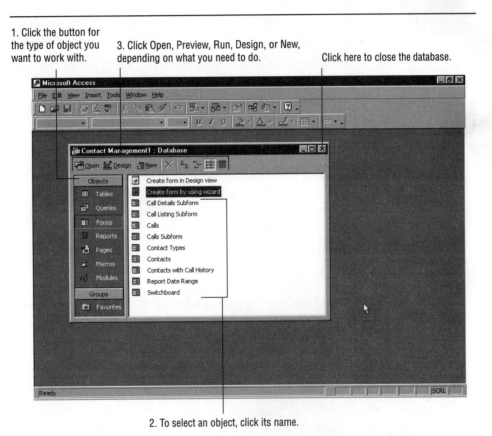

2. To select an object, click its name.

FIGURE 1.12: The Database window for a Contact Management database. From this window, you can create new objects, revise their designs, or open them for viewing.

The Database window for a project has different buttons under Objects than those for a database. See Appendix B for more information on what you'll see in the Database window for a project.

Create a New Object

There's more than one way to create a new object when the Database window is open:

- Click the Database window button for the type of object you want to create and then click New.

- Click the drop-down arrow on the New Object toolbar button and select the type of object you want to create.

- Choose Insert from the Access menu bar and select an object type.

Don't worry about the details of what to do next for specific types of objects. The important thing now is just to know how to use the Database window to start a new object.

Open an Object

To open an object:

1. In the Database window, click the button for the type of object you want to work with. (You can also click the Favorites button, or you can choose another group if you've added the object to a group as described a little later in this chapter.)

2. Highlight the object's name in the Database window.

3. Click Open.

To open a table, query, form, page, or report (or to run a macro or edit a module), double-click the object's name in the Database window. Alternatively, you can right-click the object and choose Open or Run from the shortcut menu.

Change an Object's Design

Once an object is created, you are free to change it in Design view. To open an object in Design view:

1. In the Database window, click the button for the type of object you want to work with (or click the name of any group the object may belong to).

2. Highlight the object's name in the Database window.

3. Click Design.

The tools you find in the Design view window vary depending on the type of object you are working with. You can do things like rearrange the data that's shown with the object; change the font, colors, and style of text; and add special elements like graphics and hyperlinks. You'll learn more about the Design view windows for tables, queries, forms, data access pages, reports, and macros later in this book.

TIP TIP TIP TIP TIP TIP TIP TIP TIP TIP TIP TIP TIP TIP TIP TIP TIP TIP TIP TIP TIP TIP

To open an object in Design view, you can also right-click an object's name in the Database window and select Design from the shortcut menu.

View Objects by Group

When you click one of the buttons on the Objects bar in the Database window, Access changes the objects that are shown on the list in the middle of the window. For example, in Figure 1.12, the list in the Database window shows the names of all the forms in the Contact Management1 database. If you wanted to see a list of tables in the database, you would click the Tables button under Objects.

There is a new Access feature that lets you organize objects into groups as well as by type. One group is already set up for you: *Favorites*. When you click the Favorites button (under Groups in the Database window), Access shows the objects you have added to the Favorites group, regardless of the various objects' types. In other words, the Favorites group can include references to tables, forms, queries, reports, and other types of objects all in the same place.

To add an object to the Favorites group, right-click the object and choose Add To Group ➢ 1 Favorites from the shortcut menu.

To create a new group, right-click any button on the Objects bar or the Groups bar and choose New Group from the shortcut menu. Then enter a name for the new group and click OK.

To add an object to a new group, right-click the object, choose Add To Group from the shortcut menu, and select the group for the object.

TIP TIP TIP TIP TIP TIP TIP TIP TIP TIP TIP TIP TIP TIP TIP TIP TIP TIP TIP TIP TIP TIP TIP TIP

You can create a new group and add an object to it at the same time by choosing Add To Group ➤ New Group from the object's shortcut menu.

Database Window Shortcuts

The Access 2000 Database window has its own shortcut menu, as do individual Access objects. Where you right-click in the Database window determines what you'll see on the shortcut menu that comes up.

Shortcut Menu for a Database

If you right-click the title bar or any gray area of the Database window, you'll see a shortcut menu for the database (or project) you are working with:

The Open… choice opens a dialog box from which you can select an Access database or project to open. (You can also open a few other types of files, like Web pages, from the Open dialog box.) The other menu choices won't be explored yet, but make a mental note that later on, you can probably use the shortcut menu for a database or a project to bypass menu commands.

Shortcut Menu for a Database Object

Each type of object in the Database window has its own shortcut menu. Figure 1.13 shows the shortcut menu for a form.

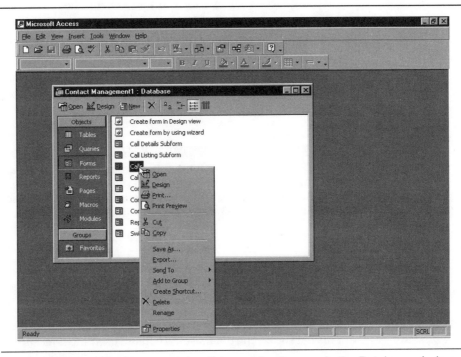

FIGURE 1.13: You can right-click an object's name in the Database window to see a shortcut menu of actions you can take with the object.

The form's shortcut menu includes Open, Design, Print…, Print Preview, Save As…, Export…, Send To, Add To Group, Delete, Rename, and other options that will be looked at in more detail later in the book. If you right-click a different type of object, like a report, you'll see a shortcut menu with slightly different choices than those that pop up for a form.

Shortcut Menu for the Database Window

The Database window has its own shortcut menu which differs from the shortcut menu for a database, a project, or a database object. Some of the choices on this menu let you change the appearance of the Database window:

View   Use this selection to display database objects with Large Icons, Small Icons, as a List alone, or with Details like file descriptions, creation dates, and modification dates.

Arrange Icons   This choice lets you choose how icons are displayed in the Database window: By Name, By Type, By (Date) Created, or By (Date) Modified. If you are currently showing icons, the Auto Arrange choice is also available. Select (check) this choice to keep icons displayed in neat rows in the Database window.

Line Up Icons   When icons are displayed, this choice straightens icons into tidy columns.

NOTE NOTE NOTE NOTE NOTE NOTE NOTE NOTE NOTE NOTE NOTE NOTE NOTE NOTE NOTE

As with the shortcut menu for databases and projects, there are other choices on the Database window shortcut menu that we don't need to bother with yet. Importing and linking tables are discussed in Skill 11, "Import, Export, and Share Data"; relationships are covered in Skill 3, "Build Tables."

Opening a Database

To open a database, you have many different options:

- Choose File from the menu and make a choice from the list just above Exit. This list shows the databases you have used most recently.

- Double-click a database name in Windows Explorer.

- Click the Open button on the toolbar.

- Right-click the title bar or gray area of the Database window and select Open.

- Choose File ➢ Open from the main Access menu.

- Press Ctrl+O.

All of these actions, except the first two, show an Open dialog box like the one in Figure 1.14 where you can select a database to work with. To choose a database from the list in the middle of the Open window, just double-click its name, or highlight it and click Open. Alternatively, use the drop-down list for File Name to select a file you opened recently.

NOTE NOTE NOTE NOTE NOTE NOTE NOTE NOTE NOTE NOTE NOTE NOTE NOTE NOTE NOTE

If you want to open a database and make sure no one else can use it at the same time, click the drop-down arrow on the Open button and select Open Exclusive.

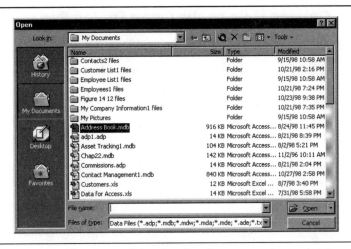

FIGURE 1.14: The Open dialog box is where you select a database or project to work with.

Changing the Look In Folder

In the Open dialog box shown in Figure 1.14, you'll find icons and buttons that are common to many Windows Open dialog boxes. The Look In box shows the location of the folders and files shown in the main part of the Open window. You can use the Look In drop-down list or the Up One Level button to change the folder Access is looking in.

The group of buttons along the left side of the Open window is new to Access and other Office 2000 programs. By clicking these buttons, you can quickly change the location shown in the Look In box. Here's what each button does:

- *History* shows the files in the Recent folder.

- *My Documents* shows the files in the My Documents folder.

- *Desktop* changes the Look In location to the Desktop and shows any short-cuts to databases.

- *Favorites* shows the files in the Favorites folder.

- *Web Folders* is for documents located on a Web server.

TIP TIP TIP TIP TIP TIP TIP TIP TIP TIP TIP TIP TIP TIP TIP TIP TIP TIP TIP TIP TIP TIP TIP TIP

To add a database to your Favorites folder, select it in the Open dialog box. Then click the Tools drop-down arrow and select Add To Favorites.

Getting Help in the Open Dialog Box

To find out more about the various parts of the Open dialog box:

1. Press F1 while the Open dialog box is open to show the Office Assistant.

2. Type **open a database** in the text box and press Enter or click Search.

3. Click Open A Microsoft Access Database on the list of topics under "What would you like to do?"

You can also view brief descriptions of the various elements of the Open dialog box without going through the Office Assistant or opening Help. Click the Help button next to the Close button in the Open dialog box, and then click the button or other element you want to learn about. Or, right-click any element in the window and choose What's This? to see a brief description pop up.

TIP TIP TIP TIP TIP TIP TIP TIP TIP TIP TIP TIP TIP TIP TIP TIP TIP TIP TIP TIP TIP TIP TIP TIP

By changing the Files Of Type setting in the Open dialog box, you can use Access to open Web pages, text files, Excel spreadsheets, and other types of files, as well as databases and projects. If you select a Web page (.htm or .html file), Access opens the file as a Data Access Page. For text files and spreadsheets, Access creates a new database and starts the Link Text File or Link Spreadsheet Wizard.

Closing a Database

There are two ways to close a database:

- Click the Close button for the Database window.

- Choose File ➤ Close from the menu bar.

If you're working with a database you created with the Database Wizard, you also have the option of going to the Main Switchboard window and clicking Exit This Database.

What's in a Relationship?

At the beginning of this chapter, there was a brief allusion to the fact that Access is a *relational database*, allowing you to use different types of information together. This chapter won't get into a theoretical discussion of what it means for a database to be relational. Instead, it takes a quick look at the benefits of a relational database, how Access relates tables, and what kinds of relationships can exist between tables.

What You Get from a Relational Database

To understand what's good about a relational database, first look at what goes on with a database that is *not* relational (called a "flat file" database). When you're working with a flat filer, you can only use one table of data at a time. For example, if you wanted to enter sales orders on your computer using a flat filer, you would have to create one table with fields for every possible bit of information that could be part of an order. You would have to include the details for order, customer, product, and tax information all in the same table. The structure of this table might look like the list of fields shown in Table 1.1.

TABLE 1.1: Fields for Orders File in a Flat File Database

Field Name
Order #
Order Date
Sales Rep
Customer #
Name
Address
City
State
Zip
Product 1
Qty 1
Price 1
Product 2
Qty 2
Price 2
Product 3
Qty 3
Price 3
Sales Tax
Freight

It is assumed that the extended price for each sales item and the order totals can be calculated by the database software.

The disadvantages of having to store all this data in one table or file are quite obvious. For one thing, you would be limited to entering a fixed, maximum number of sale items for each order (three in the example in Table 1.1). Another disadvantage is that you would have to drag all this information around together, even if you only needed to work with part of the flat file. For example, if you wanted to create letters and labels to do a mailing to your customers, you would either have to create a separate file of customer information, or use the big Orders file and weed out the duplicates, since some customers may have placed more than one order.

In contrast, with a relational database, you could store Order Header details (like the order date and order #) in one table and Order details in another, allowing for a flexible number of sales items in each order. Customer, product, and tax fields would also all be stored in their own tables, as shown in Table 1.2.

TABLE 1.2: Fields and Tables for Orders in a Relational Database

Order Header Fields	Order Detail Fields	Customer Fields	Product Fields	Tax Fields
Order #	Order #	Customer #	Product #	State
Order Date	Product #	Name	Description	Tax Rate
Sales Rep	Qty	Address	Price	
Freight		City		
		State		
		Zip		

Again, it is assumed that the extended prices and order totals can be calculated by the database software.

The advantages of working with multiple related tables like the ones listed in Table 1.2 are that:

- You only have to enter information like customer names and addresses in one place, instead of in every order for the same customer. (The names and addresses in the Customer table can be linked as needed to the Order Header table.)

- An order can have a flexible number of sales items. This is possible since line items are stored in as many records as are needed in the Order Detail table, instead of in a set number of fields in one Orders table.

- Details like tax rates and product prices can be looked up from their own separate tables, eliminating the need to enter these values altogether.

- By keeping records for orders, customers, products, and other information in their own tables, it's easier to design forms and reports for different purposes.

NOTE NOTE NOTE NOTE NOTE NOTE NOTE NOTE NOTE NOTE NOTE NOTE NOTE NOTE NOTE
In Skill 2, "Plan a Database," you'll find out how to analyze how your own information and decide how to divide it up into separate tables that can be related.

Relate Tables with Access

To show data in one table along with corresponding records in another table, Access has to be able to *relate* the tables. For tables to be related, they need to have fields with common values. For example, in the Contacts Management database that the Database Wizard created for you, both the Contacts and the Calls tables have a field for ContactID. In the Contacts table, ContactID serves as a unique identifier for each person's record, while in the Calls table, the ContactID indicates who each call record belongs to. This relationship is shown in the Relationships window in Figure 1.15. Using the linking ContactID field, Access can go to the Contacts table and look up the name of the person for each record in the Calls table.

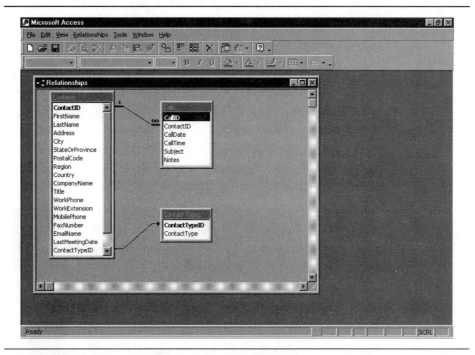

FIGURE 1.15: The Relationships window shows what fields are used to link the tables in a database. It also lets you add or change relationships.

NOTE NOTE NOTE NOTE NOTE NOTE NOTE NOTE NOTE NOTE NOTE NOTE NOTE NOTE NOTE

When you plan a database, be sure to include common fields in any tables you need to use together. You'll find some examples of how to do this in Skill 2, "Plan a Database."

Types of Relationships

Relationships between human beings are never as simple as they appear, and this applies to databases, too. A *table relationship* exists between two tables when they are related (as described above) and always falls into one of these categories, depending on how many times the linking values can occur in each table:

One-To-One   This type of relationship exists when there is only one record on each side of the relationship for each linking value. For example, there is a one-to-one relationship from an Orders table to a Customer table when they are linked on the CustomerID field (only one customer for each order).

One-To-Many   When there can be more than one record for a linking value on one side of a relationship, you end up with a one-to-many relationship. The relationship between the Contacts and Calls tables is an example of a one-to-many relationship. There is only one record in the Contacts table for each person, but you can have many records in the Calls table for each person.

Many-To-Many   This type of relationship describes the situation where linking values can appear in multiple records on both sides of a relationship. A table of Classes linked to a table of Club Members using a StudentID field would have a many-to-many relationship since a student could be in multiple classes and clubs.

In Access, the nature of a relationship between tables is determined by whether or not the linking fields are *key fields*. When a table is keyed, it means that one field, or a combination of fields, has been designated as the unique identifier for each of the table's records. Every record in a keyed table must have a unique value in the key field, or in the combination of key fields, if there is more than one. Because of this restriction, Access knows whether there can be only one possible record for a field value in a particular table. For example, if Access looks to a Customer table and finds that it is keyed on the CustomerID field, it knows that there can be only record for each CustomerID in the table.

NOTE NOTE NOTE NOTE NOTE NOTE NOTE NOTE NOTE NOTE NOTE NOTE NOTE NOTE NOTE

If key fields and relationships are still a mystery to you, don't worry. You'll learn more about them in Skill 2.

You can check what kind of relationship exists between two tables in the Edit Relationships window as shown in Figure 1.16. Just right-click the line that links two tables, choose Edit Relationship, and check the Edit Relationships dialog box. In Skill 3, you'll see how to create relationships between tables yourself and edit them in the Relationships window.

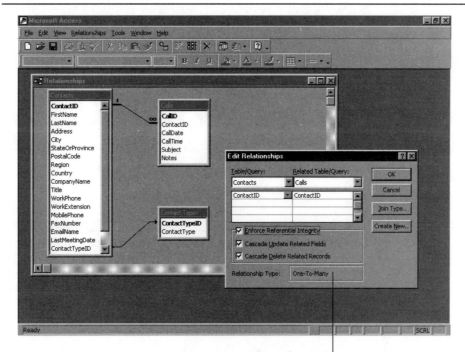

This window shows you what type of relationship exists between two tables.

FIGURE 1.16: The Edit Relationships dialog box shows you what field(s) link the tables in a relationship and what type of relationship exists.

Access, Office 2000, and the Web

Access is certainly not a database unto itself. It has lots of features that make it easy to share data with other Office 2000 programs, and it's also quite Web-aware. You might want to glance through this section to get familiar with these features, even if you're not a big user of Office 2000 or the World Wide Web. You might see something that could be useful for one of your future Access databases or projects.

Access and Office 2000

There are lots of ways you can expand the power of Access by calling on other Office 2000 applications from a database or project. You can:

- Click the OfficeLinks button on the Access toolbar to merge or publish data with Microsoft Word, or analyze a table with Microsoft Excel

- Link an Excel spreadsheet to an Access database

- Create a chart with MS Graph and show it on an Access form or report

- E-mail database information to someone via Microsoft Exchange

- Include objects like graphics, Excel spreadsheets, or Word documents in OLE fields in an Access table

NOTE NOTE NOTE NOTE NOTE NOTE NOTE NOTE NOTE NOTE NOTE NOTE NOTE NOTE NOTE

Check Skill 11, "Import, Export, and Share Data," to find out how to use the first two features on this list in your own database or project. To find out more about charting, see Skill 10, "Adding Multimedia." If you want to use OLE to include Office objects like spreadsheets and graphics in a table, see Skill 4, "Enter, View, Find, and Sort Data."

Access 2000 and the Web

You may have already noticed several Web-related features sprinkled throughout Access:

- The Web toolbar has buttons for doing things like jumping to a Web site (when you have an active Internet connection), searching the Web, and adding sites to your Favorites list.

- You can use hyperlink fields in tables to jump from database records to Web sites, Office documents, and Access objects.

- With the Insert Hyperlink tool in the Form and Report Design windows, you can include links to the Web, as well as to other documents and database objects, right in your forms and reports.

- HTML files can be imported or linked to an Access database.

- Almost any database object can be saved as an HTML document.

- The new data access pages are HTML files that can be used to browse Access data with Access or Internet Explorer.

Now that you're familiar with all the basic elements of Access, you can go on to Skill 2. It may be tempting to jump right in and start creating tables, forms, and reports right away, but spending a bit of time up front to lay a good database foundation will minimize the amount of time you have to spend revising your database later.

Are You Experienced?

Now you can...

- ☑ **Recognize the elements of an Access database**

- ☑ **Create a database**

- ☑ **Use the Access Database window to create new database objects**

- ☑ **Utilize the Database window shortcuts**

- ☑ **See how Access relates tables**

- ☑ **Be aware of how Access can work with Office 2000 and the Web**

Plan a Database

- ➔ Use the Database Wizard
- ➔ Create a database yourself
- ➔ Choose tables for your database
- ➔ Decide on fields
- ➔ Consider how you want data entered
- ➔ Plan your forms, reports, and queries
- ➔ Think about hyperlinks, command buttons, and macros

The Database Wizard

For some of us, it's hard to get started on a new task. If you fall into this group, just hearing the word "plan" may make you nervous, but this time you don't need to worry. The first decision you have to make when planning a database is actually pretty easy: whether you should use the Access Database Wizard to create the foundation for your database, or whether you should start from scratch. Once you know what the Database Wizard can do for you, it usually becomes obvious which way you should go. This section offers some guidelines on how to make a choice.

The *Database Wizard* is a powerful tool that can build a foundation for many different types of databases. All you have to do is select the kind of database you need (asset tracking, contact management, donations, and so on), and the Wizard will create tables, forms, reports, queries, macros, and even switchboards for you. You get the chance to include optional fields for some tables and choose styles for forms and reports before the Database Wizard does its stuff, but otherwise the Wizard does its work unassisted.

The key question in determining whether the Database Wizard will save you time or not is this: What are the tables and fields that the Database Wizard will include in the database? There's no way to check out the structure of a database created by the Database Wizard other than to start the wizard, choose a database, and examine the field list in the step that lets you choose fields for each table.

Start the Database Wizard

Here's how to start the Database Wizard:

1. Click the New icon on the toolbar, or press Ctrl+N.

2. Select the Databases tab in the New dialog box.

3. Scroll through the list of databases to see if any of them fit your project. If you don't find a good candidate, you might want to make a choice anyway and create a database, just to get some ideas about what Access can do. Highlight the database you are interested in.

4. Click OK to open the File New Database dialog box.

5. Change the database name, if you like, and click Create to start the wizard.

Check the Tables and Fields in the Wizard's Database

To see what tables and fields are in the database the wizard will create:

1. Click Next in the first Database Wizard dialog box.

2. To see the fields in each table, highlight a table name under Tables In The Database and check the list under Fields In The Table. You can scroll through the list to see what's included.

3. If you can see that the database you chose in the New dialog box is a hopeless candidate, click Cancel in any Database Wizard dialog box. Otherwise, continue on with the steps that follow to do more exploring.

Figure 2.1 shows the tables in the Event Management database the wizard creates. In the figure, you can see some of the fields the wizard includes in the Event Information table.

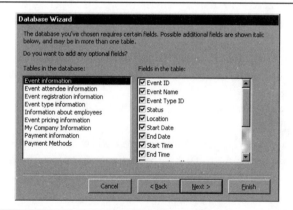

FIGURE 2.1: In this step of the Database Wizard, you can see the tables and fields that will be part of a new database. The Database Wizard is creating an Event Management database in this example.

Check for Optional Fields

Any field with a check mark on the Fields In The Table list is automatically included in the database. At the end of each field list, you may see unchecked fields with italicized names. These are optional fields that you can elect to add to the highlighted table. Just click an optional field's check box to include it in the database.

Choose Styles and Finish the Database

The next few steps of the Database Wizard are pretty self-explanatory:

1. Choose a style for forms and click Next.

2. Choose a style for reports and click Next.

3. Enter a title for the database, include a picture if you like, and click Next.

4. Click Finish to have the Database Wizard do its thing and open the new database.

Explore the Forms and Reports in the Database

It will take a little while for the Database Wizard to do its work. Once it's finished, it may ask you to enter some company information. Whether it asks for these details depends on the type of database you chose to create. Next, the Database Wizard will display a switchboard that serves as a menu for the new database. Click the buttons on the switchboard to explore the forms and reports in the new database.

Why look at the forms and reports? Sometimes it's hard to visualize what a database does just by looking at its tables and fields. Reviewing the sample forms and reports will help you evaluate whether the Database Wizard will work for your project. It's a lot easier to see how tables work together when you're viewing them in a form or report.

Figure 2.2 shows a form created by the Database Wizard for an Event Management database. This form includes data from two tables in the database: Attendees and Registration. The top part of the form shows fields about an individual attendee, while the middle section of the form displays records for any events the attendee is registered for. This is an example of how related tables can be used together in one object. A field called AttendeeID links the tables behind the scenes but is not shown on the form.

Create a Database Yourself

As you look through a database created by the wizard, check how closely the wizard's database structure matches what you need. If it looks like you will have to make only a few changes (maybe delete a few fields, add a couple of fields the wizard didn't know you would need, and perhaps change some field names), the

Database Wizard is probably a good place to start. But, if it appears that you will end up spending lots of time revising the wizard's database to fit your project, it will most likely be better to start from scratch.

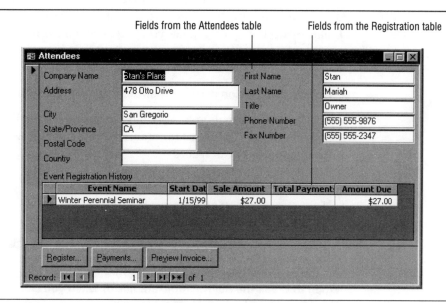

FIGURE 2.2: A form created by the Database Wizard for the Event Management database

If you decide to design a database yourself, it's best to spend some time planning before you actually get started creating objects like tables, forms, and reports. The rest of this skill will give you some ideas for things to consider as you go through the planning process. You'll find information on:

- Choosing tables for your database

- Deciding on the fields for tables

- Considering how you want data entered

- Planning your forms, reports, and queries

- Thinking about how you can use hyperlinks, command buttons, and macros to automate your database

Decide What Tables You'll Need

As with many projects, you should work from the outside in when designing a database. Before you get engrossed in details like what should go where on a form and how a report should be sorted, which will be discussed later in this skill, start by deciding what tables you will need. Following is a simple example to see what things you should think about in this phase of designing a database.

In brief, you will need to:

- Gather information on how your database will be used

- Look at the information to see what kind of records it describes (people, projects, orders, line items for orders, products, employees, etc.) and plan a table for each type of record

- List the details you will need to include in each type of record

- Make sure you don't have repeating details in a table

NOTE NOTE NOTE NOTE NOTE NOTE NOTE NOTE NOTE NOTE NOTE NOTE NOTE NOTE NOTE

In some situations, it's better to break this last rule than to force data in your tables into a theoretically proper structure. See the section later in this skill, "When to Break the Rules," for examples of when you should ignore database theory and go with common sense instead.

Gather Information

The first step in designing any database involves gathering information about how the database will be used. You should make notes on:

- What information will go into the database

- How the data needs to be updated, summarized, or otherwise acted upon

- The reports or charts you will need to print or view

If you're lucky, you may have samples of the forms and reports now being used to do the tasks that will be managed with the database. You can use this information as a jumping-off point for your plan.

When you're gathering information for a database, be sure to consider what changes to your current system should be incorporated into the new database plan. Ask questions to find out if the current system tracks everything it should, or if it's lacking in some way. You may need to add fields that are not part of the forms and reports now being used.

SKILL
2

To see how all this theoretical planning works, create a plan for an Access database called Timekeeper that will track how much time people in a department are spending on various projects. Here's what your notes might look like after we go through the information gathering stage.

How Data Is Gathered

In the current system, each department member sends a spreadsheet to the boss that looks something like this:

Jan's Hours.xls						
	A	B	C	D	E	F	G
1	Jan's Hours	Week Ending 1/9/99				
2						
3	Project	Hours		Description		
4						
5	Training	10		Update training guides for new hires		
6	Collections	6		Call "Over 90"s		
7	AR	20		Regular tasks		
8	Month End	8		Finish month end reports		
9						
10						
11						
12						

Even though there are rules for entering the data, each person ends up doing it a bit differently.

What Happens to the Data

The boss copies and pastes each person's spreadsheet into a master spreadsheet that has rows for each current project in the department. The master has formulas that sum the hours by project and looks something like the following spreadsheet:

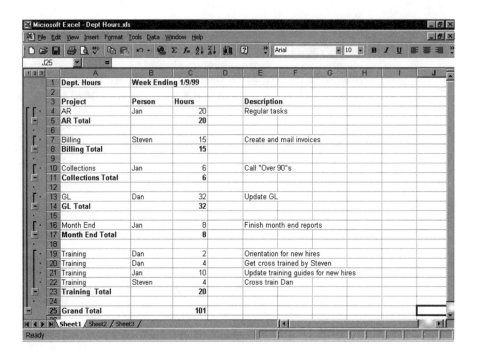

A copy of the spreadsheet is made and the records are rearranged to show totals by person. The totals for both summary spreadsheets are saved to a file of historical information.

Reports That Need to Be Printed

Two reports are currently printed each week:

Total Hours by Project

Total Hours by Person

Ideas for Changes

One problem with the current system is that it's not easy to keep a history of the records for each week. If too many records are left in the master spreadsheet, it becomes unwieldy. It's also difficult to report on the data for a selected week when there are records for more than one week in the file. Ideally, the new system should be able to easily handle an unlimited number of records.

Another desperately needed change involves data entry. It would be great to eliminate the need for the boss to consolidate everyone's spreadsheets. Each person should be able to enter their data in the same place.

It would also be nice to be able to print reports for user-specified time periods by project or person. That way summary information could be viewed by week, month, quarter, year, or whatever makes sense.

Review Your Research to Decide on Tables

When the information-gathering stage is complete, the next step is to decide which tables to use in the database. Look at all the information that will be recorded in the database to see what groups of records the data describes. Figure 2.3 shows the spreadsheet used to enter hours by project, with notes on how the pieces of data can be logically grouped.

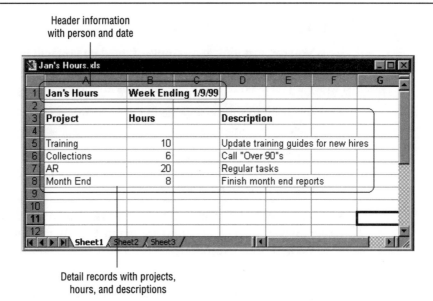

Header information
with person and date

Detail records with projects,
hours, and descriptions

FIGURE 2.3: The data-entry spreadsheet with the data grouped logically into two types of records

Looking at Figure 2.3, you can see that it makes sense to have at least two separate tables in Timekeeper:

- Weekly Records to hold records for each person/week-ending date combination

- Project Hours for the detail records for each weekly record: projects, hours, and descriptions

These two tables will be the backbone of the Timekeeper database plan. In the next section, you'll see how to set up these tables so they can be related and used together in forms and reports.

Decide on Fields

Once you decide on the tables you'll use in a database, you can move to the next level of work and choose fields for the tables. There's nothing difficult about this task, as long as you keep a few simple rules in mind.

Rules for Deciding on Fields

Usually you can just look at a sample of the data you will be entering to figure out what fields to include in a table. Jot down the list of fields and then review the list to see if you need to make any changes after considering these rules:

- If you want to sort on a value like Last Name, make it a distinct field instead of including it in a larger field like Name.

- Don't duplicate sets of fields in a table. If you have sets of repeating fields (like the project/hours/descriptions for each person/date), they probably belong in their own table.

- Avoid duplicating data in a table. It's easier to link in descriptive information like product names from a separate table than to enter it over and over again in repeated records.

- Be sure to include one or more common fields in related tables; it often works best to use an arbitrary ID # field for linking fields. For example, each record in the Weekly Records table can have a unique ID #. Then this field can be included in the Project Hours table to link detail records to a master weekly record.

Looking back at Figure 2.3, you can begin with these field lists for the Timekeeper database:

Fields for the Weekly Records Table	Fields for the Project Hours Table
WeeklyRecordID	Weekly Record ID (linking field)
Person	Project

Fields for the Weekly Records Table	Fields for the Project Hours Table
WeekEndingDate	Hours
	Description

After looking at some of the other elements of database design, you may alter this structure a bit, but the basic layout here will serve well as a jumping-off point for the rest of the plan.

When to Break the Rules

As with most rules, there are times when it makes sense to throw out the rule book and go with what seems natural. Here's one example of when common sense should prevail over theory: If you have a small number of repeating fields, don't bother with a separate table.

For example, say you have an address book where you may need to enter multiple phone numbers for a person: a home phone, a work phone, a fax line, a cell phone, and a pager number. Based on the rule that says you should avoid duplicating fields for the same type of data in a table, you could decide to keep phone numbers in their own table and link them to a table of people records. The table structures might look like this:

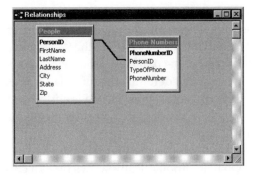

Is this worth the effort, though? When you break information down into separate, related tables, creating reports and queries gets more complicated. In this case, it might be more practical to create fields for three or four phone numbers and enter the rest in a catch-all field for notes. Even though more and more people can be contacted using many numbers, you may not want to make your phone book as complicated as their lives. You could keep it simple and use a structure like this:

Fields for a Simple Address Book Database

PersonID

FirstName

LastName

Address

City

State

Zip

HomePhone

WorkPhone

Fax

Notes (use this field for cell phone, pager, and so on when there are extra numbers)

Add Fields to Log Actions or Status

In most databases, it's a good idea to use fields to flag when certain actions occur or to note conditions like the status of an order. In the Timekeeper database, you could add a field called Entry Date to the Weekly Records table to show when each record was entered in the database. Don't worry about having to fill in another field—you can assign a default value of today's date to Entry Date to have Access fill in the field whenever a new record is added to the table. Default values are discussed later in this skill in "Consider How You Want Data Entered," and in Skill 3, "Build Tables.")

Yes/No fields are good for any field that can have values of True or False. A Yes/No field automatically shows up as a check box in a table or a form, so it's a handy way to mark things like whether a letter has been sent.

Choose Field Types

After you choose fields for a table, the next step is to select *field types*. Field types determine what can be entered in a field, how the values can be formatted, and what can be done with the data.

Access Field Types

Access has many field types. They are listed here with some notes on how each can be used:

AutoNumber   Access automatically assigns a number to this field when a record is added to a table.

Currency   This type of field is for money values.

Date/Time   Dates, times, or date/time combinations go in Date/Time fields.

Hyperlink   These fields hold hyperlink addresses that jump to Web sites, database objects, or other files.

Lookup Wizard   A Lookup field starts a wizard that places lookup constraints on a field; the lookup values can come from a list you enter, a table, or a query.

Memo   This type of field holds an unlimited amount of text.

Number   Numbers formatted in various ways can go in a Number field.

OLE Object   Objects like pictures and Word documents go in OLE (Object Linking and Embedding) Object fields.

Text   This type of field holds text: letters, numbers, and other characters.

Yes/No   Values of True or False are stored in this kind of field; the values can be shown as Yes/No, True/False, Male/Female, etc.

You can see many of these field types in the form shown in Figure 2.4. Skill 3, "Build Tables," will show you how to include each one of these field types in a table.

Field Types for the Timekeeper Database

Assign some field types to the Timekeeper database just for practice. You won't end up using all the field types yet; you'll add fields for some of the more exotic field types later.

Fields in Weekly Records Table	Field Type
WeeklyRecordID	AutoNumber
Person	Text
WeekEndingDate	Date/Time
RecordID	AutoNumber
WeeklyRecord ID	Number (link to Weekly Records table)

Fields in Weekly Records Table	Field Type
Project	Text
Hours	Number
Description	Text (or Memo if you want to keep long notes)

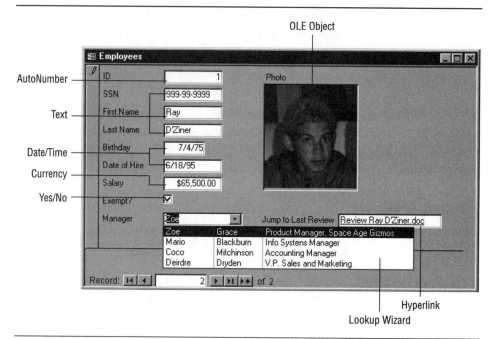

FIGURE 2.4: The table in this form includes many of the Access field types.

Fields for Relationships

If tables are going to be related, they need to have one or more fields in common. For the Weekly Records and Project Hours tables, you already planned to link the tables using a WeeklyRecordID field. Figure 2.5 shows another example of two tables linked by a common field. In the figure, the Contributors and Pledges tables in the Donations database are linked by a field called ContributorID.

This line shows how the
ContributorID field links the
Contributors and Pledges tables.

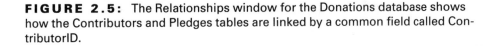

FIGURE 2.5: The Relationships window for the Donations database shows how the Contributors and Pledges tables are linked by a common field called ContributorID.

Key Fields

A *key* consists of one or more fields whose values uniquely identify each record in a table. Key fields provide some special functions in a database:

- They are often used to link tables. They also determine the nature of a relationship. See Table 2.1 to see how key fields affect table relationships.

- Access automatically builds a *primary index* using any key fields in a table. This index makes it easier for Access to find key values and speeds up any searches or other operations that look for values in the key fields.

In Figure 2.5, ContributorID is the key field, or *primary key*, for the Contributors table. This field is called a *foreign key* in the Pledges database. Because there can be only one record for each ContributorID in the Contributions table, but any number of records for the same ID in the Pledges table, a one-to-many relationship exists. The little symbols at either side of the line linking the tables in Figure 2.4 indicate the nature of the relationship.

NOTE NOTE NOTE NOTE NOTE NOTE NOTE NOTE NOTE NOTE NOTE NOTE NOTE NOTE NOTE
In Skill 3, you'll see how to specify key fields in a table.

TABLE 2.1: How Keys Fields Determine the Nature of a Relationship

Linking Field Keyed In. . .	Results in This Type of Relationship
Both tables	One-to-one
One table	One-to-many
Neither table	Many-to-many

Indexes

As mentioned just above, Access automatically builds a primary index for a table using the key fields in the table's structure. You can create additional indexes to speed up searches on other fields you think you will search frequently. For example, in the Donations database, the Database Wizard creates an index for the DonorName field in the Contributors table. This results in quicker searches by name than if the DonorName field was unindexed.

NOTE NOTE NOTE NOTE NOTE NOTE NOTE NOTE NOTE NOTE NOTE NOTE NOTE NOTE NOTE
When you create a database yourself, you can add indexes to tables in the Table Design view window. You'll see how to do this in Skill 3.

One exception to this suggestion to create indexes applies when you are working with a small table. Adding an index to a non-key field in a table with hardly any records is probably not worth the effort it takes to set it up. If you are working in a table with lots of records, however, indexes will make a big difference in how long it takes to search non-key fields.

While you are planning a database, make a note of any fields you think you should index when you create your tables.

Consider How You Want Data Entered

The next task in planning a database involves defining rules for how you want data entered in your tables. It's important to enter data consistently for these reasons:

Linking Values   Values in linking fields need to be controlled so you don't end up with orphan records. For example, Access won't match records where the Product ID is "a1234" in one table and "A 1234" in another.

Grouping and Sorting Records   If values like names are entered differently in different records, Access won't be able to group or sort the records as you might expect. To Access, "Los Angeles" is a completely different value than "L.A." or "Hollywood."

Appearance   When data is entered inconsistently, there's not too much you can do to make it look good on a form or in a report.

There are some tricks you can use to doctor data after it's entered in a table, but it's much easier to set up limits on field values ahead of time. Fortunately, Access has several features you can use to control data entry. Some of them are described next. Skill 3 shows how to actually implement these features when you are creating tables.

NOTE NOTE NOTE NOTE NOTE NOTE NOTE NOTE NOTE NOTE NOTE NOTE NOTE NOTE NOTE

See Skill 8, "Master Advanced Queries," for examples of how to reformat data using Update queries. For example, you can use an Update query to change all the values in a field to uppercase letters or do things like split names into separate values for FirstName and LastName fields.

Fill In Default Values

If a field will usually, but not always, hold the same value, you can assign a *default value* for it. When you plan a database, peruse your list of fields to see if using a default value for any of them would save data-entry time. For example, in the Project Hours table, you could assign a default value of "Regular work" to the Description field. You can also use Access Visual Basic functions for default values. If you use Date( ) as the default value for a field, Access will put today's date in that field in any new record. See Skill 3 for some examples of handy default values.

SKILL
2

Check Data against Input Masks

Input masks provide a couple of different kinds of data-entry checks. They can:

- Make sure a field value matches a pattern, such as 000-00-0000 for a social security number

- Automatically fill in constant characters like dashes (-) or parentheses (())

- Optionally show placeholders to make data entry easier

- Store data with or without constants, depending on your preference

Adding an input mask to a field is easy because there's a wizard to guide you through the process. Skill 3 shows you how to add a predefined input mask, or one you define yourself, to a field.

Look Up a Value from a List or Table

To get good summary information from a database, some fields usually need to be limited to a certain set of values. For example, in the Timekeeper database, it would be a good idea to verify that a valid set of initials from a table of Employee records is entered in the Person field. You could also check that anything entered in the Project field has a matching entry in a table of Projects. There are a couple ways to do this with the Lookup Wizard when you are designing a table. You can:

- Limit a value to those that appear in a field in a table or query

- Check a value against a list of allowable entries that you define

Lookup fields have another benefit in addition to checking what's entered in a field against a set of values. When you create a lookup field that gets its possible values from a table, Access automatically defines a relationship between the main table and the lookup table. This makes it easy to include descriptive fields from the lookup table in forms and reports. For example, if you add a table for Projects to the Timekeeper database, you can include fields like Project Start Date, Project Manager, and so on, in the new table. Then you can show these fields in any report for the Project Hours table, assuming the Projects and Projects Hours tables are linked on a common field like ProjectID.

TIP TIP TIP TIP TIP TIP TIP TIP TIP TIP TIP TIP TIP TIP TIP TIP TIP TIP TIP TIP TIP TIP TIP TIP TIP

When you are still in the planning phase, look to see which fields in your database should be checked using a lookup against a table, a query, or some other list of values. Skill 3 explains how to use the Lookup Wizard to add these controls.

Validation Rules

There's another data-entry check you can apply to a field called a *validation rule*. A validation rule is a statement that checks whether data conforms to some rule after it is entered. When you set up a validation rule, you can also specify a message for Access to show when a value is entered that violates the rule. This book won't go into detail on how to use validation rules (they can be pretty tricky to set up), but you can look them up in Access Help if you think they would be useful for your database.

A Working Plan for Tables and Fields

With the previous information in mind, you can create a fairly detailed plan for the tables and fields that are needed in a database. Table 2.2 lists the fields for the Timekeeper database along with special properties, like indexes and lookups, the fields should have.

TABLE 2.2: Fields for the Timekeeper Database

Table	Field	Type	Key	Index	Default Value	Input Mask	Lookup
Weekly Records	Weekly-RecordID	AutoNumber	Yes				
	Person	Text		Yes		LL?*	Employees table
	WeekEnding-Date	Date/Time					
	EntryDate	Date/Time			Date( )		
Project Hours	RecordID	AutoNumber	Yes				
	Weekly-RecordID	Number					Weekly Records table
	ProjectID	Number		Yes			Projects table
	Hours	Number					
	Description	Text (or Memo)			"Regular work"		
Employees	EmployeeID	Text	Yes			LL?*	
	FirstName	Text					

TABLE 2.2: Fields for the Timekeeper Database *(continued)*

Table	Field	Type	Key	Index	Default Value	Input Mask	Lookup
	LastName	Text					
Projects	ProjectID	AutoNumber	Yes				
	Name	Text					
	Start Date	Date/Time					
	Project Manager	Text					

*The input mask LL? allows for two or three letters to be entered in a field.

Plan Your Forms and Reports

Once you have a plan for your database tables, you can start on the forms and reports. First, gather any samples that are available to you and match the information on them to the fields in your tables to make sure you haven't forgotten a critical field or two. Also make notes on any calculated or summary fields that are needed on the forms or reports.

NOTE NOTE NOTE NOTE NOTE NOTE NOTE NOTE NOTE NOTE NOTE NOTE NOTE NOTE NOTE

If you need to show fields from more than one table on the same form or report, make sure that the tables have common fields. Then you can set up relationships between the tables. With the proper relationships in place, the Form and Report Wizards will let you include fields from multiple tables.

You don't have to answer the next couple of questions right away, but at some point you will have to consider them. You may want to wait until after you design your tables and start experimenting with the Form and Report Wizards and the Form and Report Design windows.

Can the Wizards Do the Job?

You may be able to use the Form and Report Wizards to create many of your database objects. If you can't use the wizard designs as is, you will probably be able to use them as a foundation for your work instead of starting from scratch. (Designing a form or report from a blank design window can be a tedious, thankless task.)

The key here is to select the right wizard design as the basis for each form or report. Check Skill 5, "Use AutoForms and the Form Wizard," and Skill 9, "Create and Customize Reports," to see examples of what the Form and Report Wizards can do for you.

Do You Need to Show Selected Data?

Sometimes, maybe most times, you will have to show a form or print a report for selected records in your database. There's more than one way to do this. You can:

- Base a form or report on a query. (See Skill 1 to find out what a query is, if you don't remember.)

- Include a filter in your form or report design. (Again, check Skill 1 if you want to find out what a filter is.)

- Use a WHERE statement to limit the records that you see. (Check Access 2000 Help for details on WHERE statements; they are not covered in this book.)

Review your list of forms and reports and make notes of how you want to limit the records that each document includes. Keep in mind that you can also prompt someone to enter criteria for a query. Skill 8, "Master Advanced Queries," explains how to do this with a parameter query.

NOTE NOTE NOTE NOTE NOTE NOTE NOTE NOTE NOTE NOTE NOTE NOTE NOTE NOTE NOTE
Remember: If you are using an Access project instead of a database, you will not be able to create queries from Access. You will have to set up SQL Server views to work with selected table records. You can create views with whatever SQL Server tools you are accustomed to working with, or using the Client Server Visual Design Tools that come with Access 2000.

Consider Whether You Need to Browse Data from the Web

If you want to let people browse the data in your Access database from the Web, you can use data access pages. (These objects were described briefly in Skill 1.) Data access pages are similar to Access forms, but they let you browse Access data using Internet Explorer 5. These pages are stored in their own HTML files, but can be viewed from within Access as well as with Internet Explorer.

If you decide you will need to create some of these special purpose objects, check Skill 13, "Create Web Pages with Access," for details on what to do next.

Think about Automation

This part of a database is really optional at this point, so you may want to move on to Skill 3 and check back here when you are ready to add time-saving razzle-dazzle to your database. But if you have the patience to continue planning, read these sections now to get some ideas on how you can automate your database with hyperlinks, command buttons, and macros.

Use Hyperlinks to Create a Mini Info Highway

Hyperlinks were briefly described in Skill 1, "Access Basics." To refresh your memory, you can use a hyperlink to do all these things:

- Jump to another object in the database you're working in.
- Jump to an object in another database.
- Open another Office file, like a Word document or an Excel spreadsheet.
- Jump to a site on the Web.

Even if you don't need to browse the Web from your database, you may want to use hyperlinks to create your own personal information highway. Look at how you will be working with your database to see if you will want to do things like open one form from another or view a report while you have a form open.

What Will You Be Doing Over and Over Again?

Some database tasks can get pretty boring when you do them repeatedly. Thankfully, you can automate many of these tedious jobs with *command buttons* and *macros*. As part of your database plan, make a list of the jobs you'd like to automate after all your tables, forms, queries, reports, and any data access pages are in place. You may want to use command buttons and macros to:

- Print a report while you're viewing a form
- Print an entire group of reports with one mouse click
- Print a report for selected records and note the action in each record
- Open a form and show a specific record
- Update a field value conditionally after another field changes
- Close a form and return to what you were doing

- Perform a series of calculations on records in one or more tables and then view the results in a report

- Close the database you're working with and leave Access

Actions like the last one seem pretty easy (just click the Close button!), so you may wonder why it would be worth the effort to set up a command button. The main reason is to make it easy for someone who's not familiar with Access to use the database. Clicking a command button labeled "Add record" is easier for a new Access user than hunting through the toolbar to find the built-in button that does the same job.

NOTE NOTE NOTE NOTE NOTE NOTE NOTE NOTE NOTE NOTE NOTE NOTE NOTE NOTE NOTE

You'll find out how to create command buttons in Skill 14.

Now that you've gone through a whirlwind tour of how to plan a database, you can really get started using Access. Get ready to do some hands-on work in Skill 3, "Build Tables."

Are You Experienced?

Now you can. . .

- ☑ **Use the Database Wizard to create a new database**

- ☑ **Create a database yourself**

- ☑ **Choose tables for your database**

- ☑ **Decide on fields for your tables**

- ☑ **Plan how to make the best use of key fields and indexes when you create tables**

- ☑ **Consider whether to use default values, input masks, lookup tables, or other controls to make sure data is entered consistently**

- ☑ **Plan forms, reports, and data access pages**

- ☑ **Think about how to use hyperlinks, command buttons, and macros in your database**

Build Tables

- ⊖ **Find your style for creating tables**
- ⊖ **Use the Table Design window**
- ⊖ **Add key fields to a table**
- ⊖ **Use the Lookup Wizard to create drop-down lists**
- ⊖ **Include data checks in a table design**
- ⊖ **Add indexes to a table**
- ⊖ **Change a table's design**
- ⊖ **Define relationships between tables**

Find Your Style for Creating Tables

After you create a new database and formulate a plan for the objects you think you'll need to work with, the next step is to make some tables to hold your information.

If the data you need for your database already exists in another file, you may be able to import it or even link the existing file directly to your database. See Skill 11, "Import, Export, and Share Data," to see if you can use these features to save time you would otherwise spend creating tables and entering data. If you need to change tables that you import, see "Change a Table's Design" later in this chapter.

There's more than one way to create a table. You can use:

The Database Wizard to create a database that includes tables, forms, reports, queries, macros, and switchboards.

The Table Wizard to select a table design from a set of business or personal table templates. You are free to select and rename fields, and the wizard helps you define relationships if there is more than one table in the database.

Design view to have complete freedom to create the fields, keys, indexes, lookups, and other data-entry checks you need in a table.

Datasheet view to enter data into a spreadsheet-type view and have Access make its best guess as to the data types for the fields (columns) of the new table.

The Import Wizards to get help bringing data outside your database into Access tables.

With all these options, you may wonder which one is best for your project. Before exploring the primary skill covered in this chapter, using the Table Design window, take a quick look at each of these tools, except for the Import Wizards, which are covered in Skill 11. See Table 3.1 for a summary of what these options have to offer.

TABLE 3.1: Comparing the Database Wizard, the Table Wizard, and the Table Design Window

Can You. . .	With the Database Wizard	With the Table Wizard	With the Table Design Window
Choose fields	Optional fields only	Yes	Yes
Rename fields	No (you can do this later in Design view)	Yes	Yes
Move fields	No (you can do this later in Design view)	Yes	Yes
Create a key field	Automatically	Optionally	Manually
Relate tables	Automatically	Optionally	Manually
Add your own data-entry checks	No (you have to add them in Design view)	No (you have to add them in Design view)	Yes
Get forms, reports, switchboards	Yes	No (you have to create them yourself)	No (you have to create them yourself)

SKILL
3

The Database Wizard

As you learned in Skill 2, "Plan a Database," the Database Wizard can create an entire database for you, complete with tables, forms, reports, queries, switchboards, and even relationships defined behind the scenes. You do have to trade some flexibility, though, to get all this work done for you. The designs for the forms and reports created by the Database Wizard expect to find certain fields in the database tables. Because of this, you don't get a chance to rename or delete fields while the Database Wizard creates a new database for you.

You are free to add optional fields to some tables, but you can't alter the backbone of a table's design until the Database Wizard completes its work. Once a database is created by the Database Wizard, you can make changes to its tables using the Table Design window. If you opt to do this, though, be careful not to change any fields that are used to link tables. You can see which fields are linked in a database by using Tools ➤ Relationships.

The Database Wizard can create several different database projects for you. You can choose from these databases in the New dialog box shown in Figure 3.1.

Asset Tracking	Ledger
Contact Management	Order Entry
Event Management	Resource Scheduling
Expenses	Service Call Management
Inventory Control	Time and Billing

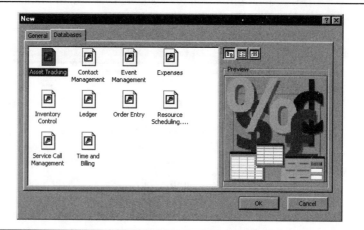

FIGURE 3.1: If you click the Databases tab in the New dialog box, you can select from several different projects.

NOTE NOTE NOTE NOTE NOTE NOTE NOTE NOTE NOTE NOTE NOTE NOTE NOTE NOTE

The process of creating a database with the Database Wizard was described in Skill 2, "Plan a Database." If you need detailed instructions on using the Database Wizard, please refer back to that skill. If you're still not sure whether the Database Wizard will work for you, refer back to Table 3.1 for a comparison of what you can do with the Database Wizard, the Table Wizard, and the Table Design window.

If the Database Wizard is too limiting for your needs, you can turn to the Table Wizard or go directly to the Table Design window to work on your own. The Table Wizard is discussed next.

The Table Wizard

The Table Wizard can be a great time-saver when you are creating tables. It lets you:

- Choose a table from lists of business or personal samples
- Select fields for a table
- Rename the fields and change their order
- Choose a key field
- Get help relating a table to other tables in the same database

Try creating a few tables with the Table Wizard to see how it works. To begin, create a new database called Timekeeper to hold your work:

1. Click New and choose File ➤ New from the menu, or press Ctrl+N.

2. Leave Database highlighted on the General tab in the New dialog box and click OK.

3. Enter **Timekeeper** in the File New Database dialog box and select Create.

Access will open a Database window:

Create a Table with the Table Wizard

To start the Table Wizard, follow these steps:

1. Click the Tables button in the Database window.

2. Double-click Create Table By Using Wizard in the middle of the window. You'll see the opening dialog box of the Table Wizard.

3. Select Business or Personal to narrow down the Sample Tables list. For this example, leave it set to Business.

4. Highlight your choice on the Sample Tables list. This will change the selections on the Sample Fields list. Select Employees to create one of the tables we need for the Timekeeper database.

5. To add a field to the Fields In My New Table list, highlight its name on the Sample Fields list and click the > button. You can click the >> button to add the entire list of sample fields at once, if you think you want to use all or most of them. For the Employees table in the Timekeeper database, select

the fields shown in Figure 3.2. There are a few extra fields that weren't in the plan you came up with in Skill 2, but it's fine to add them at this point. Title, EmailName, and WorkPhone are fields from the sample table that may end up being useful in the Timekeeper reports.

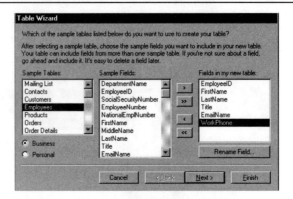

FIGURE 3.2: When you select a table in the first step of the Table Wizard, it changes the fields you can select on the Sample Fields list. This Table Wizard dialog box shows fields selected for a table called Employees.

6. If you want to rename a field, highlight the field on the Fields In My New Table list and click Rename Field. In the Rename Field dialog box, change the name as you like and click OK. (The rules for naming fields are discussed later in this chapter.)

7. Click Next after you complete the Fields In My New Table list.

8. Change the table name in the next step if you need to. For the Timekeeper example, leave it as Employees.

9. If you want to choose your own key field(s), select No, I'll Set The Primary Key. Otherwise, leave Yes, Set A Primary Key For Me selected. For the Employees table, let the Table Wizard make the choice for you.

10. Click Next.

11. In the last step, you can choose how you want to open the new table. Select:

> **Modify the table design** to open the table in Design view so you can make changes.

Enter data directly into the table to open the table in Datasheet view so you can enter data.

Enter data into the table using a form. . . to have the wizard create a basic form and open the table in Form view so you can enter data.

For the Employees table in the Timekeeper database, select the last choice to create a new form.

12. Click Finish after choosing how you want the new table opened.

If you followed along with the example, you'll see a form window called Employees open on the Access Desktop. You don't need to enter data into this table yet, since there is more to learn about table design. So just click the form's Close button, select Yes, and choose OK to save the new form.

NOTE NOTE NOTE NOTE NOTE NOTE NOTE NOTE NOTE NOTE NOTE NOTE NOTE NOTE
Skill 4, "Enter, View, Find, and Sort Data," explains the ins and outs of entering data in a table.

Relate Tables with the Table Wizard

As mentioned in Skills 1 and 2, Access lets you create relationships between tables so you can use them together. The Table Wizard can assist you with this process. To see how this works, create another table called Weekly Records for the Timekeeper database with the wizard's help. Because another table already exists in the database, the Table Wizard will give you a chance to relate the new table to the other one:

1. Click the Table button in the Database window if it's not already selected.

2. Double-click Create Table By Using Wizard, or click the New button and double-click Table Wizard in the New Table dialog box.

3. In the first Table Wizard step, leave Business selected and highlight Projects on the Sample Tables list.

4. Add these fields to the Fields In My New Table list and rename them as noted:

ProjectID   Rename this field WeeklyRecordID.

EmployeeID

ProjectEndDate   Rename this field WeekEndDate.

You should end up with a dialog box that looks like this:

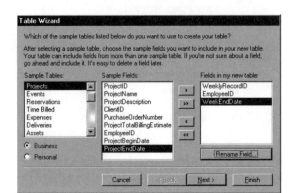

You may have noticed that the field names being used here vary slightly from the plan in Skill 2. This is fine, as it is helpful to work with the wizard's default names as much as possible.

5. Click Next.

6. Change the table name to Weekly Records and click Next.

7. This next step is where the Table Wizard helps you relate the new table to other tables in the database. Because the new table includes a field called EmployeeID, the Table Wizard will automatically establish a relationship to the Employees tables you created earlier:

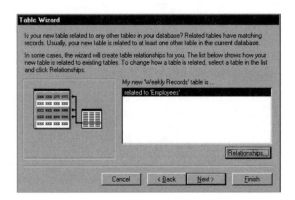

To see how the wizard has related the tables, click the Relationships button. Figure 3.3 shows that the Employees table has a one-to-many relationship to the new table. The Table Wizard comes to this conclusion because the EmployeeID field is keyed in the Employees table. This means that the Employees table can have only one record for each EmployeeID. However, there can be any number of records in the Weekly Records table for the same EmployeeID with different week-ending dates.

8. Click OK when you are finished checking the Relationships dialog box.

9. Click Next when you return to the Table Wizard.

10. Select Enter Data Into The Table Using A Form… and click Finish.

11. Click the Close button for the new form.

12. Choose Yes and then OK to save the new form with the same name as the new table, Weekly Records.

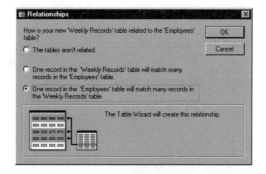

FIGURE 3.3: The Relationships dialog box, which you open from the Table Wizard, lets you change the way the wizard has chosen to relate tables.

You still need to make a few changes to the Employees and Weekly Records tables in keeping with the plan outlined in Skill 2. In the Design window, you need to:

- Add a field called Entry Date to the Weekly Records table

- Tell Access to automatically place today's date in the Entry Date field

- Change the data type for the EmployeeID field to text and the length to 3, if the Table Wizard assigned AutoNumber or some other type that won't allow us to enter initials

- Add a data-entry check in the form of an input mask to the EmployeeID field to make sure that two or three uppercase letters are entered for the employee's initials

The "Use the Table Design View Window" section later in this chapter contains all the information you need to figure out how to make these changes yourself. If you want to follow along with the examples in the rest of this book on your own computer, you should use the Table Design view window (described next) to create the other tables for the Timekeeper database you planned in Skill 2.

Table Design View

The Table Design view window is another place you can create new tables with Access. It's a completely different kind of tool than the Table Wizard. Instead of choosing fields from a predefined list, you enter whatever fields you like and select the data types for each field. The Table Design window is also the place where you add properties like default values, input masks, and lookups to fields.

Figure 3.4 shows the Table Design window for the Weekly Records table that was created with the Table Wizard in the last example.

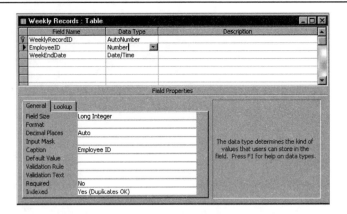

FIGURE 3.4: In Table Design view, you can create a new table or change a table's design. This window shows the design for the Weekly Records table created by the Table Wizard.

 TIP TIP TIP TIP TIP TIP TIP TIP TIP TIP TIP TIP TIP TIP TIP TIP TIP TIP TIP TIP TIP TIP

No matter what method you use to create a table, you can always open it later in Table Design view to make changes or check its structure.

The Table Design view window will be used in another example to create a new table from scratch. You'll also see how to use it to make changes to a table's design.

Before you get into all the features of the Table Design view window in "Use the Table Design View Window" later in this chapter, take a quick look at one other way to create tables in Access.

Datasheet View

When you open a table in Access, you see your data arranged in rows (records) and columns (fields). This is called *Datasheet view*. Access has a neat feature that lets you enter data directly into an empty Datasheet view window to create a new table. You can bypass the Database Wizard, the Table Wizard, and even the Table Design view window, if you're lucky. When you create a table this way, Access takes a look at the data you enter in the various columns of the Datasheet view window, and then makes its best guess as to what types of fields the new table should have.

To create a table in Datasheet view:

1. Select the Tables button in the Database window.

2. Double-click Create Table By Entering Data. (You can also click the New button and double-click Datasheet View in the New Table dialog box.)

3. Access will open an empty Datasheet view window that looks like this:

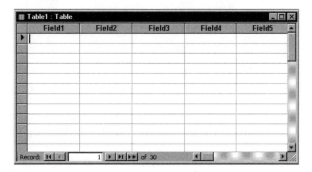

4. Start entering data in the Datasheet view, making sure you enter the values for each field in their own column. For example, to create the Weekly Records table for the Timekeeper database using this technique, enter initials for EmployeeIDs in Field1, WeekEndDates in Field2, and EntryDates in Field3. (Don't bother entering values for a WeeklyRecordID field. Access

can add ID numbers for you, as you'll see in a minute.) You'll end up with a datasheet like this:

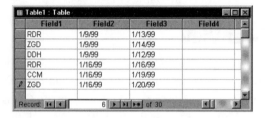

5. To give a column a more descriptive name than the default Field*n*, right-click the field header and choose Rename Column. Edit the field name right in the field header area and press Enter. You can change the field names shown in the last step to EmployeeID, WeekEndDate, and EntryDate. The Datasheet view now has field names as shown here:

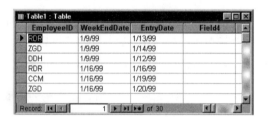

6. To create the new table, click the Close button for the Datasheet view, choose Yes, enter a table name, and click OK.

7. Access will ask if you want to create a primary key. Click Yes to have Access add a key field called ID with the AutoNumber type.

Figure 3.5 shows the Table Design view window for a table created in Datasheet view using the field names shown in step 4 above. As you can see, Access has included a key field called ID. The EmployeeID field has the Text field type, and the WeekEndDate and EntryDate fields both have the Date/Time field type. Access was able to assign these field types by looking at what was entered in each column of the Datasheet view.

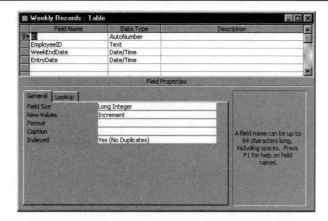

FIGURE 3.5: This table was created in Datasheet view. Access added the ID field automatically and assigned the Text and Date/Time field types to the other fields after looking at what was entered in each column.

Use the Table Design View Window

In the Table Design view window, you can create a new table or change a table's design. Next you'll see how to:

- Create a new table

- Add fields to a table, insert them, delete them, and move them

- Define key fields and remove them, in case you change your mind about the fields that should be keyed for a table

- Assign input masks, default values, or validation rules to fields

- Set up indexes

- Use the Lookup Wizard to make sure a field's values match those in another table or query (or in some list of values you enter)

Create a New Table in Design View

To create a new table with the Table Design view window, follow these steps:

1. Select the Tables button in the Database window.

2. Double-click Create Table In Design View(or click New to open the New Table dialog box and double-click Design View). You'll see an empty Table Design view window like the one in Figure 3.6.

3. Add fields and field properties as described in the next few sections.

4. Click the Close button for the Table Design view window, choose Yes, enter a name for the new table, and click OK.

5. If Access asks if you want to define a primary key, choose Yes to add an AutoNumber key field. Choose No if you want to create your own key field later or leave the table unkeyed. In either case, you will be returned to the Database window. The new table name will appear on the list of objects in the Database window when Tables is selected.

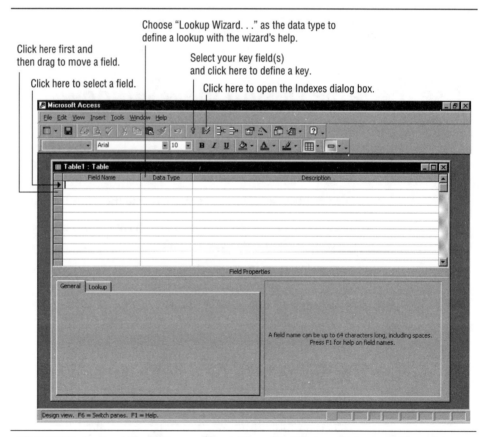

FIGURE 3.6: When you create a table using Design view, you will work in a Table Design view window that looks like this.

Add a Field

The first thing you need to do in an empty Table Design view window is add some fields. It's easy to do:

1. Enter a name in the first row under Field Name. A field name can be up to 64 characters long and can contain letters, numbers, spaces, and other characters except for periods (.), exclamation points (!), accent graves, (`), and brackets ([ ]). For other naming restrictions, see Access Help.

2. Move to the Data Type column and choose a data type for the field. You can enter a type yourself or choose it from the drop-down list of data types. (The arrow for this drop-down list is visible only after you move the cursor to a box in the Data Type column.) The Access data types are described in Skill 2 in the section on choosing fields for a table.

3. If you choose Text or Number for the data type, the field will have a Field Size property. The default length for Text fields is 50; the default Field Size setting for Number fields is Long Integer. To change this property, make sure the General tab is selected in the bottom half of the Table Design view window. Then, for a Text field, click the line after Field Size and change the size. For a Number field, click the Field Size line and use the drop-down arrow to choose a different setting (Byte, Integer, Long Integer, Single, Double, or Replication ID).

4. To add another field, move the cursor to the Field Name column in the next row and repeat steps 1–3.

TIP TIP TIP TIP TIP TIP TIP TIP TIP TIP TIP TIP TIP TIP TIP TIP TIP TIP TIP TIP TIP TIP TIP TIP

To change the default size for Text and Number fields, choose Tools ➢ Options, click the Tables/Queries tab, and change the settings for Default Field Sizes.

WARNING WARNING WARNING WARNING WARNING WARNING WARNING WARNING

If you join a Number field to an AutoNumber field to relate two tables, leave the Field Size for the Number field set to Long Integer. Otherwise, Access will not be able to link the fields.

Move a Field

Once a field is added to a table's design, you are free to move it to a new location:

1. Click the row selector to the left of the field's name to select the field. (You can click and drag at this point to select multiple fields.)

2. Point your mouse to the selected field(s) and drag to a new spot. A small dotted rectangle will appear to the lower right of the mouse pointer while you are dragging, and you will see a thin horizontal line above the last selected field.

Insert a Field

To insert a field in the field list, instead of adding a field to the end of the list:

1. Click the row selector of the field that will appear below the inserted field.

2. Press Insert or click the Insert Rows button on the toolbar.

3. Enter a field name and data type for the new field in the blank row that is inserted.

TIP TIP TIP TIP TIP TIP TIP TIP TIP TIP TIP TIP TIP TIP TIP TIP TIP TIP TIP TIP TIP TIP TIP TIP TIP
You can also insert or delete fields in Datasheet view. See "Make Changes in Datasheet View" later in this chapter for details.

Delete a Field

It's easier to delete a field than to add one!

1. Select the field(s) you want to delete.

2. Press Delete or click the Delete Rows button on the toolbar.

If you make a mistake, you can use Edit ➤ Undo Delete right after you delete to get the fields back. If you make another change, however, you will not be able to use Undo to get the field back. The only way to recover the field, if the table was previously saved, is to close the Table Design view window and cancel all your changes to the table's design.

Add Key Fields

Key fields were covered in Skill 2. In a nutshell, the *key* for a table must have a unique value for each record in the table. A key can consist of more than one field and is used to generate a *primary index* for the table. The primary index speeds up searches on the key field(s) and is used to determine the nature of a relationship when it is used to join tables (one-to-one or one-to-many).

With that speedy review out of the way, let's see how to actually key one or more fields in a table:

1. Click the row selector for the field you want to key. (Click and drag if you want to select contiguous fields for the key, or hold down the Ctrl key while you click fields that do not follow each other.)

2. Click the Primary Key button on the toolbar or choose Edit ➢ Primary Key.

When a field is keyed, it will have a small key in its row selector, as does the WeeklyRecordID field shown here:

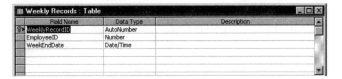

NOTE NOTE NOTE NOTE NOTE NOTE NOTE NOTE NOTE NOTE NOTE NOTE NOTE NOTE NOTE

When you use a query to append records into a table that has an AutoNumber key field, Access will automatically assign key values to the new records. However, if you append records to a table with another type of key field(s), you will have to make sure that each new record has a unique value in the key field(s). If there are records that don't have unique keys, Access will not append them.

Remove Key Fields

To remove a key field or fields:

1. Click the row selectors to select the key field(s).

2. Click the Primary Key button on the toolbar or choose Edit ➢ Primary Key.

The small key in the row selector(s) will disappear. The Primary Key button on the toolbar, just like the Edit ≻ Primary Key menu command, works as a toggle to turn key fields on or off.

Add Drop-Down Lists with the Lookup Wizard

If you want to use a drop-down list to limit what can be entered in a field, it's time to use the Lookup Wizard. The Lookup Wizard can help you create a drop-down list from values in a table or a query, or from a list of values you specify.

In addition to limiting the values that can be entered in a field, a drop-down list also offers these benefits:

- You don't have to remember the valid entries for a field since they are shown on the drop-down list.

- If you bypass the drop-down list and start typing, Access fills in the first value from the list that matches the character(s) you enter. As you continue typing, Access changes the value to reflect your changes. This saves data-entry time.

- You can type the first few characters of a value and then open the drop-down list to move to the first entry that matches what you type. This allows you to avoid scrolling through a lengthy list and is a convenient way to navigate through a long list of values that are sorted alphabetically.

- Using a drop-down list ensures that data gets entered in a uniform manner.

Let's use the Lookup Wizard to show the EmployeeID field in the Weekly Records table in the Timekeeper database as a drop-down list. The list will only show values that already exist in the EmployeeID field in the Employees table.

NOTE NOTE NOTE NOTE NOTE NOTE NOTE NOTE NOTE NOTE NOTE NOTE NOTE NOTE NOTE

Before following the steps below, make sure that you have created an Employees table like the one described in "Create a Table with the Table Wizard" earlier in this chapter. You will also have to open the table in Table Design view and change the data type of the EmployeeID field from AutoNumber to a Text field with a length of 3. Then open the Employees table and add records for any EmployeeIDs you have already entered in the Weekly Records table. Otherwise, Access will not allow the old records to remain in the Weekly Records table after the lookup is added to the EmployeeID field.

NOTE NOTE NOTE NOTE NOTE NOTE NOTE NOTE NOTE NOTE NOTE NOTE NOTE NOTE
If you haven't yet entered records in the Weekly Records table, you don't have to worry about entering matching records in the Employees table.

1. Open the Weekly Records table in Table Design view. (Right-click the table's name in the Database window and choose Design.)

2. Move to the Data Type for the EmployeeID field.

3. Select Lookup Wizard. . . from the list of Data Types to start the wizard.

4. In the first step, make sure the first option, "I Want the Lookup Column to Look Up the Values in a Table or Query," is selected and click Next.

5. Select Employees on the list of tables in the next dialog box and click Next.

6. Highlight EmployeeID on the Available Fields list and click the > button to move this field over to the Selected Fields list. Add the FirstName and Last-Name fields, too, to show them on the drop-down list. Then click Next.

7. In the next dialog box, you can change the column widths that will show up on the drop-down list. (Drag the right border of a field's header to resize it or double-click the right border to have the column fit all its values.) You can also "unhide" the key field (the EmployeeID field) so it will appear on the drop-down list. If you want to see the EmployeeID, uncheck the Hide Key Column option and click Next.

8. If you unchecked Hide Key Column in the last step, you will be asked to select a field that uniquely identifies each record. Leave EmployeeID selected and click Next. If you don't see this step, don't worry.

9. Change the label for the lookup column, if you want, and click Finish in the last step of the Lookup Wizard.

10. Choose Yes when Access asks if you want to save changes to the table before it creates relationships.

To see how the new lookup works, click Datasheet View on the toolbar (assuming you are still in Design view) and move the cursor to the EmployeeID field. You will see a drop-down arrow appear at the right side of the field. Click this arrow to see a list of the records in the Employees table. If you get an empty drop-down list, the Employees table has no records. Add some names to the Employees table and try the drop-down list for the Weekly Records table again. Figure 3.7 shows the

EmployeeID drop-down list after it was opened in Datasheet view for the Weekly Records table.

FIGURE 3.7: This drop-down list for the EmployeeID field in the Weekly Records table was created with the Lookup Wizard. It draws its values from the EmployeeID, FirstName, and LastName fields in the Employees table.

 NOTE NOTE NOTE NOTE NOTE NOTE NOTE NOTE NOTE NOTE NOTE NOTE NOTE NOTE NOTE

If you want to sort the values on a drop-down list, use a query that includes a sort as the basis of the list. See Skill 7, "Find Data with Queries and Filters," to see how to sort records with a query.

Create Your Own Values for a Drop-Down List

In the first step of the Lookup Wizard, you can choose to create your own list of lookup values instead of using a table or query for the list. To create your own list, follow these steps:

1. In the Table Design view window, choose Lookup Wizard. . . as the data type for the field you want to add a lookup to.

2. In the first step of the Lookup Wizard, select "I Will Type in the Values that I Want" and click Next.

3. In the next step, enter the number of columns you want to see on the drop-down list (the default is 1). Then enter the values for the drop-down list in the columns shown in the dialog box. Click Next when you are finished.

4. If you used more than one column in step 3, choose the field that uniquely identifies each record on the lookup list and click Next.

5. Change the label for the drop-down list, if you like, and click Finish.

TIP TIP TIP TIP TIP TIP TIP TIP TIP TIP TIP TIP TIP TIP TIP TIP TIP TIP TIP TIP TIP TIP TIP TIP

It's best to use this option when the number of lookup values is small and the values won't change frequently. If the lookup values for a field are likely to change, or you have a long list of possible values, you should probably take the time to enter them in a table before starting the Lookup Wizard. It's easier to edit a long list of lookup values in a table than in the Table Design view window.

If You Need to Revise the Lookup Wizard's Work

After you set up a drop-down list with the Lookup Wizard, you can revise the resulting list two ways. You can do either of the following:

- Open the table in Design view and rerun the Lookup Wizard.

- Use the Lookup tab in the bottom of the Table Design view window and edit the various lookup properties.

If you need to change the source of lookup values or the columns that are shown on the drop-down list, it's probably best to rerun the Lookup Wizard. To do this, just click the Data Type box for the field you want to change and select Lookup Wizard from the list of data types. Then follow the wizard as described just above.

If you need to edit a list of values you supplied, or perhaps change the width of a column on the drop-down list, you can edit the Lookup properties directly:

1. Select the field with the lookup to make sure you are looking at the right stuff.

2. Click the Lookup tab in the bottom half of the Table Design view window.

You'll see some cryptic properties like Bound Column and other not-so-mysterious entries like Column Count and Column Widths. It's OK to edit these entries directly if you are cautious. Adjusting the column width property is not too dangerous, but be careful if you play with the others. You may have to start the Lookup Wizard over again if you end up with a mess!

Specify a Default Value for a Field

If you have a field that will hold the same value all the time, or most of the time, you can use the *Default Value* property to fill in the field automatically whenever a new record is added to a table.

To assign a default value to a field:

1. In the Table Design view window, click the field you want to define a default value for.

2. Select the General tab in the bottom half of the Table Design view window.

3. On the General tab, click the line for Default Value.

4. Enter the value you want to use for the default. You can use either a constant value or a Visual Basic function as explained below.

Figure 3.8 shows a default value in the Table Design view window for a field called Description. The Description field is selected in the top half of the window and "Regular work" is entered for the Default Value on the General tab.

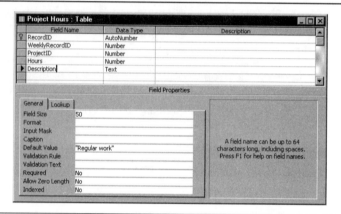

FIGURE 3.8: In this Table Design view window for the Project Hours table, a default value of "Regular work" is assigned to the field Description.

Use a Constant for a Default Value

The default value for the Description field in Figure 3.8, "Regular work," is called a *constant*. A constant value always remains the same. To enter a constant in the Default Value box for a field, just type it in, unless it includes punctuation like periods or commas. If this is the case, you need to enclose the value in quotes as in "L.A." to make sure Access doesn't try to interpret it as a Visual Basic function. Otherwise, don't worry about the quotes. Access will add them to whatever value you enter as soon as you leave the Default Value box.

Use a Function to Derive a Default Value

You can also use a Visual Basic function for a default field value. A *function* is a bit of programming code that is designed to return a certain type of value. For example, the function Date() returns the current date from your computer's clock. The Now() function is similar to Date(), but it returns the current date and time. To automatically timestamp a Date/Time type field with today's date, just use Date() as the field's default value, as shown for the WeekEndDate field in Figure 3.9.

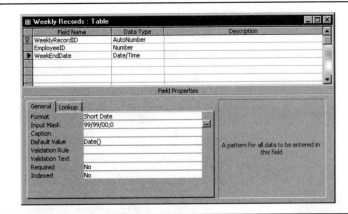

FIGURE 3.9: The Visual Basic function Date() is used as the default value for the WeekEndDate field in this example. Whenever a new record is added to the Weekly Records table, Access places the current date in the WeekEndDate field.

Create Input Masks

Using an *input mask* is another way to limit what can be entered in a field. An input mask can do a couple of different things:

- It forces you to enter field values in a pattern such as 999-99-9999 or 415-555-5543.

- It can fill in constant characters like dashes (-) and slashes (/), and optionally store these characters as part of the field value so you don't have to enter them yourself.

Figure 3.9 (see above) shows an input mask for the WeekEndDate field that automatically fills in the slashes as dates are entered.

To add an input mask to a field:

1. In the Table Design view window, click the field that the input mask will belong to.

2. In the bottom half of the window, click the line for Input Mask.

3. You can enter an input mask yourself or click the ". . ." at the end of the Input Mask line to get help from the Input Mask Wizard for Text and Date/Time fields.

Use the Input Mask Wizard

The Input Mask Wizard lets you choose from a list of built-in masks that are included with Access. The list the wizard shows you depends on the type of field you are setting up a mask for. For a Text field, you'll see a list like this:

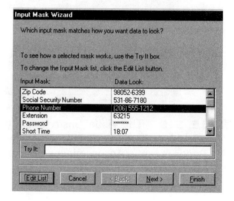

To use the Input Mask Wizard, follow these steps:

1. Start the Input Mask Wizard for a Text or Date/Time field as described in the last section.

2. Highlight the mask you want to use (e.g., Zip Code, Phone Number, etc.).

3. Click Next.

4. In the next dialog box, change the input mask and the placeholder character, if you need to. (The rules for creating input masks are outlined in the next section, "Create Your Own Input Masks.") Then click Next.

5. The next step asks whether you want Access to store constant characters like dashes and slashes with the field value. Make your choice and click Finish. (There's nothing else to do in the last step, so you may as well finish here.)

See the Warning below for details on how your choice in this step can affect what happens when you look for data later.

WARNING WARNING WARNING WARNING WARNING WARNING WARNING WARNING

If you tell the Input Mask Wizard not to store constants with field values, you need to remember to leave out the constants when you do finds or queries. For example, if you have an input mask that automatically displays a zip code with a dash like this, *94002-0000*, but the dash is not stored in the Zip Code field, you have to enter *940020000* when you look for this zip code with a query or a find.

Create Your Own Input Masks

The built-in masks you can select using the Input Wizard are handy for zip codes, phone numbers, dates, and times. There's also a mask for entering hidden passwords. Beyond that, though, you're on your own. If you need to format other kinds of values (maybe product codes or tax codes), you'll have to create your own masks.

Creating an input mask is not difficult once you are familiar with the rules for setting one up. Basically, there are two things to be aware of:

- The three possible parts of a mask

- The way Access uses special characters in a mask to impose limits on what can be entered in a field

Check the sections below, "The Parts of an Input Mask" and "Input Mask Characters," if you need help formulating a mask.

The Parts of an Input Mask

An input mask can have up to three parts, separated by semicolons (;):

- The first part is the mask itself.

- The second part tells Access whether to store any constant characters with the field values. A 0 tells Access to store constants; a 1 or blank says not to.

- The third part lets you change the placeholder from an underscore (_) to some other character.

Take a look at the parts of the input mask in Figure 3.9, *99/99/00;0*. The *99* tells Access to check that numbers, not other characters, are entered in the first two places of the Date field value. The *9*, as explained in the next section, also says that the entry of the character is optional. (In this case, because the input mask is for a Date field, this means you can omit either the first or second character before the slash (/), but not both since you need at least one character each for the month and for the day.) The slashes are shown automatically, and the *00* says that two numbers must be entered after the second slash. Finally, the *;0* after the input mask tells Access to store the slashes with the field values. Since there is no third part in this example, the default placeholder (_) is used.

That's a lot of words to explain how a short input mask works. The best way to see how an input mask affects data entry is to try it. In the first dialog box of the Input Mask Wizard, select any input mask, click the Try It box, and enter a value to see how it gets checked by the mask.

Input Mask Characters

When you create an input mask, special characters tell Access how to limit the data that gets entered in a field. Table 3.2 lists the characters you can include in an input mask and describes their functions. To see some examples of how these characters work in a mask, check Table 3.3.

TABLE 3.2: Input Mask Characters

Use This Character. . .	To Check For. . .
0	Required number (0–9), no plus or minus signs
9	Optional number (0–9) or space, no plus or minus signs
#	Optional number or space, plus and minus signs allowed
L	Required letter (A–Z)
?	Optional letter (A–Z)
A	Required letter or number
a	Optional letter or number
&	Required character or space
C	Optional character or space
. , : ; - /	Decimal placeholder, number, and date/time separators; characters used depend on Windows Control Panel settings
<	Character that gets converted to lowercase
>	Character that gets converted to uppercase
!	A mask that displays from right to left, characters always entered left to right
\	Next character in mask to display as a constant

TABLE 3.3: Sample Input Masks

This Mask. . .	Allows These Field Values
(999)000-0000	(650)555-9999
	( )555-9999
>LL0000	AB0932
AAa	123
	12
	AB1
	AB
	1a
00000-9999	94000-0000
	94000-
000-00-0000	999-99-9999
>L<??????????	Melanie
	Benjamin

Enter Your Own Mask

Once you formulate an input mask, you can enter it two ways.

If you don't need the mask for other fields, just select the field the mask will belong to in the top half of the Table Design view window. Then, in the bottom half of the Table Design view window, click the General tab and type your mask on the Input Mask line on the General tab.

If you want to use the mask for other fields, add it to the Input Mask Wizard's list as described next.

Add a Mask to the Input Wizard's List

To add a mask you create to the Input Mask Wizard's list so you can use it for other fields in the future:

1. Start the Input Mask Wizard as described earlier.

2. In the first step of the Input Mask Wizard, click the Edit List button to show the Customize Input Mask Wizard dialog box:

Click here to add a mask to the Input Mask Wizard list.

3. To add a new mask, click the New Record navigation button (the one with the asterisk at the bottom of the Customize Input Mask Wizard window). You'll see a blank record (except for Mask Type) where you can enter your input mask and a description.

4. Type in a description and the input mask. If you want to show placeholders in the field for the mask, enter an underscore or other character in the box labeled Placeholder. Whatever you enter in the box for Sample Data will be shown in the Data Look column of the Input Mask Wizard dialog box. If you are creating a mask for a Date/Time field, change the setting for Mask Type to Date/Time. Otherwise, leave it set to Text/Unbound.

5. Click the Close button to return to the Input Mask Wizard dialog box.

When you return to the Input Mask Wizard dialog box, your new input mask will appear on the scrollable list in the middle of the window. You can then select it and try it out, just like one of the built-in masks.

Add Indexes to a Table

Access uses *indexes* to speed up finds and other operations where it has to look for data in one or more fields. Any table that is keyed automatically has a primary index created for its key field(s). You may want to create your own indexes for other fields that you search frequently to find records. Indexes are also good for non-key fields that you use to join tables or sort records. You can index using fields that have the Text, Number, Currency, or Date/Time type.

Create an Index Using One Field

To create an index for one field:

1. Select the field to be indexed in the top half of the Table Design view window.

2. In the bottom half of the window, select the General tab and click the line for Indexed.

3. Open the drop-down list for Indexed and select "Yes (Duplicates OK)" or "Yes (No Duplicates)," depending on whether there will be more than one record with the same value in the indexed field.

Create an Index with More Than One Field

You can create an index using up to ten fields. This type of multifield index is useful for queries or filters that search more than one field at the same time, and for tables that are joined on more than one field. To create a multifield index:

1. Click the Indexes button on the toolbar in the Table Design view window. You'll see an Indexes dialog box that looks something like this:

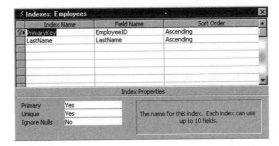

The Index Names you see will depend on the table you are working with. This Indexes dialog box for the Employees table shows a primary index based on the EmployeeID field and another index called LastName for the field with the same name.

2. To add an index, enter a name on the next blank line in the Index Name column.

3. Move to the next column, Field Name, and select the first field for the index from the drop-down list of field names.

4. Move down a row in the Field Name column and choose the second field for the index. You don't need to enter anything under Index Name on this line; just leave it blank.

5. Repeat step 4 for each additional field you want to include in the index.

6. If you want to make sure that the index does not have duplicate values, change the setting for Unique to Yes in the bottom half of the Indexes window. If there will be lots of records with blanks in the indexed fields, change Ignore Nulls to Yes to save disk space.

7. Close the Indexes dialog box to return to the Table Design view window.

Delete an Index

If you have many indexes for a table, it may actually slow down certain operations (like append queries) because of the time it takes Access to maintain the indexes. Also, if you index a field with many repeated values, the index may not do you much good. To get rid of an index that doesn't appear to be useful:

1. Click the Indexes button on the toolbar in the Table Design view window.

2. Click the row selector to the left of the name of the index you want to delete. If you are deleting a multifield index, hold down Shift and click the first and last rows for the index.

3. Press Delete.

4. Close the Indexes dialog box.

Save a Table's Design

To save your work in the Table Design view window, you can do any of the following:

- Choose File ➤ Save from the menu and enter a table name if the table hasn't already been named.

- Press Ctrl+S.

- Close the Table Design view window, choose Yes when Access asks if you want to save your changes, and enter a table name if needed.

- Click the View button to switch to Datasheet view and choose Yes to save your changes.

Change a Table's Design

Once you create a table, you are free to change its design. There are two different places you can make design changes:

> **Table Design view**   Use this view for any kind of revision including field name changes, field moves, data type and length changes, field additions and deletions, and index changes.

> **Datasheet view**   Use this view to insert or delete fields, rename fields, or add lookup fields.

Make Changes in the Design Window

To change a table's design in the Table Design view window, right-click the table's name in the Database window and choose Design from the shortcut menu that pops up. Or:

1. Click the Tables button in the Database window.

2. Select the name of the table you want to change. (Click it to highlight it.)

3. Click Design.

If you want to change a table that's already open in Datasheet view, just click the View button on the toolbar to switch to Design view.

Once you're in Design view, you can add, move, insert, or delete fields as described earlier in the "Use the Table Design View Window" section. You can also work with input masks, indexes, or any other table properties.

> **WARNING** WARNING WARNING WARNING WARNING WARNING WARNING WARNING
>
> **Access won't let you delete a field that is used to relate tables unless you delete the relationship first. (See "Define Relationships" later in this chapter for information on deleting and changing relationships between tables.)**

Rename a Field in Design View

To rename a field, just click the field's name and make your changes.

Be careful about changing field names if you've already created forms, reports, and queries. Access won't recognize the renamed fields and you'll have to do some repair work on your designs. To avoid this problem, turn on the new AutoCorrect feature before you make any changes to field names. Choose Tools ➢ Options, click the General tab, and click the boxes for Track Name AutoCorrect Info and Perform Name AutoCorrect under Name AutoCorrect. Then click OK to close the Options window.

Make Changes in Datasheet View

Some changes can be made to a table's design from a Datasheet view window. You can:

- Insert a field

- Delete a field

- Rename a field

- Insert a Lookup field

The quickest way to make these changes in Datasheet view is through the shortcut menu that comes up when you right-click a field header:

When you make changes to a table's design in Datasheet view, you won't be able to cancel your changes when you close the window. Each change is saved as soon as you make it.

Insert a Field in Datasheet View

To add a field to a table while you are working with it in Datasheet view:

1. Right-click the header (field name) of the field that will follow the new field.

2. Choose Insert Column from the shortcut menu that comes up. Access will create a new field called *Field1* (or *Fieldn* where *n* is the next available number).

3. Right-click the header of the new column (field) and choose Rename Column from the shortcut menu, or double-click the field name. The field name will be highlighted and the cursor will appear to the left of the field name.

4. Type in the name you want to use for the new column and press Enter.

After you start entering data in the new field, Access will make its best guess as to what data type should be assigned to the field. You can check the data type, and change it if need be, in the Table Design view window.

Skill 3

Delete a Field in Datasheet View

You can bypass going to the Design view window if you want to delete a field while you're working in Datasheet view:

1. Right-click the header of the field you want to delete.

2. Choose Delete Column from the shortcut menu.

3. Choose Yes to delete the field and all the data it contains from the table.

Rename a Field in Datasheet View

It's easy to rename a field in Datasheet view. Just double-click the field name to highlight it and make your changes. Or you can:

1. Right-click the field name you want to change.

2. Choose Rename Column from the shortcut menu.

3. Click the field name if you want to edit it, or just start typing to replace the name completely.

Insert a Lookup Field in Datasheet View

You can start the Lookup Wizard to create a drop-down field right from Datasheet view:

1. Right-click the header of the field after the place you want to insert the lookup field.

2. Choose Lookup Column. . . from the shortcut menu.

3. Follow along with the Lookup Wizard as described in "Add Drop-Down Lists with the Lookup Wizard" earlier in this chapter.

Define Relationships

In Skill 2's section on planning a database, you learned about table relationships and how Access uses them to link tables. You also learned about the types of relationships that can exist between tables (one-to-one, one-to-many, and many-to-many) and how they are determined by whether linking fields are keyed.

If you use the Database Wizard or the Table Wizard to create tables, you may not need to define any table relationships on your own. Also, when you use the Lookup Wizard to create a drop-down list that draws its values from a table, Access creates a relationship for you. Sometimes, though, you need to relate tables yourself. This task is performed in the Relationships window.

To open the Relationships window, choose Tools ➤ Relationships from the menu, or right-click anywhere in the Database window and select Relationships.

Figure 3.10 shows the Relationships window with two tables from the Time-keeper database used in some of the examples in this chapter: Employees and Weekly Records. The Table Wizard created this relationship between the Employees and Weekly Records tables using the EmployeeID field.

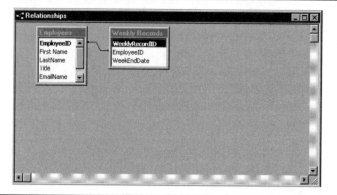

FIGURE 3.10: In the Relationships window, you can see how tables are related as well as define relationships, change referential integrity rules, and join types.

Add a Relationship

Now add another relationship to the window shown in Figure 3.10 to see how you can do this yourself. The following steps relate the Project Hours table to the Weekly Records table.

1. Open the Relationships window as described in the last section.

2. Click the Show Table button on the toolbar.

3. In turn, double-click the names of the tables you want to work with if they are not already visible in the Relationships window.

4. When all the tables you need have been added to the window, click Close in the Show Table dialog box.

5. Click the linking field in one table and drag the mouse pointer to the linking field in the related table. When you release the mouse, you'll see an Edit Relationships dialog box like this:

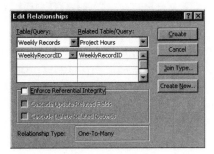

6. If you need to relate tables using more than one field, click the second row under Table/Query and choose the next field for the relationship from the drop-down list. Choose the linking field in the second row under Related Table/Query. Repeat this step for any additional pairs of fields you need to define the relationship.

7. Click Create to create the relationship. You'll see a line for the new relationship added to the Relationships window as in Figure 3.11.

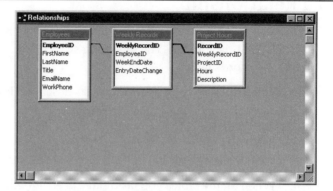

FIGURE 3.11: The line between the Weekly Records table and the Project Hours table shows that these tables are related on the WeeklyRecordID field.

Set Rules for Referential Integrity

In the Edit Relationships dialog box, you may have noticed a check box for Enforce Referential Integrity. *Referential integrity* is a way to protect data in linking fields so you don't end up with orphan records. You can turn this feature on or off in the Edit Relationships dialog box and set the rules for how referential integrity is enforced.

To turn referential integrity on:

1. Right-click the line that shows the relationship between two tables and choose Edit Relationship.

2. In the Edit Relationships dialog box, click the box for Enforce Referential Integrity.

3. Check any rules you want enforced:

   Cascade Update Related Fields changes the values in related records when the linking value in their master record is changed.

   Cascade Delete Related Fields deletes related records when the master record in a relationship is deleted.

4. Click OK to close the Edit Relationships dialog box.

If you have trouble getting a shortcut menu with the Edit Relationship choice, click the relationship line first to select it. It will appear as a bold line. Then right-click the line again. You should see a shortcut menu with the choices Edit Relationship and Delete.

Change the Join Type

When you do things like run queries to find records in related tables, by default Access looks for records that have matching values on both sides of the relationship. When records are matched up this way, it is referred to as an *inner join*. You can change the join type to an *outer join* so that Access includes all records from one side of the relationship, whether or not there are matching values in the linking fields on the other side of the relationship.

To change the join type:

1. Open the Edit Relationships dialog box as described earlier.

2. Click the Join Type button to show this dialog box:

3. Click 2 or 3, depending on which table you want to show all the records for.

4. Click OK to return to the Edit Relationships dialog box. Click OK again if you want to go back to the Relationships window.

Delete a Relationship

To delete a relationship:

1. In the Relationships window, right-click the line for the relationship you want to get rid of.

2. Choose Delete from the shortcut menu.

3. Choose Yes.

If you have trouble getting a shortcut menu with a selection for Delete, click the relationship line first to select it and right-click again.

Save Your Relationship Changes

To save any work you do in the Relationships window, just close the window and choose Yes.

Are You Experienced?

Now you can...

- ☑ **Find your own style for creating tables**
- ☑ **Use the Table Design window**
- ☑ **Add key fields to a table**
- ☑ **Use the Lookup Wizard**
- ☑ **Create input masks and use the Input Mask Wizard**
- ☑ **Add indexes to a table**
- ☑ **Save a table's design**
- ☑ **Change a table's design**
- ☑ **Define relationships between tables**

SKILL 4

Enter, View, Find, and Sort Data

- ➔ **Move through a table**
- ➔ **Use Subdatasheet views to see related records**
- ➔ **Edit a table**
- ➔ **Edit special fields like memos and date/times**
- ➔ **Enter hyperlink addresses and use them to jump to various types of documents**
- ➔ **Work with OLE objects**
- ➔ **Customize a Datasheet view**
- ➔ **Find records**
- ➔ **Sort records**

Once you create tables for a database, you can start entering data in them using Datasheet view or Form view. (To find out more about the differences between these views, see Skill 1.) In this skill, you'll learn how to work in Datasheet view to enter, view, find, and sort data. Later on, in Skills 5 and 6, you'll find out how to create forms and use them for the same purposes.

To open a table in Datasheet view from the Database window:

1. Click the Tables button if it's not already selected.

2. Double-click the name of the table you want to view.

You can also highlight a table's name and click Open, or right-click a table and choose Open. You'll see a Datasheet view window like the one in Figure 4.1.

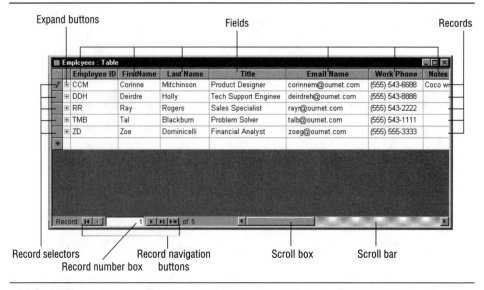

FIGURE 4.1: The Employees table is shown here in Datasheet view. Each row represents a record in the table, and each column corresponds to one of the table's fields.

Move through a Table

There are lots of ways to move around a table in Datasheet view. Some of them are pointed out in Figure 4.1. Use the:

- Horizontal scroll bar to scroll sideways through a table to change the fields that are visible, if they don't all fit in the window

- Vertical scroll bar to scroll through the records in a table if there are more records than will fit in the Datasheet view window

- Record navigation buttons to create a new record or move to the first, next, previous, or last record in the table

- Record Number box to enter the number of a record to move to

- Cursor movement keys like Tab, Enter, Page Up, Home, and End as described in Table 4.1

- Go To Field box on the Formatting (Datasheet) toolbar to move to a field you choose

You can probably figure out how to use these options on your own, but here are some brief descriptions anyway.

**SKILL
4**

Scroll Bars

Access includes scroll bars in a Datasheet view window if it can't display all the records or fields of a table at the same time. If you see a horizontal scroll bar, it means there are additional fields in the table. A vertical scroll bar means there are more records than you can see in the window.

The scroll bars can be used in these ways:

- Click the light area to scroll to the next group of records or fields that can be shown in the window.

- Click the arrow at the beginning of the scroll bar to scroll back one field or record.

- Click the arrow at the end of the scroll bar to scroll forward one field or record.

- Drag the scroll box along the scroll bar to move to a specific record. (The record number is shown just below the scroll box as you drag.)

NOTE NOTE NOTE NOTE NOTE NOTE NOTE NOTE NOTE NOTE NOTE NOTE NOTE NOTE NOTE

When you use the scroll bars to change the fields or records shown in Datasheet view, the cursor position doesn't change. Click the mouse on a new field, click the Record Navigation buttons, or use the cursor keys to move the cursor.

Record Navigation Buttons

Every Datasheet view window has a set of Record Navigation buttons in its lower-left corner that looks like this:

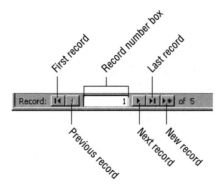

Click the First, Next, Previous, Last, or New Record button to move the cursor to a different record.

TIP TIP TIP TIP TIP TIP TIP TIP TIP TIP TIP TIP TIP TIP TIP TIP TIP TIP TIP TIP TIP TIP TIP TIP TIP TIP TIP

If you know the number of the record you want to move to, click the Record number box, change the record number and press Enter.

Cursor Movement Keys

If you prefer to leave your hands on the keyboard, you can press various keys to move the cursor instead of using your mouse. Table 4.1 lists the cursor movement keys you can use in Datasheet view and explains what each key does.

TABLE 4.1: Keys You Can Use to Move in Datasheet View

Press This Key. . .	To Move to the. . .
Enter	Next field
Tab	Next field
Shift+Tab	Previous field
Right arrow	Next field
Left arrow	Previous field
Up arrow	Same field in the previous record
Down arrow	Same field in the next record
Home	First field in current record
End	Last field in current record
Ctrl+Home	First field in first record
Ctrl+End	Last field in last record
Page Down	Same field in the first record of the next group of records
Page Up	Same field in the first record of the previous group of records

The Go To Field Box

When you have lots of fields in a table, it may be tedious to use the horizontal scroll bar to find the field you need to work with. Here's a shortcut you can use to get there quickly, assuming you know the name of the field you want:

1. If the Formatting toolbar is not visible, right-click any toolbar that you can see and select Formatting (Datasheet). You'll see a new toolbar added to the Access Desktop:

Go To Field box

2. Click the drop-down arrow for the Go To Field box on the Formatting (Datasheet) toolbar. This box is the on the left side of the toolbar and displays the name of whatever field the cursor is in.

3. Select the name of the field you want to move to.

TIP TIP TIP TIP TIP TIP TIP TIP TIP TIP TIP TIP TIP TIP TIP TIP TIP TIP TIP TIP TIP TIP TIP
You can type a field name directly into the Go To Field box instead of choosing it from the drop-down list of field names. Click once in the box to highlight the current name, then type in the name of the field you want to move to.

View Related Records in a Subdatasheet

If you look back at Figure 4.1, you'll see that there are Expand buttons (+) on the left side of each record shown in the Datasheet view. These buttons are a new feature in Access that let you open a *subdatasheet* from a datasheet to see related records in another table. When there is a one-to-one or a one-to-many relationship between two tables, Access automatically adds Expand buttons to any Datasheet view for the table on the one side of the relationship. You can also add subdatasheets to a table open in Datasheet view yourself, as you'll see shortly.

Open a Subdatasheet

To open a subdatasheet for a record, click the record's Expand button (+). A subdatasheet will open that shows the related records in the table on the many side of the relationship. Since the Employees tables in the Timekeeper database has a one-to-many relationship to the Weekly Records tables, you can click the Expand button for the first Employees record to show a subdatasheet like this:

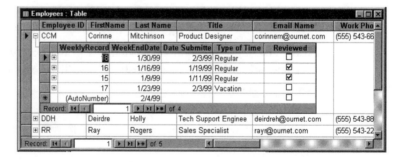

As you can see, the subdatasheet shows only the records in the Weekly Records table that belong to Corinne Mitchinson, the first employee in the Employees table. If there are too many fields to show at one time in a subdatasheet, a horizontal scroll bar will appear within the subdatasheet window. If the subdatasheet has more records than will fit in the Datasheet view window it belongs to, you will have to use the vertical scroll bar for the Datasheet window to bring the additional related records into view.

You may have noticed that the records in the subdatasheet for Weekly Records all have their own Expand buttons. Since the Weekly Records table is related to the Project Hours table in the Timekeeper database, you can view any related records in Project Hours from each record in the Weekly Records subdatasheet as shown here:

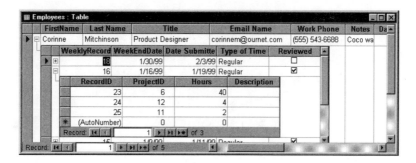

SKILL
4

> **NOTE** NOTE NOTE NOTE NOTE NOTE NOTE NOTE NOTE NOTE NOTE NOTE NOTE NOTE NOTE NOTE
>
> **In a subdatasheet, you are free to edit data as well as add, delete, sort, and filter records. All the instructions for working with tables in the rest of this chapter also apply to tables shown in subdatasheets.**

Close a Subdatasheet

When you're finished using a subdatasheet, click its Collapse button (-) to close it. You don't need to close all the levels of subdatasheets that might be open under a record. You can just click the Collapse button for the topmost record in the Datasheet view window to close any Subdatasheet views open under it. When you do this, Access remembers which sub-subdatasheets, if any, were opened for the subdatasheet and will open them if you expand the topmost subdatasheet again.

Expand All Subdatasheets at the Same Time

Instead of opening one subdatasheet at a time for a table, you can expand all of them at once. Choose Format ➤ Subdatasheet ➤ Expand All from the Access menu. You'll end up seeing a Datasheet view window with several subdatasheets open like this one for the Employees table:

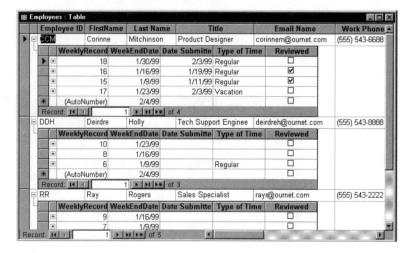

If you want to collapse all open subdatasheets, choose Format ➢ Subdatasheet ➢ Collapse All. Any subdatasheets for the active table will close. For example, if you choose Collapse All after clicking a field in the Employees table, all open subdatasheets for the Weekly Records and the Project Hours tables will close. If the current field is in a Weekly Records subdatasheet when you choose Collapse All, only the subdatasheets for the Project Hours table will close.

Remove a Subdatasheet

Access lets you remove a subdatasheet from a datasheet altogether instead of just closing it. Choose Format ➢ Subdatasheet ➢ Remove from the Access menu. All the Expand buttons for the Subdatasheet view window will disappear from the datasheet. Once you remove a subdatasheet, you can add it back using the instructions discussed next. Or, when you close the main Datasheet view window, you can cancel your changes. This will save the original Datasheet view properties and keep the subdatasheet that's associated with the main table.

Add a New Subdatasheet

Even if there is no relationship defined between two tables, you can add a subdatasheet to one table for the other, as long as the tables can be linked with a common field. When you open the Project Hours table in the Timekeeper database, for example, Access does not automatically include Expand buttons to open sub-datasheets for the Projects table. But you can add a subdatasheet for Projects yourself this way:

1. Open the Project Hours table in Datasheet view.

2. Choose Insert ➢ Subdatasheet from the menu to open the Insert Subdatasheet window:

SKILL
4

3. Click Projects on the list of tables.

4. Use the drop-down lists to select ProjectID for both the Link Child Fields and the Link Master Fields. (The child table is the table for the subdatasheet; the master table belongs to the main Datasheet view.)

5. Click OK.

When you return to the Datasheet view window, you'll see Expand buttons for each record in the window. You can then click these buttons to open subdatasheets for the table you chose in the Insert Subdatasheet window.

NOTE NOTE NOTE NOTE NOTE NOTE NOTE NOTE NOTE NOTE NOTE NOTE NOTE NOTE NOTE

If you need to change the table for a subdatasheet, follow the instructions above and select a new table in the Insert Subdatasheet window.

Edit a Table

Check the sections that follow for instructions on how to:

- Add a record to a table
- Delete a record from a table
- Enter values in a field
- Change values in text and number fields
- Find and replace data

You'll also find some quick editing tips. For instructions on editing fields with data types other than text or numbers, such as hyperlinks or memos, see "Editing Special Field Types" later in this chapter. As noted a little earlier, all the techniques outlined here apply to tables shown in Datasheet views or subdatasheets.

Add Records

If you are working with a new table that has no records, just click any field in the empty record in the Datasheet view window and start entering information. To add another record to a table, you may use any of the following procedures:

- Click the New Record button on the Table Datasheet toolbar.
- Choose Edit ➢ Go To ➢ New Record from the menu.
- Press the Down arrow key while you are in the last record of the table, or the Right arrow key when you are in the last field of the last record in the table.
- Press Ctrl++ (the Control key with the plus sign key).
- Click the New Record navigation button at the bottom of the Datasheet view window (the button with the * on it).

NOTE NOTE NOTE NOTE NOTE NOTE NOTE NOTE NOTE NOTE NOTE NOTE NOTE NOTE

If you are working in a table that has an AutoNumber field, you will always see an empty record at the end of the table with *(AutoNumber)* in that field. After you enter data in at least one field of the new record, Access will assign a value to the AutoNumber field and add another empty line to the Datasheet view.

Delete a Record

To delete a record from a table, use any of the following actions:

- Click the Delete Record button on the Table Datasheet toolbar.

- Click the record's record selector (the gray box to the left of the record as shown in Figure 4.1) and press Delete.

- Choose Edit ➤ Delete Record from the menu.

- Press Ctrl+– (the Control key and the minus key).

Choose Yes when Access asks if you really want to delete the record(s). Be careful, though: You can't undo a delete if you change your mind later.

Delete Multiple Records

To delete a group of records all at the same time, just select the records as a group before you click Delete Record or press Delete. Click the record selector for the first record in the group you want to delete, then hold down Shift while you click the last record in the group. You'll see all the records in the group highlighted with a black background.

Enter Field Values

To enter a value in a field, just move to the field and start typing. Access checks whatever you enter to make sure it conforms to the data type and size of the field. See "Editing Special Field Types" a little later in this chapter for details on entering data in Memo, Date/Time, Yes/No, Hyperlink, and OLE Object fields.

Change Field Values

If you want to change a field value, click wherever you want to make your edits and start typing. To replace an entire field value, point with the mouse to the beginning of the field value. When the mouse pointer changes to a large plus sign, click to highlight the field and type in the new value. It will replace the current field contents.

TIP TIP TIP TIP TIP TIP TIP TIP TIP TIP TIP TIP TIP TIP TIP TIP TIP TIP TIP TIP TIP TIP TIP TIP

Use Enter, Tab, or other cursor movement keys to land in a field and select it at the same time.

Undo Changes

Before you leave a field or a record, you can undo your last change with the Esc key as noted in Table 4.2.

TABLE 4.2: How To Undo Field and Record Changes

Press. . .	Before You Leave a. . .	To Undo Your Last Changes to. . .
Esc	Field	The field
Esc	Record	The record
Esc twice	Field	The field and the record

Find and Replace

You can *find and replace* data in a table instead of making time-consuming, repetitive changes one at a time:

1. If you want to replace values in one field only, click that field in any record.

2. Click Find on the toolbar and click the Replace tab. (You can also choose Edit ➤ Replace from the menu or press Ctrl+H.) You'll see a Find And Replace dialog box like this, without the Find What and Replace With values entered:

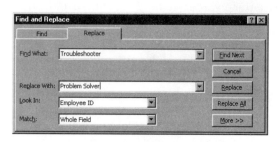

3. Enter the value you want to change in the Find What box, and the replacement value in the Replace With box.

4. If you want to change the Find What values in every field in the table and not only the current field, change the setting for Look In to the table's name.

5. Change the setting for Match to Any Part Of Field, Whole Field, or Start Of Field, as needed.

6. Click Replace All to change all instances of the Find What value without further ado. If you want to make your changes one at a time, click Find Next, and then Replace if needed, until you're finished with the job.

7. Click Cancel or the Close button (X) to return to the Datasheet view window.

Change How Access Finds Values

There are some options you can change in the Find And Replace dialog box to tell Access how it should look for the Find What values. Begin by clicking More to bring these options into view. Then, check:

Match Case if you want Access to look for values that match the case of letters entered in the Find What box. For example, with this setting turned on, a search for "Wendy Smith" finds Wendy Smith, but not WENDY SMITH or wendy smith.

Search Fields As Formatted to have Access search for data using its display format, instead of the way it's stored.

You can also use the Search drop-down list to change the direction of a search: Up searches backward from the current record, Down continues from the current record, and All checks all the records in the table.

Use Wildcards to Find Values

If you don't quite know what name or phrase you're looking for, or you just don't want to type the whole thing in, you can use *wildcards* in the Find And Replace dialog box. Wildcards are also useful when you want to search for values that match some pattern instead of a constant. Table 4.3 shows the wildcards Access recognizes and gives some examples of how they work.

TABLE 4.3: Wildcards You Can Use in the Find And Replace Dialog Box

This Wildcard. . .	Matches. . .	This Example. . .	Finds. . .
*	Any characters	C*	Coco, Connie, and Carl
		*son	Carlson and Jenson
?	Any one letter	D?n	Den, Din and Don
[ ]	Any one character in the brackets	S[aio]ng	Sang, Sing, and Song
!	Any character not in the [ ]	S[!aio]ng	Sung
-	Any character in a range	A[a-c]	Aa, Ab, and Ac
#	Any one number	AB#	AB1, AB5, and AB0

SKILL 4

NOTE NOTE NOTE NOTE NOTE NOTE NOTE NOTE NOTE NOTE NOTE NOTE NOTE NOTE NOTE

If you need to find an *, ?, #, [, or -, enclose it in [ ].

Quick Editing Tips

While editing a table, you can use lots of shortcut keys to speed up your data entry. Check Table 4.4 for a list of the ones you might use most often. For details on a few others, open the Office Assistant, enter **use shortcut keys,** and click the topic *Keyboard shortcuts.*

TABLE 4.4: Shortcut Keys for Editing Table Data

Use This Shortcut. . .	To. . .
Ctrl+Left arrow	Move back a word
Ctrl+Right arrow	Move forward a word
End	Move to the end of the line
Ctrl+End	Move to the end of a multi-line field value
Home	Move to the beginning of the line
Ctrl+Home	Move to the beginning of a multi-line field value
Ctrl+C	Copy the selected text to the Clipboard
Ctrl+X	Cut the selected text to the Clipboard
Ctrl+V	Paste what's on the Clipboard to the insertion point
Delete	Delete selected text
Ctrl+Z	Undo typing
Alt+Backspace	Undo typing
Esc	Undo changes before leaving a field or record
Ctrl+;	Enter current date
Ctrl+:	Enter current time
Ctrl+'	Copy value from the same field in the last record
Ctrl+Alt+Spacebar	Enter default value for the field
Ctrl++	Add a new record
Ctrl+-	Delete the current record
Shift+Enter	Save your changes to the current record
Spacebar	Switch between the values in a check box or option list
Ctrl+Enter	Add a new line in a memo field
F2	Switch between insert and overwrite mode in a field
Shift+F2	Open a Zoom window for editing a field

Edit Special Field Types

The next examples show you how to enter and edit data in fields with these data types:

- Memo
- Date/Time
- Yes/No
- Hyperlink
- OLE Object

If you want to follow along with the examples, add a field for each of the above data types to one of your tables. You can use the Employees table in the Timekeeper database, if you created it in an earlier chapter. Figure 4.2 shows the structure of the Employees table with these fields added:

Field	Data Type	Purpose
Notes	Memo	For miscellaneous notes
Date of Hire	Date/Time	Shows the employee's date of hire
Trained	Yes/No	Indicates whether an employee has been trained
Last Review	Hyperlink	Jumps to Word document for last review
Photo	OLE Object	Opens Paint to show employee's picture

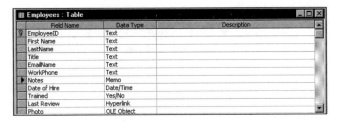

FIGURE 4.2: The Employees table with fields added for these special data types: Memo, Date/Time, Yes/No, Hyperlink, and OLE Object

If you haven't already created an Employees table, don't worry. Either create one now or add the fields for the examples to another table in your database. You can always delete the fields after you finish experimenting with them.

NOTE NOTE NOTE NOTE NOTE NOTE NOTE NOTE NOTE NOTE NOTE NOTE NOTE NOTE NOTE

You may have noticed that some of these field names have spaces, even though the ones created by the Wizards don't. Spaces are allowed in field names, but they can cause problems if you convert the table to some different types of database files later.

Memos

When you add text to a Memo field, you can enter it directly into the field in the Datasheet view window. You will probably prefer to open a Zoom window, though, so you can see the entire contents of the field. To open a Zoom window:

1. Click anywhere on the memo field or use one of the other methods (described above) to move to it.

2. Press Shift+F2.

Figure 4.3 shows a Zoom window opened for the Notes memo field in the Employees table. The Zoom window has a scroll bar that you can use to move through the contents of the field, if they are not entirely visible.

TIP TIP TIP TIP TIP TIP TIP TIP TIP TIP TIP TIP TIP TIP TIP TIP TIP TIP TIP TIP TIP TIP

Use Ctrl+Enter to create a new line in a Memo field. If you press Enter, you will close the Zoom window and return to the Datasheet view window.

WARNING WARNING WARNING WARNING WARNING WARNING WARNING WARNING

Be careful not to start typing in the Zoom window when all the contents are highlighted unless you really want to overwrite the entire memo.

When you are finished with the Zoom window, either click OK to save your edits or click Cancel to abandon your changes

Dates and Times

Working with Date/Time fields is pretty straightforward. The only things that can hang you up are the date separators (the slashes in a date that are shown like this: 12/1/99) and the time portion. If you pay attention to these couple of things, you shouldn't have any problems:

- If the Date/Time field doesn't have an input mask that enters the date separators for you, be sure to enter them yourself. If you don't, you'll get a message that the value (for example, 120199) isn't valid for the field.

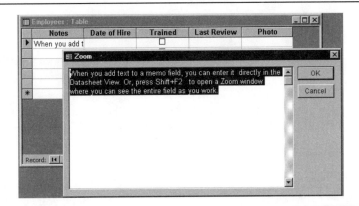

FIGURE 4.3: Press Shift+F2 while you are in a Memo field to open a Zoom window where you can view the field's contents more easily.

- If you enter an hour without any minutes (for example, 10), be sure to enter an A.M. or P.M., otherwise you will get an invalid data message.

- You can leave the A.M. or P.M. off a time, but Access will use A.M. for the default.

NOTE NOTE NOTE NOTE NOTE NOTE NOTE NOTE NOTE NOTE NOTE NOTE NOTE NOTE NOTE

If you enter a date in a format different from the default display format for the field, Access 2000 will automatically reformat the date for you. For example, if you enter **January 1, 1999** in a Date/Time field where the format is set to *mm/dd/yy*, Access will show the date as 1/1/99.

WARNING WARNING WARNING WARNING WARNING WARNING WARNING WARNING

When you enter only two digits for a year, Access assumes that 00 through 29 are years in the 21st century. If you use a value from 30 through 99, Access assumes that the date is in the 20th century. For more information on how Access handles dates in the year 2000 and beyond, use the Office Assistant to search for help on "enter dates," and click the topic *Handling dates in the Year 2000 and beyond*.

Yes/No Fields

It's easy to enter a value in a Yes/No field because Access automatically shows the field as a check box like the Trained field in this Datasheet view:

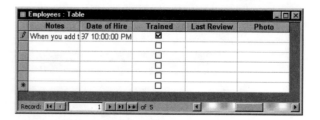

To enter a "Yes" in the field, just click the check box in the field. To change the value to "No," just click again to remove the check mark. You can also press the spacebar to toggle a Yes/No check mark on or off.

NOTE NOTE NOTE NOTE NOTE NOTE NOTE NOTE NOTE NOTE NOTE NOTE NOTE NOTE NOTE
When you query a table with a Yes/No field, you can use Yes or True as the criteria to find all records with check marks in the Yes/No field. Similarly, No or False finds all records without check marks.

Hyperlinks

Hyperlink fields are special fields where you can store *hyperlink addresses* that jump to Web sites, database objects, or other Office documents. You can also use a hyperlink field to store an e-mail address that, when clicked, opens a New Message window with the recipient's address already filled in.

The Parts of a Hyperlink Address

A hyperlink address can have up to three parts:

Optional display text that appears in the hyperlink field instead of the actual hyperlink address.

An **address** that consists of the path to the jump document. For example, C:\My Documents\Trip Report, http://www.mywebsite.com, or mailto:Me@mynet.com.

A **subaddress** that optionally points to a location in the jump document; this could be a bookmark in a Word document or an object in an Access database.

These parts are separated by number signs (#) in an address like this: SYBEX Home Page#http://www.sybex.com#. If you include the optional display text, that's all you will see in the hyperlink field in the Datasheet view window. For addresses that point to objects in the open database or another database, Access automatically creates display text that consists of the object name.

TIP TIP TIP TIP TIP TIP TIP TIP TIP TIP TIP TIP TIP TIP TIP TIP TIP TIP TIP TIP TIP TIP TIP TIP

If you want to check the address that's stored behind the scenes in a hyperlink field showing optional display text, move to the field (without clicking it) and press F2. Access will show you the entire hyperlink address instead of the display text alone.

SKILL
4

Table 4.5 shows some examples of hyperlink addresses and how they appear after they are entered in a hyperlink field.

TABLE 4.5: Examples of Hyperlink Addresses

This Hyperlink Address. . .	Appears Like This. . .	And Jumps to. . .
SYBEX Home Page#http://www.sybex.com#	SYBEX Home Page	www.sybex.com
#C:\Expenses\Trip Report.doc#	C:\Expenses\ Trip Report.doc	C:\Expenses\Trip Report.doc
#Review for DDH.doc#[1]	Review for DDH.doc	C:\My Documents\Review for DDH.doc
#Review for DDH.doc# NextReview	Review for DDH.doc	The bookmark called Next-Review in C:\My Documents\ Review for DDH.doc
Employees##Form Employees	Employees	The Employees form in the open database
Addresses#Address Book. mdb#Table Addresses	Addresses	The Addresses table in the Address Book database
Me@Mynet.com#mailto: Me@Mynet.com#	Me@Mynet.com	New Message window with the message addressed to Me@Mynet.com

1. This address doesn't include the folder name, so, by default, the path is the same as for the open database. Use File ➤ Data Properties and use Hyperlink Base on the Summary tab to change the relative path.

Enter Hyperlink Addresses

Some of the addresses in Table 4.5 look pretty complicated. You don't have to get bogged down with the rules for entering valid addresses, though. There are lots of shortcuts for entering an address in a hyperlink field. You can:

- Use the Insert Hyperlink button on the Table Datasheet toolbar
- Copy and paste a hyperlink address
- Drag and drop an Internet shortcut
- Type in a hyperlink address

In the examples that follow, you'll see how to use the Insert Hyperlink button or type addresses in yourself. We don't have room to go into the other options for entering hyperlink addresses here, but you can find step-by-step instructions in the Access Help. Use the Office Assistant to search for help on "Enter a hyperlink address in Form view or Datasheet view" and click the topic *Enter a hyperlink address in Form view or Datasheet view*.

TIP TIP TIP TIP TIP TIP TIP TIP TIP TIP TIP TIP TIP TIP TIP TIP TIP TIP TIP TIP TIP TIP TIP TIP TIP

The Insert Hyperlink dialog box has been revamped in Access 2000 and has new tools and options for entering hyperlink addresses. One feature lets you create a new document from the Insert Hyperlink window. The new Screen Tip button lets you enter a message that will appear as bubble help when someone points to the hyperlink field and pauses without clicking.

Enter an Address for an Office Document

A hyperlink address field can point to Office files like Word documents, Excel spreadsheets, and other Access databases. This example shows you how to enter an address for a Word document in a field called Last Review in the Employees table.

1. Click the Hyperlink field you want to enter an address in. The field in this example is called Last Review.

2. Click the Insert Hyperlink button on the Table Datasheet toolbar.

3. In the box labeled Type The File Or Web Page Name, enter the name of the file you want to jump to. Or you can click the button for Existing File Or Web Page (if it's not already active) and click the File button under Browse

For. Figure 4.4 shows the Insert Hyperlink dialog box with the name of a Word document entered, `C:\My Documents\Review DDH 020299.doc`.

4. Click OK to insert the hyperlink address in the field.

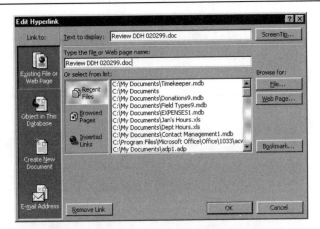

FIGURE 4.4: When you click the Insert Hyperlink button on the toolbar, this dialog box opens. The hyperlink address in this example jumps to a Word document.

When you return to the Datasheet view window, you'll see an address entered in the hyperlink field like this:

Email Name	Work Pho	Notes	Date of Hire	Trained	Last Review
⊞ corinnem@ournet.com	(555) 543-	Coco wa	6/15/97	☑	
⊞ deirdreh@ournet.com	(555) 543-		11/3/97	☐	Review DDH 020299.doc
⊞ rayn@ournet.com	(555) 543-		1/1/95	☐	
⊞ talb@ournet.com	(555) 543-		5/14/96	☑	
⊞ zoeg@ournet.com	(555) 555-		6/18/95	☑	
*				☐	

Record: ◄◄ ◄ 2 ► ►► ►* of 5

TIP TIP TIP TIP TIP TIP TIP TIP TIP TIP TIP TIP TIP TIP TIP TIP TIP TIP TIP TIP TIP TIP TIP

The Edit Hyperlink window (Figure 4.4) has several tools to help you enter a Web page or filename. First, click Existing File Or Web Page button in the upper-left corner of the window. Then use the Browse For buttons, or click one of the buttons for Recent Files, Browsed Pages, or Inserted Links, to narrow down the list in the middle of the window.

Jump to an Office Document

To jump to an address for an Office document, just click the field. Figure 4.5 shows what happens after you click the jump to C:\My Documents\Review DDH 020299 in the Last Review field in the Employees table. When you are finished with the document you jumped to, just close it to return to the Datasheet view window. You can also click anywhere in the Access window, if it's visible, to minimize the application opened with the jump. To restore the minimized application, click its icon on the Windows Taskbar.

Click here. . .

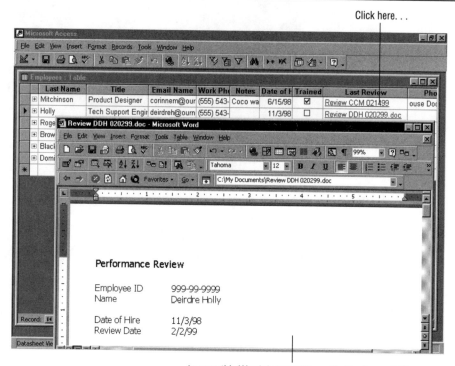

. . . to open this Word document from the Employees table.

FIGURE 4.5: This Word document was opened by clicking the Last Review hyperlink field in the Employees table.

By default, a hyperlink address is shown as blue underlined text until you use it to jump. After you follow an address, it appears as purple, underlined text.

NOTE NOTE NOTE NOTE NOTE NOTE NOTE NOTE NOTE NOTE NOTE NOTE NOTE NOTE

To change the way hyperlinks appear by default, choose Tools ➢ Options, select the General tab, and click the Web Options button. A dialog box will open where you can change the color for hyperlinks, before and after they are followed, and turn off their underlining, if you like.

Enter a Web Site Address or a URL

In this example, we'll type in an address that jumps to the SYBEX home page:

1. Click the empty hyperlink field you want to enter an address in.

2. Enter **www.sybex.com**. (If you want to show SYBEX Home Page instead of the actual Web address in the hyperlink field, enter **SYBEX Home Page# http://www.sybex.com#.**)

This address is easy to enter without going through the Insert Hyperlink dialog box. For a lengthier address, though, open the Insert Hyperlink window and use the tools there to select a Web page or URL. These tips should help you find your way around this busy dialog box:

- If you've recently browsed the Web page you want to enter as the hyperlink address, make sure the button for Existing File Or Web Page is selected. Then click the button for Browsed Pages and select the Web page from the list in the middle of the Insert Hyperlink window.

- To browse for a Web page, make sure you are connected to the Internet. Then, in the Insert Hyperlink dialog box, click the button for Existing File or Web Page. Under Browse For, click the Web Page button to launch your browser. When you find the Web page you want the hyperlink to jump to, go back to the Access window. You'll see the URL for the open page in your browser's box for the Type The File Or Web Page Name.

TIP TIP TIP TIP TIP TIP TIP TIP TIP TIP TIP TIP TIP TIP TIP TIP TIP TIP TIP TIP TIP TIP

If you begin a hyperlink address with www, Access 2000 will recognize it as a Web site and add the http:// to the beginning of the address for you. It will also create a section of display text for the address that begins with the www instead of showing the complete address with http://.

SKILL
4

Jump to a Web Site

To jump to a Web site from an Access table:

1. Make sure you have a connection to the Internet established.

2. In the Access window, click the address you want to jump to.

3. If you don't see a window open for your Web browser, check the Windows Taskbar and click the browser's icon there to view the Web site.

Figure 4.6 shows the SYBEX home page after it was opened from the Employees table.

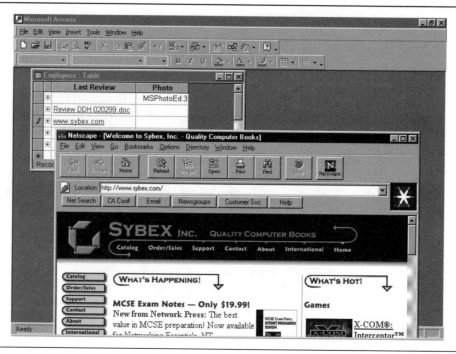

FIGURE 4.6: To open the SYBEX home page from an Access table, enter the address www.sybex.com in a hyperlink field. Then make sure your Internet connection is established and click the address.

Enter an Address for an Object in Your Open Database

You can enter an address for an object in your open database directly into a hyperlink field as shown in Table 4.5, or you can use the Insert Hyperlink button like this:

1. Move the cursor to the hyperlink field that the address will go in.

2. Click the Insert Hyperlink button on the Table Datasheet toolbar.

3. Under Link To, click the Objects In This Database button. The Insert Hyperlink dialog box will look like the one in Figure 4.7.

4. Click the Expand button (+) for the type of object you want to jump to (Tables, Queries, Forms, and so on).

5. Double-click the name of the object for the hyperlink address.

SKILL
4

Click the Expand button (+) for the
type of object you want to jump to.

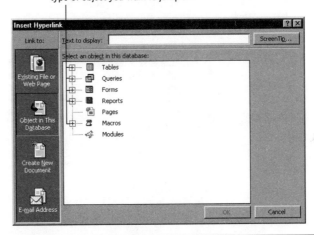

FIGURE 4.7: This shows the Insert Hyperlink dialog box as it appears after clicking the Objects In This Database button.

Enter an Address for an Object in Another Database

You can enter an address for a database object by following the example shown in Table 4.5. You can also use the Insert Hyperlink dialog box like this:

1. Move to the hyperlink field you want to enter an address in.

2. Click Insert Hyperlink on the toolbar.

3. Click Existing File Or Web Page, if it's not already active.

4. If you recently opened the database holding the object you want to jump to, click the Recent Files button in the middle of the window and select the database from the list in the middle of the Insert Hyperlink window. If you want to browse for the database, click the File button, browse for the database, and double-click its name in the Link To File window.

5. In the Insert Hyperlink window, click the button for Bookmark. This will open a dialog box where you can choose an object in the database you selected in step 4.

6. Click the Expand button for the type of object you want to jump to.

7. Double-click the name of the object for the hyperlink.

8. Click OK in the Insert Hyperlink dialog box.

Figure 4.8 shows the Edit Hyperlink dialog box after it was used to create an address that will jump to the Addresses table in a database called Address Book.

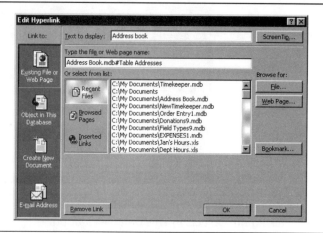

FIGURE 4.8: This Edit Hyperlink dialog box will create an address that jumps to the Addresses table in a database called Address Book.

Enter an E-Mail Address

A new feature of the Insert Hyperlink dialog box lets you enter an e-mail address for a hyperlink field. When you click this type of hyperlink, a New Message window opens so you can compose a message. The recipient information in the To box is already filled in with the e-mail address you entered in the hyperlink field, along with a subject if you want.

To create this kind of hyperlink:

1. Click the E-Mail Address button in the Insert Hyperlink dialog box. You'll see a window similar to this one:

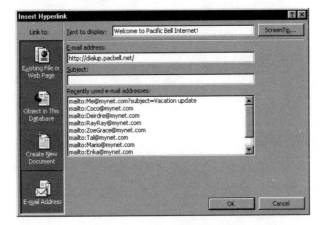

2. In the E-Mail Address box, enter the e-mail address of the person to whom you want to send a message when the New Message window opens. You can also select an address from the list under Recently Used E-Mail Addresses in the middle of the Insert Hyperlink dialog box.

3. If you would like the message to have a subject, enter one in the Subject box.

4. Click OK to return to the Datasheet view window.

Access will fill the e-mail address into the hyperlink field. If you press F2 to view the field's contents, you'll see that the address looks something like this: *#mailto:Me@mynet.com?subject=Vacation update#* where *Me@mynet.com* is the e-mail address you entered and *Vacation update* is the subject you entered in the Insert Hyperlink window.

Figure 4.9 shows an example of what happens when you click an e-mail address hyperlink. In this case, Microsoft Outlook Express has opened a new message window with the subject that was entered in the Insert Hyperlink dialog box. The To box is filled in, too.

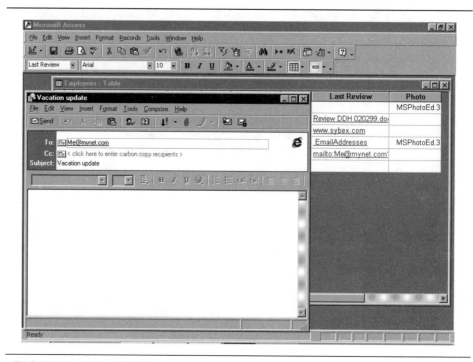

FIGURE 4.9: Clicking an e-mail address in a hyperlink field will open a New Message window that's already addressed.

When a message window is opened from Access this way, complete the message as you normally would. Then click Send, or close the window to save the message as a draft. The message window will close and you'll be returned to the Access datasheet.

Edit an Address in a Hyperlink Field

To edit a hyperlink address, you can do any of the following:

- Right-click the Hyperlink field and choose Hyperlink ➤ Edit Hyperlink from the shortcut menu.

- Move the cursor to the Hyperlink field (without clicking it) and click the Insert Hyperlink button on the toolbar to open an Edit Hyperlink window.

- Move the cursor to the Hyperlink field (without clicking it) and press F2 to get an insertion bar in the address so you can make changes.

If you use one of the techniques that opens the Edit Hyperlink dialog box, use any of the instructions outlined in the last several sections for working with the Insert Hyperlink dialog box. Then click OK to close the window and return to the Datasheet view window.

Create a New Object from the Insert Hyperlink Window

Another new hyperlink feature lets you create a new document for a hyperlink right from the Insert Hyperlink dialog box. To do this:

1. Open the Insert Hyperlink dialog box (or the Edit Hyperlink box if you are changing the address for a hyperlink that already has a value entered).

2. Click the Create New Document button to make the Insert Hyperlink window look like this:

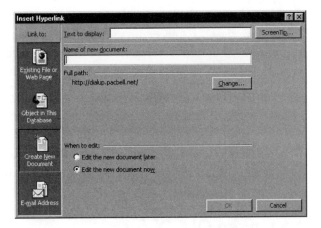

3. The name of the folder the new document will be located in is shown under Full Path. If you need to change the folder name, click the Change button to open a Link To File dialog box where you can navigate to a different location. (Don't select an object here since you're creating a new one; just select a folder.)

4. In the box for Name Of New Document, enter the name you want to assign to the new document. This name will appear in the hyperlink field unless you enter something else in the Text To Display box. Be sure to include the file extension for the type of document you want to create so Access knows which program to launch.

NOTE NOTE NOTE NOTE NOTE NOTE NOTE NOTE NOTE NOTE NOTE NOTE NOTE NOTE

If you don't include a file extension in the new document's name, Access will assume that you are creating a Data Access Page.

5. Under When To Edit, select Edit The New Document Now if you want to launch the program for the new document upon closing the Insert Hyperlink dialog box. Otherwise, choose Edit The Document Later. With this option selected, Access will wait to open the document's program until you click the hyperlink field.

6. Click OK to close the Insert Hyperlink window and return to the Datasheet view window.

OLE Objects

Fields with the OLE Object data type can hold pictures, Word documents, sound, or other kinds of data that are created in programs outside of Access. When you enter data in an OLE Object field, you can do it two ways. You can create:

- A *linked object* where a reference to the picture, document, or other OLE object is stored in the Access table. When you double-click the OLE Object field, Windows will open the program for the object so you can change it.

- An *embedded object* where Access stores a copy of an OLE object right in the table. Changes made to the original object do not affect the object stored in the database.

Insert a Linked OLE Object

The Photo field in the Employees table has the OLE Object data type. Let's insert a linked picture (one that already exists as a `.bmp` file) into this field to see how this works:

1. Move the cursor to the Photo field for the record you are editing in Datasheet view.

2. Either right-click the field and select Insert Object or use Insert ➤ Object. You'll see a dialog box something like the one below. The objects you see on the Object Type list will vary depending on the programs you have on your computer.

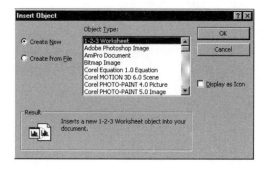

3. Click Create From File.

4. Click the Browse button that appears when the dialog box changes.

5. Select the file for the picture you want to link using the Browse dialog box. `C:\\My Documents\NewCoco.bmp` was used for this example.

6. Back in the Insert Object dialog box, click the check box for Link to select it.

7. If you prefer to display the object as an icon in the OLE Object field in Datasheet view, check Display As Icon. This shows the icon instead of the name of the object type.

8. Click OK to return to the Datasheet view window.

In the Datasheet view window, you will see a reference to the type of object you linked in the OLE Object field. For example, if `.bmp` files are associated with Corel Photo House on your computer, the OLE Object field looks like this:

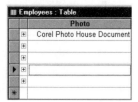

See "Open an OLE Object" a bit later in this chapter to see how the photo looks when it's opened with Corel Photo House from the Datasheet window.

SKILL
4

Insert an Embedded OLE Object

If you want to store a copy of the photo NewCoco.bmp in the Employees table (instead of linking a live copy of it to the table), you need to insert it as an embedded object in the Photo field:

1. Move to the Photo field (or whatever OLE Object field you are working with).

2. Right-click the field and choose Insert Object.

3. Click Create From File.

4. Click Browse and select the file for the picture.

5. Click OK in the Insert Object dialog box without checking Link.

When you return to the Datasheet view window, the OLE Object field will look like the linked example shown in the previous section. You can open the picture and edit it, but your changes will only be made to the copy stored in the field. Nothing will happen to the original picture.

View an OLE Object

To see the contents of an OLE Object field, double-click it to open it in its source application. For example, if you have inserted a Word document in an OLE Object field as a linked object, when you double-click the document, a Word window will open with the document ready for editing. Figure 4.10 shows the file NewCoco.bmp opened with Corel Photo House from the OLE Object field called Photo.

Edit an OLE Object

If you are working with an object in an OLE field, simply double-click the field to open the object in its source application as described just above. Then you can edit the object using the tools available in the OLE object's window. If you save your changes to the OLE object when you close its window, they will be reflected the next time you open the object from Access.

The main difference between editing linked and embedded objects is this: Any changes you make to a linked OLE object are made directly to the object that was inserted into the field. If you change an embedded OLE object, any changes affect only the copy of the object that is stored in Access. The original object that you inserted into the OLE field will not be changed.

FIGURE 4.10: Double-click an OLE Object field to open its contents with the program it is associated with. In this example, NewCoco.bmp was inserted into a field called Photo and opened with Corel Photo House from the Employees table.

Customize a Datasheet View

When you open a table in Datasheet view, there are lots of things you can do to customize what you see. You can:

- Resize columns to show more or fewer fields in the window

- Change row height to show more or fewer records in the window

- Move columns around

- Freeze columns so they are always in view, even when you scroll through other columns

- Hide columns from view

NOTE NOTE NOTE NOTE NOTE NOTE NOTE NOTE NOTE NOTE NOTE NOTE NOTE NOTE NOTE

Access lets you resize and move columns and rows in a subdatasheet, just like you can in Datasheet view. You can also freeze or hide subdatasheet columns.

Resize a Column

To resize a column in a Datasheet view:

1. Point the mouse to the right side of the column's header until it shows up as a two-headed arrow:

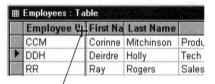

The mouse pointer looks like this when you are ready to resize a column.

2. Drag with the mouse until the column is the desired width.

TIP TIP TIP TIP TIP TIP TIP TIP TIP TIP TIP TIP TIP TIP TIP TIP TIP TIP TIP TIP TIP TIP TIP TIP

Double-click the right side of a column's header to automatically size the column to show all the column's data, including the field name.

Change the Row Height

You can change the height of rows in Datasheet view to show more or less space between records. To do this:

1. Point with your mouse to one of the lines between rows until the mouse pointer looks like this:

Employee ID	First Name	Last Name	Title
CCM	Corinne	Mitchinson	Product Designer
DDH	Deirdre	Holly	Tech Support Engineer
RR	Ray	Rogers	Sales Rep

The mouse pointer looks like this when you are ready to change the row height.

2. Drag the row divider up or down until the rows are the size you want.

In the previous graphic, the row divider was dragged down slightly to increase the space between records.

Move Columns

You can move a column or a group of adjacent columns to a new spot in a datasheet. To move your column(s):

1. Point in the header of the first column you want to move until the mouse pointer looks like this:

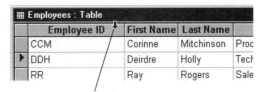

Wait until the mouse pointer looks like this
before you click to select the columns.

2. Click the column to select it, or drag and then release the mouse to select adjacent columns. The selected columns show up with a black background:

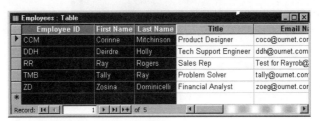

3. Hold down the mouse key in any of the selected column headers so the pointer looks like this:

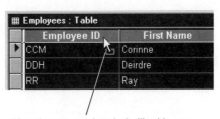

When the mouse pointer looks like this, you
can drag the selected column(s) to a new location.

4. Drag the selected column(s) to their new location. Drag until you see a heavy black vertical line along the right side of the column that will precede the moved column(s).

Freeze Columns

If you need to keep some columns in view while scrolling through others (called *freezing*), use the Freeze Columns command. To lock one or more columns on the left side of the datasheet view window:

1. Select the column(s) you want to freeze. (Check the first two steps for "Move Columns" if you need details on selecting columns in a datasheet.)

2. Choose Format ➢ Freeze Columns from the menu.

Figure 4.11 shows the Employees table with its first three columns frozen. After scrolling, the last three columns of the table are visible alongside the EmployeeID, First Name, and Last Name.

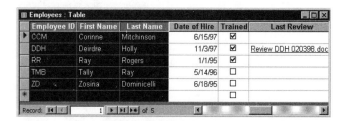

FIGURE 4.11: In this Datasheet view window, the first three columns of the Employees table are frozen in place. The last three columns of the table have been scrolled into view without moving the frozen columns.

Unfreeze Columns

To "unfreeze" columns that are locked in place, choose Format ➢ Unfreeze All Columns from the menu.

Hide Columns

Access lets you hide columns from view altogether. To hide one or more columns:

1. Select the column(s) you want to hide.

2. Choose Format ➢ Hide Columns from the menu.

Unhide Columns

To bring hidden columns back into view:

1. Choose Format ➣ Unhide Columns from the menu.

2. Click the check box of any column you want to bring back into view. (Any column that is hidden will not have a check mark.)

3. Repeat step 2 for all the columns you want to unhide.

4. Click Close to return to the Datasheet view window.

Figure 4.12 shows the Unhide dialog box. As you can see, the Last Review field is unchecked indicating that this field is currently hidden in the datasheet view.

FIGURE 4.12: The Unhide dialog box uses check boxes to show which fields are currently hidden. Click an empty check box to bring a field back into view.

Find Records

When you are working in a datasheet, it's easy to look for records that have a certain value in a particular field, or even in any field:

1. If you want to look for a value in a certain field, click anywhere in the field.

2. Click the Find button on the Table Datasheet toolbar to open the Find And Replace dialog box.

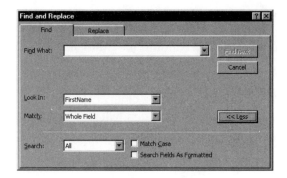

3. Enter the value you want to look for in the Find What box.

4. If you want to search every field instead of the current field only, change the setting for Look In to the name of the table.

5. Select Match To Any Part Of Field, Whole Field, or Start Of Field, depending on how you want Access to look for matches.

6. Click Find Next.

7. Continue to click Find Next to find additional matches, if you need to.

8. Click Close to return to the Datasheet view window.

NOTE NOTE NOTE NOTE NOTE NOTE NOTE NOTE NOTE NOTE NOTE NOTE NOTE NOTE NOTE

When you use the Find feature, Access searches for matching records and shows them to you one at a time. If you want to limit the Datasheet view so it shows only the records that match your search criteria, use a *filter* or a *query*. Skill 7, "Find Data with Filters and Queries," explains how to set up these searches.

Change the Search Direction

Unless you tell it differently, Access will look in all the table records for matches to the Find What value. To look only for records above or below the current record, click the More button if the Search drop-down is not already visible at the bottom of the Find And Replace window. Then change the Search option from All to Up or Down.

Look for Part of a Field Value

When you open the Find dialog box, the setting for Match is normally set to Whole Field. Change the Match option to:

- Start Of Field to find records where the field begins with the Find What value

- Any Part Of Field if you are looking for a match any place in the field

TIP TIP TIP TIP TIP TIP TIP TIP TIP TIP TIP TIP TIP TIP TIP TIP TIP TIP TIP TIP TIP TIP TIP TIP TIP

If you find yourself changing the Match option to Start Of Field often, you may want to set this as the default. Choose Tools ➢ Options, click the Edit/Find tab, and check Start Of Field Search under Default/Find Replace Behavior.

Skill
4

Search All Fields

You can search all the fields shown in a Datasheet view instead of just the current field. All you have to do is change the setting for Look In. By default, Look In is set to the name of the current field. Change it to the name of the open table to search all fields.

Do Case-Sensitive Searches

In the More section of the Find And Replace window, there's a Match Case check box. Check this if you want Access to look for values that match the case of the Find What value. For example, in a case-sensitive search, "BLACK BEANS" finds only BLACK BEANS and not Black Beans or black beans.

Use Wildcards to Search for Values

You can use wildcards in the Find What box to look for values that match some pattern. This is really useful when you don't remember how something is spelled or exactly how it appears. Perhaps you need to find someone whose first name is Derrick, but you're not sure how they spell it. It might be *Derek* or maybe it's *Derick*. You can use the * wildcard like this, *Der*k*, in your Find What value to find the name.

Table 4.3 in the "Find and Replace" section earlier in this chapter lists the wildcards you can use in the Find And Replace dialog box along with examples of how they work.

Search Fields Using Data As It's Displayed

When you enter a search value, Access ordinarily compares what you enter to the values that are stored in the field. But what you see on the screen is not always the same as what's stored, because you can format values to be displayed differently. For example, you can format a date so it appears as 01-Jan-99, but it will be stored as 1/1/99 in the database. To have Access look for values that match display values, open the More section of the Find And Replace dialog box. Then check the box for Search Fields As Formatted.

Sort Records

You can quickly sort the records in Datasheet view in ascending or descending order.

NOTE NOTE NOTE NOTE NOTE NOTE NOTE NOTE NOTE NOTE NOTE NOTE NOTE NOTE
You can also sort records with a filter or a query. Skill 7 has information on how to do this.

Sort Records in Ascending Order

To sort records in ascending order, from A to Z:

1. If you want to sort by more than one field, move the datasheet columns so the second sort column follows the first, the third column follows the second, and so on.

2. Select the fields you want to sort by.

3. Click the Sort Ascending button on the Table Datasheet toolbar.

NOTE NOTE NOTE NOTE NOTE NOTE NOTE NOTE NOTE NOTE NOTE NOTE NOTE NOTE
You can sort records with a query or in a report, so don't worry about sorting records before you open these objects.

Sort Records in Descending Order

To sort records in descending order, from Z to A, follow the instructions in the last section for an ascending sort, but click the Sort Descending button in step 3.

If you've mastered all the steps in this skill, you should be able to handle any data-entry task in Access. You're probably pretty adept with moving around in a Datasheet view window and changing it to suit your needs. The next few skills explore the Form view window. First you'll see how to create forms with the various Form Wizards. Then you'll learn how to use the Form Design window to make changes to the instant forms. By customizing the forms created by the wizards, you can make them more attractive and more suitable for your particular needs.

SKILL
4

Are You Experienced?

Now you can. . .

- ☑ **Move through a table**
- ☑ **Use subdatasheets to see related records**
- ☑ **Edit a table**
- ☑ **Edit special fields like Memos and Date/Times**
- ☑ **Enter hyperlink addresses and use them to jump to various types of documents**
- ☑ **Work with OLE objects**
- ☑ **Customize a Datasheet view**
- ☑ **Find records**
- ☑ **Sort records**

Use AutoForms and the Form Wizard

- → **Understand what AutoForms are**
- → **Create an AutoForm**
- → **Know what the Form Wizard can do**
- → **Create a single table form with the wizard**
- → **Create multi-table forms with the wizard**

In Skill 4, you learned how to work with data in Datasheet view. This simple presentation of information in rows and columns is okay for some tasks. It definitely falls short, however, when you need to view all the fields of a record at the same time, or view a group of related records together for something like an order. This is when you need to turn to a *Form view*.

Skill 1 showed some examples of simple forms that were created with the Auto-Form feature and the Form Wizard. This skill explores how to use both of these techniques to create basic forms quickly without having to do a lot of tedious work in the Form Design window. Later, in Skill 6, "Customize Forms," you'll find out how to add personal touches to the basic forms you'll learn about here.

Understand AutoForms

The quickest way to create a form for a table or a query is with the *AutoForm* feature. An AutoForm is an instant form that Access creates for you without stopping to prompt you for information as the Form Wizard does. There are three varieties of AutoForms:

- Columnar
- Tabular
- Datasheet

Before you go through the simple steps of creating an AutoForm, take a quick look at what each type looks like.

Columnar Forms

A *columnar AutoForm* shows one record at a time in the Form view window. The fields are arranged in columns as in Figure 5.1.

You can see that the picture in the Photo field is not placed nicely in its frame. This is one of the situations where it's helpful to know how to change the instant forms that Access creates for you.

NOTE NOTE NOTE NOTE NOTE NOTE NOTE NOTE NOTE NOTE NOTE NOTE NOTE NOTE NOTE

In Skill 6, you'll see how to resize field objects and do other tasks in the Form Design window.

FIGURE 5.1: A columnar AutoForm shows all the fields from one record arranged in columns.

Tabular Forms

A *tabular AutoForm* can show several records in the Form view window with the fields arranged in rows. Figure 5.2 shows the Projects table displayed with a tabular AutoForm.

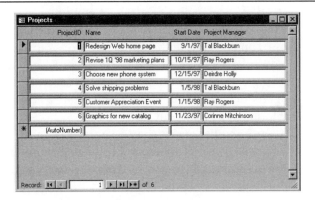

FIGURE 5.2: In a tabular AutoForm, records are shown with the fields arranged in rows.

If you created a tabular AutoForm for the Employees table shown in Figure 5.1, you would end up with only one record visible in the Form view window because of the size of the Photo field. This is another case where you might want to open the AutoForm in the Form Design window after it's created and nudge the size of objects so you can see more data at once.

Datasheet Forms

In a *datasheet AutoForm*, like the one in Figure 5.3, records are shown the same as they appear in a Datasheet window. In fact, you can resize, move, hide, and freeze columns just as you can in Datasheet view.

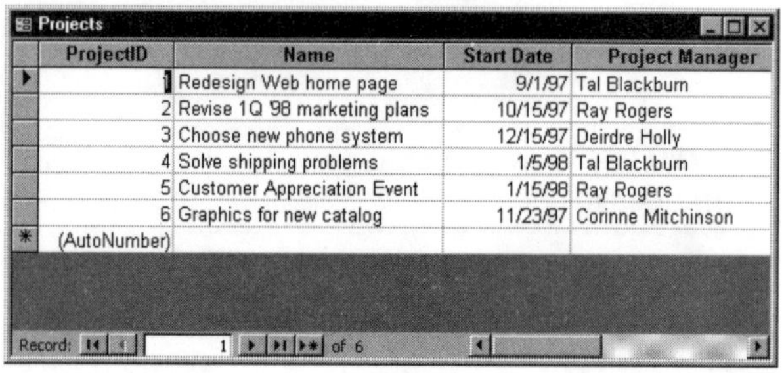

Projects

ProjectID	Name	Start Date	Project Manager
1	Redesign Web home page	9/1/97	Tal Blackburn
2	Revise 1Q '98 marketing plans	10/15/97	Ray Rogers
3	Choose new phone system	12/15/97	Deirdre Holly
4	Solve shipping problems	1/5/98	Tal Blackburn
5	Customer Appreciation Event	1/15/98	Ray Rogers
6	Graphics for new catalog	11/23/97	Corinne Mitchinson
(AutoNumber)			

Record: 1 of 6

FIGURE 5.3: In this datasheet AutoForm, records appear the same as they do in Datasheet view.

You might wonder why you would ever bother with a datasheet AutoForm instead of just opening a Datasheet window. One reason is that a datasheet AutoForm is often a good way to show detail records in a form that shows data from more than one table at the same time. For example, the top part of a form could show Order #, Order Date, and Customer # from an Orders table. The bottom part could show a datasheet AutoForm for an Order Line Items table with fields like Product #, Qty, and Price. You'll create a multi-table form like this in "Add a Subform to an AutoForm" later in this skill.

There's another reason to use a datasheet AutoForm instead of Datasheet view: If you want to use graphics and command buttons, you can add them to an AutoForm (or any other type of form) in the Form Design window. You can't include these objects in a regular Datasheet view window.

Create an AutoForm

This section goes through the steps needed to create several different types of AutoForms, including two forms that show data from more than one table.

Create a Columnar AutoForm

Columnar AutoForms are the easiest type of AutoForm to create:

1. In the Database window, click the Tables button (or the Queries button) and click the name of the object you want to show in an AutoForm. The Employees table is highlighted in Figure 5.4.

2. Select AutoForm from the New Object drop-down button on the Database toolbar.

That's it! You'll see a form like the one for the Employees table in Figure 5.4.

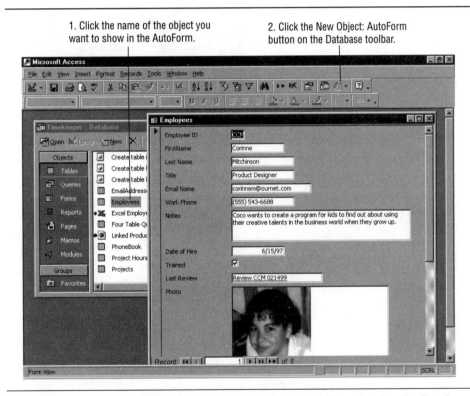

FIGURE 5.4: This Columnar AutoForm was created by selecting the Employees table in the Database window and clicking the AutoForm button.

Create a Tabular or Datasheet AutoForm

To create a tabular or datasheet AutoForm:

1. Click the Forms button in the Database window.

2. Click New to open the New Form dialog box:

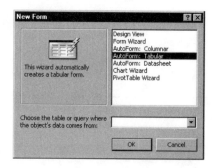

3. Select AutoForm: Tabular or AutoForm: Datasheet.

4. Choose a table or query from the drop-down list in the dialog box.

5. Click OK.

Access will work a bit and open the AutoForm in a Form view window.

Save an AutoForm

When you create an AutoForm, it doesn't get saved until you close the new Form view window:

1. Close the Form view window for the AutoForm.

2. Choose Yes when Access asks if you want to save the form.

3. Enter a name for the form.

The name of this new AutoForm will now appear in the Database window when the Forms button is selected.

Show Data from Two Tables with an AutoForm

Even though AutoForms are super easy to create, they aren't limited to showing data from just one table. If you create an AutoForm using a query that joins two or more tables, you end up with a form that shows data from more than one table at the same time. Next you'll see how to create an AutoForm for the Weekly

Records table (introduced in Skill 3, "Build Tables") that shows fields from the Employees table along with the information from Weekly Records.

First look at what happens when you create an AutoForm for the Weekly Records table by itself. After you select the Weekly Records table in the Database window and choose AutoForm from the New Object toolbar drop-down menu, you end up with a form that looks like this:

It shows all the fields from the Weekly Records table, but the Employee ID field is kind of cryptic. It would be better to see the employee name along with the ID like this:

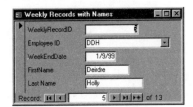

**SKILL
5**

You can create a form like this using AutoForm, but you have to create a query that links the Employees table to the Weekly Records table first.

NOTE NOTE NOTE NOTE NOTE NOTE·NOTE NOTE NOTE NOTE NOTE NOTE NOTE NOTE NOTE NOTE
Skill 7, "Find Data with Filters and Queries," explains in detail how to create queries.

If you already see a name instead of an ID number, you probably used the Lookup Wizard to create a drop-down list for the EmployeeID field that shows the names in the Employees table, as described in Skill 3. If so, you don't need to use a query in this case. But, if you want to show fields other than those shown on the drop-down list, you can use the technique outlined in this example.

Create a Query for an AutoForm

You haven't worked with queries yet, but this one is easy. It links the Weekly Records and Employees tables so you can see fields from both tables at the same time.

1. Click the Queries button in the Database window.

2. Click New.

3. In the New Query dialog box, leave Design View selected and click OK.

4. Click Weekly Records and then Add. Repeat this for the Employees table.

5. Click Close to open a Query Design window:

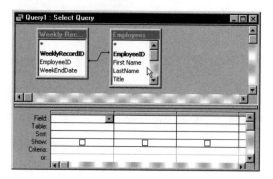

6. If you don't see a line that links the tables using their EmployeeID fields, drag between the fields to establish a link.

7. Drag the asterisk on the Weekly Records field list to the Field column in the first row of the grid in the bottom half of the window. The asterisk tells Access to include all the fields from the Weekly Records table in the query result.

8. Drag FirstName and LastName from the Employees field list in the top half of the Query Design window to the second and third columns of the grid. (You can also double-click each field in turn to move it to the next available column in the query grid.)

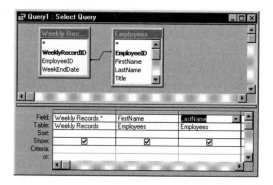

9. Close the Query Design window, choose Yes, and enter **Weekly Records with Names** for the query name.

Create an AutoForm with a Query

Now that you have the query you need, you can create an AutoForm for it with a couple of clicks:

1. In the Database window, highlight the query you created in the last section.

2. Click the New Object: AutoForm button on the Database toolbar.

3. To save the form, close the Form view window, choose Yes when Access asks if you want to save the form, and enter a name.

If you prefer to have the FirstName and LastName fields follow the EmployeeID field, instead of appearing after the last Weekly Records fields, you can rearrange the AutoForm layout in the Form Design window. Or you can use the Form Wizard as described a little later in this chapter in the section "Create a Form with the Wizard."

SKILL
5

Add a Subform to an AutoForm

A *subform* is a form that is included on another form to show information from another table. You can take the AutoForm you created in the last example for the Weekly Records table and quickly add a subform for the Project Hours table to create a multi-table form. You may feel as if you're getting a bit ahead of yourself here since you'll have to work in the Form Design view window, but this exercise will give you an idea of how you can build on an AutoForm to create a more complex form like the one in Figure 5.5.

NOTE NOTE NOTE NOTE NOTE NOTE NOTE NOTE NOTE NOTE NOTE NOTE NOTE NOTE NOTE
The details of using the Form Design view window are covered in Skill 6.

To add a subform to the AutoForm created in the last example:

1. In the Database window, click the name of the AutoForm you just created for the Weekly Records table to select it. Then click Design. (You can also right-click the form's name and select Design from the shortcut menu.)

2. Drag the lower-right corner of the Form Design view window to make it larger.

This section of the form was created with AutoForm.

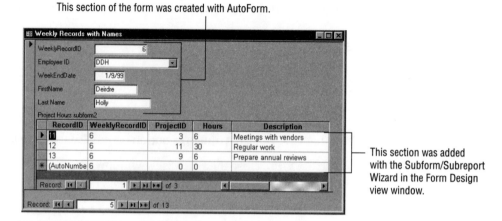

FIGURE 5.5: This form was created by adding a subform for the Project Hours table to an AutoForm for the Weekly Records table.

3. Point to the lower-right corner of the form (the area with the grid) and drag to make it longer and a bit wider:

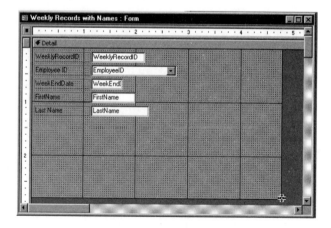

4. Move the Form Design view window, if necessary, to make the Database window visible.

5. Click the Tables button in the Database window.

6. Drag Project Hours from the Database window to the new space you created in the Form Design view window to start the Subform/Subreport Wizard.

7. Click Next to use the link that's displayed or use Define My Own to pick the linking fields. WeeklyRecordID is the field that is common to both tables in this example.

8. Change the subform name, if you want to, and click Finish.

9. Change the size of the subform if you need to make it longer. (Click the View button on the toolbar to switch between Form view and Design view so you can check and change the subform size and position until it's right.)

10. Click View on the toolbar to see what the AutoForm looks like with the subform for Project Hours added.

11. If you need to, resize the columns in the subform so you can see the field values clearly.

12. Close the Form view window and choose Yes to save the file. (Use File ≻ Save As in the Form Design view window first if you want to save the form with a different name from the original AutoForm.)

SKILL
5

TIP TIP TIP TIP TIP TIP TIP TIP TIP TIP TIP TIP TIP TIP TIP TIP TIP TIP TIP TIP TIP TIP TIP

If the subform shows detail records that don't belong to the record displayed in the top part of the form, this means that the subform is not properly linked to the master form. See Skill 6 to learn how to specify the linking fields for a subform.

Use the Form Wizard

The Form Wizard is another tool you can use to create an "instant form" for a table or a query. It takes a little more work than using AutoForm, but it gives you more control over the final result. The Form Wizard lets you:

- Select the fields for a form, from more than one table if you like
- Choose the order in which fields appear on the form
- Choose the "master" table for the form (which determines the order of the form's records), when the form includes fields from more than one table
- Pick a layout for the form: columnar, tabular, datasheet, or justified
- Choose a style (Blends, International, Standard, Stone, and so on)

The Form Wizard is a series of dialog boxes that walk you through all the steps needed to create a form. First you select the table or query you want to use. Then, in the following steps, you choose the fields and other elements you would like in your form. In the next group of examples, you'll use the Form Wizard to create a single table form and forms that show fields from two related tables. You'll go through a couple of multi-table form examples to see what happens when you choose tables on different sides of a one-to-many relationship for the form's master table.

Create a Single Table Form

This example shows you how to create a form for the Employees table with the Ricepaper background:

1. In the Database window, click the Forms button.

2. Double-click Create Form By Using Wizard. You'll see the first step of the Form Wizard:

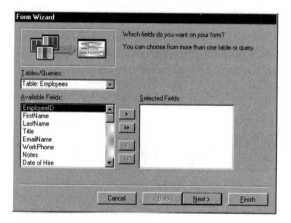

3. Under Tables/Queries, select Table: Employees from the drop-down list.

4. Click the >> button to add all the fields from Employees to the form and click Next.

5. Choose the Columnar layout and click Next.

6. When the Form Wizard asks which background you would like, select Ricepaper and click Next.

7. In the last step, enter a name for the form and click Finish.

Figure 5.6 shows the end result of these steps.

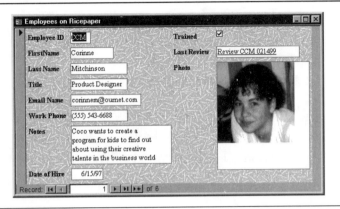

FIGURE 5.6: This form for the Employees table was created with the help of the Form Wizard.

TIP TIP TIP TIP TIP TIP TIP TIP TIP TIP TIP TIP TIP TIP TIP TIP TIP TIP TIP TIP TIP TIP TIP TIP

If you choose fields in the Form Wizard individually instead of using the >> button to add all the fields at once, you can control their order on the form.

Create a Multi-Table Form

Earlier in the section on AutoForms, you saw how to show fields from two tables by creating an AutoForm based on a query. It worked fairly well, except that there was no way to control the order in which the fields appeared on the form, short of going into the Form Design window and rearranging things. You can use the Form Wizard to avoid this problem and get a more attractive form than the rather plain one created by AutoForm at the same time.

The next example uses the Form Wizard to create a form for the Weekly Records table that also includes the FirstName and LastName fields from the Employees table. One of the Form Wizard's features is used to position the FirstName and LastName fields from the Employee's table right after the EmployeeID field from the Weekly Records table. In contrast, AutoForm places the FirstName and Last-Name fields after the last field in the Weekly Records table (WeekEndDate) rather than after the EmployeeID field.

1. Click the Forms button in the Database window.

2. Double-click Create Form By Using Wizard.

3. In the first step of the Form Wizard, select Table: Weekly Records from the Tables/Queries drop-down list.

4. Click the > button twice to move the first two fields from Weekly Records to the Selected Fields list.

5. Go back to the Tables/Queries drop-down list and choose Table: Employees.

6. Highlight FirstName on the Available Fields list and click the > button.

7. Repeat step 7 for the Last Name field.

8. Again, select Table: Weekly Records from the Tables/Queries drop-down list.

9. Click the > button to add WeekEndDate to the Selected Fields list.

10. Click Next to continue to the next Form Wizard dialog box:

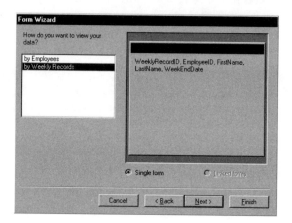

11. The dialog box shown above allows you to choose the "master" table for the form. For this first example, leave By Weekly Records selected. This tells Access to create a form that shows one form for each record in the Weekly Records table. (A later example that illustrates what happens when you choose Employees as the master table.) Click Next.

12. Choose Columnar or whichever layout you like and click Next.

13. Select Stone or the style you prefer and click Next.

14. Change the form name, if you need to, and click Finish. You'll see a form like the one in Figure 5.7.

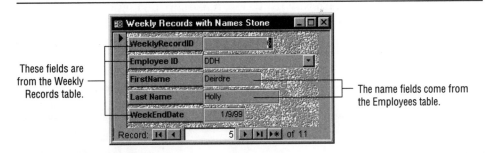

These fields are from the Weekly Records table.

The name fields come from the Employees table.

FIGURE 5.7: This form, created with the Form Wizard, shows fields from both the Weekly Records and the Employees tables.

A Multi-Table Form with a One-to-Many Relationship

In the last example, the Weekly Records table was the master table for the multi-table form created by the Form Wizard. Because there is a one-to-one relationship from Weekly Records to Employees, the Form Wizard shows one form for each record in Weekly Records, finds the related employee name information in the Employees table, and adds it to the form.

This next example creates another form with the Form Wizard for the same two tables. But this time, you'll select the Employees table as the master for the form. Because there is a one-to-many relationship from Employees to Weekly Records, the final form will look different from the one in Figure 5.7. (A one-to-many relationship exists because there can be multiple records in the Weekly Records table for each Employee record.)

1. Click the Forms button in the Database window.

2. Double-click Create Form By Using Wizard.

3. In the first step, select Table: Employees from the Tables/Queries drop-down list.

4. Add the EmployeeID, FirstName, and LastName fields to the Selected Fields list.

5. Use the Tables/Queries drop-down list to select the Weekly Records table.

6. Add all the fields from Weekly Records, except EmployeeID, to the Selected Fields list. Then click Next.

7. In the next wizard step, make sure By Employees is selected on the left side of the wizard's window. On the bottom right, you can choose either Form With Subform(s) or Linked Forms. If you leave the default, Forms With Subform(s), selected, the dialog box will look like this:

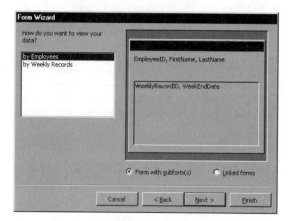

8. Follow the rest of the Form Wizard's steps, choosing a layout for the subform and a style, and providing a name for the two forms (the main form and the subform) in the last step.

9. Click Finish to view the finished form.

Figure 5.8 shows the result of the last exercise with the Form Wizard. As you can see, the form has two parts: the main part of the form, which shows records from the Employees table, and the subform that displays related records from Weekly Records. The form could benefit from a little work in the Form Design window. You'll find out how to use all the features of the Form Design window in Skill 6.

NOTE NOTE NOTE NOTE NOTE NOTE NOTE NOTE NOTE NOTE NOTE NOTE NOTE NOTE NOTE
There are several ways you can limit the records that you see with a form. See the techniques described in Skill 7 to learn how to filter records and to base a form on a query instead of a table.

In this skill, you've learned how to create forms with Access 2000 using Auto-Forms and the Form Wizard. In the next skill, you'll see how to use Form Design view to turn these instant forms into exactly what you need.

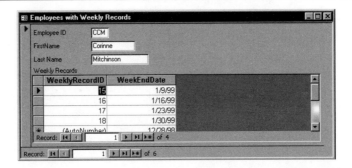

FIGURE 5.8: This form for the Employees table includes a subform that shows related records from the Weekly Records table. It was created with the Form Wizard.

Are You Experienced?

Now you can...

- ☑ **Understand what AutoForms are**

- ☑ **Create an AutoForm**

- ☑ **Use the Form Wizard**

- ☑ **Create a single table form with the wizard**

- ☑ **Create a multi-table form with the wizard**

- ☑ **Choose the master table for a multi-table form**

Customize Forms

- → **Know the elements of the Form Design view window**
- → **Change the layout of a form**
- → **Do basic maneuvers like move, resize, and align form objects**
- → **Add fields and text to a form**
- → **Include option groups, check boxes, combo boxes, and list boxes**
- → **Add pictures, lines, and boxes to a form**
- → **Create a tabbed form**
- → **Add a subform**
- → **Change the record source for a form**
- → **Create your own form template**

If you're lucky, you may never need to customize a form. The forms you get from the Database Wizard or the Form Wizard just might work perfectly for your database projects. But chances are you'll end up in the Form Design view window at some point. You may need to do practical things like move fields around or add command buttons. Or you might want to change the form's colors and add graphics to create your own style. This skill includes step-by-step instructions for doing all these form design tasks and more.

The Form Design View Window

The *Form Design view window* is the place to make changes to a form's design. It has several tools available to help you with your design work:

- The Form Design toolbar
- The Formatting (Form/Report) toolbar
- The Toolbox
- The Field List
- The properties sheet
- Various Control Wizards

Before you start working on some forms, take a quick look at each of these tools. First we have to open the Form Design view window.

Open the Form Design View Window

The best way to open the Form Design view window depends on where you are:

- If you are creating a form with the Form Wizard, choose the option to open the new form in Design view when you get to the last step of the wizard.
- If you are in the Database window, click the Forms button, highlight the form you want to change, and click Design. Or you can right-click the form you want to work with and choose Design from the shortcut menu.
- If you are viewing a form, click the Design View button on the toolbar.

Figure 6.1 shows a form called "Weekly Hours with Project Hours" open in Design view. As pointed out in the figure, there are two special toolbars in Design view: Form Design and Formatting (Form/Report).

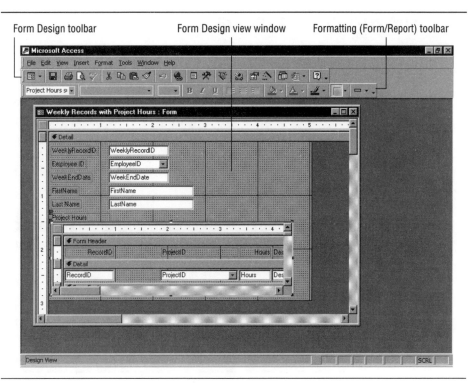

FIGURE 6.1: A form open in Design view.

The Form Design Toolbar

The *Form Design toolbar* has buttons for common tasks like View, Save, and Print. It also has special buttons to open Design tools like the Toolbox and the Field List.

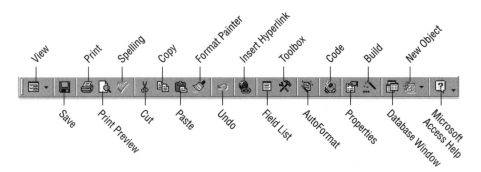

The Formatting Toolbar

The *Formatting (Form/Report) toolbar* appears in both the Form Design view and Report Design view windows. Most of the buttons are for typical formatting jobs like changing font sizes and colors. This section won't go through step-by-step instructions on how to use these buttons. (It would make for pretty boring reading.) However, you will find descriptions of how they work sprinkled through other examples later in this skill.

The first button, Object, is different from the other button on the Formatting toolbar. It lets you select an object (like a field object or a label) by choosing it from a drop-down list.

TIP TIP TIP TIP TIP TIP TIP TIP TIP TIP TIP TIP TIP TIP TIP TIP TIP TIP TIP TIP TIP TIP TIP TIP

Check the Object button to see what object is currently selected in the Design view window.

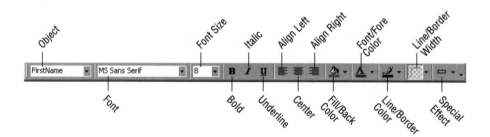

The Toolbox

The *Toolbox* has buttons for placing labels, fields, combo boxes (drop-down lists), command buttons, and other special purpose objects in a form. To open the Toolbox, just click the Toolbox button on the Form Design toolbar.

The Toolbox looks like this:

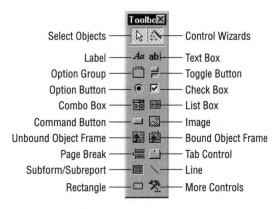

Select Objects		Control Wizards
Label		Text Box
Option Group		Toggle Button
Option Button		Check Box
Combo Box		List Box
Command Button		Image
Unbound Object Frame		Bound Object Frame
Page Break		Tab Control
Subform/Subreport		Line
Rectangle		More Controls

After going through the basics of getting around in the Design view window (moving and resizing objects, aligning objects, and so on), the next sections spend time on each of these tools to see how they work.

The Field List

The *Field List* is a handy way to reference fields in the Design view window. For example, to create an object for the LastName field on a form, you can click Text Box in the Toolbox, then drag LastName from the Field List to the design window. (Don't worry if this isn't clear; these steps are detailed in the "Add Fields to a Form" section.)

To show the Field List, click the Field List button on the Form Design toolbar. You'll see a list like the one in Figure 6.2. The Field List shows fields from the table or query that is the source of data for the form you are working on.

NOTE NOTE NOTE NOTE NOTE NOTE NOTE NOTE NOTE NOTE NOTE NOTE NOTE NOTE NOTE

The Field List doesn't show fields from subforms. To work with a subform's fields, you need to open the subform in its own Design view window. You can either open the subform from the Database window or double-click it while you are working on the design of the master form. For more information on subforms, see "Include a Subform" later in this skill.

TIP TIP TIP TIP TIP TIP TIP TIP TIP TIP TIP TIP TIP TIP TIP TIP TIP TIP TIP TIP TIP TIP TIP TIP

To select all the fields on the Field List at one time so you can drag them as a group to the form you're working on, double-click the Field List's title bar. To deselect all the fields, click one field or close the Field List and open it again.

SKILL
6

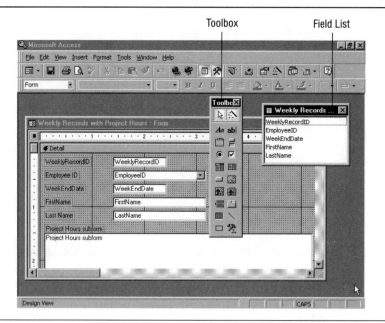

FIGURE 6.2: The Field List and the Toolbox are shown with this Form Design view window.

The Properties Sheet

Each object in a Form Design view window has its own *properties sheet*, a tabbed box that lists the properties you can change for the object.

Open the Properties Sheet

You can open an object's properties sheet with any of these methods:

- Select the object and click the Properties button on the Form Design toolbar.

- Right-click the object and select Properties from the shortcut menu.

- Double-click any object in the Form Design view.

This properties sheet shows the properties for the "Weekly Records with Project Hours" form:

TIP TIP TIP TIP TIP TIP TIP TIP TIP TIP TIP TIP TIP TIP TIP TIP TIP TIP TIP TIP TIP TIP TIP TIP TIP TIP

If the properties sheet is already open for another object, just click the object whose properties you want to check. The properties sheet contents will change to reflect the object you just selected.

The Properties Sheet Categories

The tabs you see on all properties sheets remain the same:

Format shows properties like Caption, Scroll Bars, and Border Style. It also lets you set properties that determine things, such as the way a date is displayed or the number of decimal places shown for a number.

Data properties indicate where the data for the selected form or field come from. If you're viewing the properties sheet for a form, you'll also see lines for properties, like Filter, Order By, and Allow Filters. For a field, the Data tab has lines for Input Mask, Default Value, and Enabled. Any properties you set here take precedence over similar properties set in the Table Design view window (discussed in Skill 3).

Event has lines for the different types of events that can be associated with the selected object: After Update, On Open, On Close, and so on. Typically, you use these properties to tell Access to run a macro or some Visual Basic code when an event occurs, like clicking a command button.

Other shows all properties that don't fall into the other categories: Menu Bar, Shortcut Menu, Help File, and so on.

All shows all the properties included on the other tabs.

The lines on each tab, though, vary depending on the type of object you selected in the Design view window.

Change Properties

To change a property for an object, you can simply type a new entry on the right line in the properties sheet. This isn't always as easy as it sounds, however. You might not know the valid possibilities for a property, or you may not remember how to spell a field name.

Thankfully, you can get help from Access on many lines. To see if help exists for a specific property, just click its line on the properties sheet and look for a drop-down arrow at the end of the line. If there is one, you can use the drop-down menu to select a valid value for the property. For example, if you click the Views Allowed property on the Format tab with the entire form selected, you'll see a list of possible views including Form, Datasheet, and Both.

TIP TIP TIP TIP TIP TIP TIP TIP TIP TIP TIP TIP TIP TIP TIP TIP TIP TIP TIP TIP TIP TIP TIP TIP TIP
Repeatedly double-click a line on the properties sheet to cycle through its possible values.

When you click some lines, you may see a drop-down arrow and an ellipsis (. . .). The drop-down arrow opens a list of existing choices for the field, while the ellipsis opens a helper like an Expression Builder or a Macro Builder. For example, if you click a line for an Event property like On Open, you can use the drop-down arrow to see a list of the macros you have already created in the database. Or you can use the ellipsis to open a Choose Builder dialog box that lets you select the Expression Builder, the Macro Builder, or the Code Builder. You'll use these builders later on in Skill 14, "Bypass Database Drudgery with Command Buttons and Macros."

Enable the Control Wizards

When you click a button in the Toolbox to place an object like a combo box, or do something like drag a subform from the Database window to the Form Design window, you usually get some help from one of the Access wizards. For example, if you click the Option Group button in the Toolbox and drag a spot for a new control in the design window, the Option Group Wizard automatically steps in to help you.

If you're not getting help when you expect it:

1. Open the Toolbox, if it's not already visible.

2. Check the Control Wizards button in the Toolbox and make sure it's depressed, as in Figure 6.2. (The background will be lighter than that of the buttons below it.)

3. If the Control Wizards button is not depressed, click it to turn on the Control Wizards.

Customize a Form's Layout

There are some general things you can do to change the overall characteristics of a form before you start manipulating the objects it contains. You may want to:

- Adjust the size of a form

- Change the overall style

- Add headers and footers

- Display a picture for the background

Let's quickly go over how to make each of these changes to a form.

Change a Form's Width

To change a form's width:

1. Right-click the form selector in the upper-left corner of the Design view window. The mouse pointer below points to the form selector:

2. Choose Properties from the shortcut menu.

3. Click the Format tab.

4. Scroll to the Width setting and type in the desired width.

A Shortcut for Resizing a Form

Another way to change the size of a form is to drag on its right or bottom border:

1. Make the form window larger or use the scroll bars to bring the form's right and/or bottom border into view.

2. Point to one of the borders, or the lower-right corner of the form, until you see the mouse pointer change to an arrow with two or four heads:

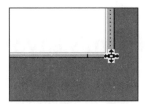

3. Drag the borders until the form is the desired size.

Use AutoFormat to Change a Form's Style

The style of a form determines its background, the colors and fonts for objects like labels and field objects, and the look for borders. In Skill 5, you saw how to select a style with the Form Wizard. Once a form is created, you are free to change its style using the AutoFormat feature.

To use AutoFormat:

1. Use the Object drop-down on the Formatting toolbar and select Form, if it is not already selected. (Just take a quick look at the Object button to see what object is currently selected.)

2. Click AutoFormat on the Form Design toolbar to open the AutoFormat dialog box:

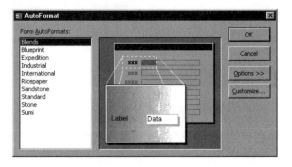

3. Double-click the style you want to use.

Click once on a style in the AutoFormat dialog box to see a preview of how the style looks.

Add Headers and Footers

You can include headers and footers on a form to hold visual elements like form titles and page numbers. There are two types of headers and footers:

- *Form headers and footers* show up at the top and bottom of Form windows; they also appear on printed forms.

- *Page headers and footers* only appear on printed forms.

To add header and footer areas to a form, choose View ➤ Form Header/Footer or View ➤ Page Header/Footer from the menu. Once you add a header or a footer to a form, you can resize it by dragging on its bottom border. Then you can add controls that show things like the date or a title.

Remove Headers and Footers

Select View ➤ Form Header/Footer or View ➤ Page Header/Footer again to remove headers and footers from a form.

Add a Background Graphic

This is one of the fun things you can do in the Form Design view window. You can take a picture stored in a graphic file and use it as a background. The types of graphic files you can use depend on the filters that you installed as part of Office 2000.

To put a picture on the background of a form:

1. Select Form from the Object drop-down list on the Formatting toolbar.

2. Click Properties on the Form Design toolbar.

3. Scroll down to the Picture property on the Format tab and click the line.

4. Type in the filename for the graphic you want to use, or click the ellipsis at the end of the line to browse for a picture.

Skill
6

5. If you want to tile the picture instead of showing just one copy of it in the window, change the Picture Tiling property a few lines down to Yes.

6. Click the View button on the Form Design toolbar to see how the new background looks.

Figure 6.3 shows the Weekly Records form with a background created from the Jungle.bmp file. The field labels are a little hard to read, even with their background color changed, but this example shows how easy it is to jazz up a form by changing its Picture property.

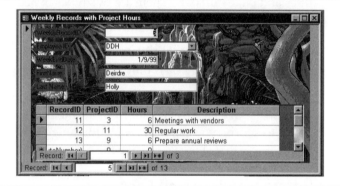

FIGURE 6.3: The Weekly Records form with a picture added to its background. The picture is taken from Jungle.bmp.

Fill a Background with a Picture

If the picture you choose doesn't fill the form's background, you can either tile it (as described in the last example) or stretch it to fill the form:

1. Open the properties sheet for the form itself.

2. Click the Format tab.

3. Change the Picture Size Mode property to Stretch.

Remove a Picture from a Form

To get rid of a picture you've added to a form, just highlight the Picture property, press Delete, and click Yes. Check the form in View mode again and the background will be gone.

The Basic Maneuvers

This section explains the basic tasks you need to be familiar with to work effectively in Design view. You'll find out how to:

- Select objects in the Design view window
- Move and resize objects
- Format objects by aligning and spacing them
- Resize form areas like headers, the detail area, and footers

Select Objects

For jobs like resizing an object in Design view, you need to select the object first. Objects can be selected in several ways:

- Click an object to select it.
- Select the object from the Object drop-down list on the Formatting toolbar.
- Tab to the object, if it's one of a group of objects contained in another object.
- Click the form selector or a section selector to select the form itself or a form section like the Detail area.
- Click the horizontal ruler to select all controls underneath the spot you click, or the vertical ruler to select all controls beside the point you click.

**SKILL
6**

Select the Form

The quickest way to select a form is via the form selector. Just click the box in the upper-left corner of the Design view window as pointed out here:

Select Multiple Objects

For design tasks like aligning objects, you'll need to select more than one object at the same time. There are two ways to do this:

- Hold down Shift while you click all the objects you want to select.

- Drag a box around or through the objects; when you release the mouse, everything in the box will be selected.

TIP TIP TIP TIP TIP TIP TIP TIP TIP TIP TIP TIP TIP TIP TIP TIP TIP TIP TIP TIP TIP TIP TIP TIP

By default, Access selects any objects that you drag around *or* through when you use the last technique described above to select objects. If you want Access to select only those objects that you drag around, instead of through, choose Tools ➤ Options, click the Forms/Reports tab and, under Selection Behavior, click Fully Enclosed. Then click OK to save your change.

Undo Changes

You can undo most changes you make in the Design view window if you catch them right away. Use any of these methods to undo changes:

- Press Ctrl+Z.

- Choose Edit ➤ Undo from the menu.

- Click the Undo button on the Form Design toolbar.

Move Objects

You can move objects with your mouse or with the keyboard.

Move Objects with Your Mouse

To move an object in the Design view window with your mouse:

1. Select the object you want to move.

2. Point to a border of the object until the mouse pointer turns into a hand like this:

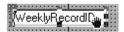

3. Drag the object to a new spot.

TIP TIP TIP TIP TIP TIP TIP TIP TIP TIP TIP TIP TIP TIP TIP TIP TIP TIP TIP TIP TIP TIP TIP

If the object you want to move isn't already selected, you can combine steps one and two above. Just point to the object and drag. When you click to start the drag, the pointer will turn into a hand.

Move Objects with the Keyboard

If you prefer to leave your hands on the keyboard, you can move objects this way:

1. Select the object(s) you want to move.

2. Hold down Ctrl while you use the arrow keys to move the selected object(s).

Undo a Move

If you move something by mistake, you can move the object back to where it belongs if you haven't made any other changes to the design. Use either of the following methods to do so:

- Press Ctrl+Z.

- Choose Edit ➢ Undo Move from the menu.

Resize Objects

As with moving objects, you can use either the mouse or the keyboard to change an object's size. You can also change an object's dimensions using its properties sheet. If you want to size a group of objects so they are uniform, use the Format ➢ Size commands as described a little later in this chapter.

Resize Objects with the Mouse

To resize an object using your mouse:

1. Select the object.

2. Point to one of the object's handles, depending on the border you want to adjust, until the mouse pointer appears as a double-headed arrow:

If you point to one of the handles at the corner of an object, you can resize both of the adjacent borders at the same time.

3. Drag until the object is the desired size.

Resize Objects with the Keyboard

You can also resize an object using the keyboard. Select the object(s) you want to resize, hold down Shift, and tap an arrow key to change the size. Choose the arrow key depending on the type of change you want to make. Use the:

- Left arrow key to reduce an object's width from its right side

- Right arrow key to widen an object along its right side

- Up arrow key to make an object shorter by moving its bottom border up

- Down arrow key to make an object taller by moving its bottom border down

TIP TIP TIP TIP TIP TIP TIP TIP TIP TIP TIP TIP TIP TIP TIP TIP TIP TIP TIP TIP TIP TIP TIP TIP

To fine-tune an object's size, use its properties sheet to change its dimensions. Right-click the object, choose Properties, click the Format tab, and change the settings for Width and Height as needed.

Align Objects

If you place a group of controls like text boxes or command buttons on a form, you will probably want to align them so they look tidy. Access has tools to help you align objects along their left or right sides, their tops or bottoms, or to the grid.

To align a group of objects in the Design view window:

1. Select the objects.

2. Choose Format ➤ Align and then Left, Right, Top, Bottom, or To Grid.

TIP TIP TIP TIP TIP TIP TIP TIP TIP TIP TIP TIP TIP TIP TIP TIP TIP TIP TIP TIP TIP TIP TIP TIP

If you find yourself using the Align commands on the Format menu frequently, you may want to add buttons for them to the Formatting toolbar. See Skill 16, "Customize Access," for instructions on changing a toolbar.

Formatting Tips

Here are a few quick formatting tips that might save you some time.

Move a Text Box Object without Moving Its Label

When you move a text box, its label usually moves along with it. To get around this, point to the top left corner of the value portion of the text box (not the part that holds the label) until the mouse pointer changes to a closed hand. Then move just the text box without dragging the label along with it. You may also want to resize the text box instead of moving it:

1. Drag the left border of the field object left or right, depending on whether you want it closer to or farther from its label.

2. Adjust the right border of the field object to the desired length.

Space Objects Evenly Horizontally

Instead of moving objects individually to space them evenly along a horizontal line:

1. Select the objects you want to align.

2. Move the leftmost object to the place you want it.

3. Move the rightmost object to the place it should be.

4. Choose Format ➣ Horizontal Spacing ➣ Make Equal.

Space Objects Evenly Vertically

Follow the above steps, but with these changes: Place the top and bottom objects as needed. Then choose Format ➣ Vertical Spacing ➣ Make Equal.

Make Objects the Same Size

Here's a quick way to make a group of objects all the same size without a lot of mouse work:

1. Select the objects that should be the same size.

2. Choose Format ➣ Size and then choose To Tallest, To Shortest, To Widest, or To Narrowest, depending on how you want the objects to match.

Resize Form Areas

When you create a form with a wizard, the form includes a Detail area with just enough room to show the form's fields. If you want to add text, graphics, or other

SKILL
6

objects, you may need to increase the area of this section. You may also want to increase the size of any footers or headers you added to a form.

To change an area's size:

1. Select the area you want to resize by clicking its background or choosing it from the Object drop-down list on the Formatting toolbar.

2. Point to the bottom border of the area until the mouse pointer appears as a double-headed arrow:

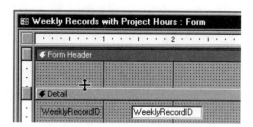

3. Drag up or down to change the area's size.

TIP TIP TIP TIP TIP TIP TIP TIP TIP TIP TIP TIP TIP TIP TIP TIP TIP TIP TIP TIP TIP TIP TIP TIP TIP
You can only add space to the bottom of an area. To make room at the top, select the area and drag its bottom border down. Then select all of the area's objects and drag them down at the same time.

Add Fields to a Form

If you add a field to a table after you've already created the forms for your database, that field will not be a part of any forms that already exist. When this happens, you will have to go back and add the new field to any forms it belongs on. This can be done in a couple of different ways. The next couple of examples show how to add a field called Date Submitted to the Weekly Records form.

Use the Field List

To use this technique:

1. Click Field List on the Form Design toolbar, if the Field List is not open.

2.   Drag Date Submitted from the Field List to the spot where you want the new field object to appear in the Design view window.

3.   Drag or otherwise move the new field object if needed.

Figure 6.4 shows the "Weekly Records with Project Hours" form with a field object added for Date Submitted.

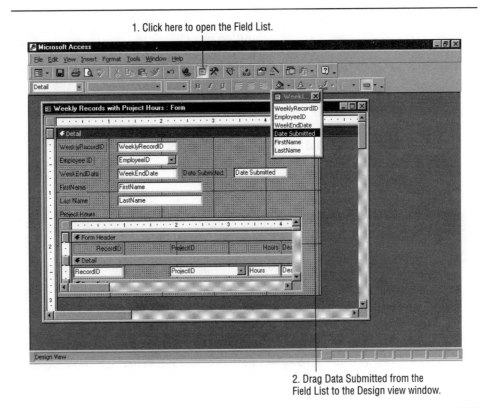

FIGURE 6.4:   A new field object for Date Submitted has been added to this form for the Weekly Records table.

Copy a Field and Change Its Data Source

Instead of using the Field List, you can simply copy a field in the Design view window and then change its properties to have it display a different field and label.

1.   Select the field you want to copy.

2. Choose Edit ➤ Duplicate from the menu.

3. Move the new, duplicated field object to the place you want it to appear.

4. Adjust the borders of the text box (the part that shows the field values) if needed to change its distance from the field label.

5. Right-click the new field object and choose Properties from the shortcut menu.

6. Click the Data tab.

7. Choose Date Submitted from the drop-down menu for the Control Source property.

8. Right-click the label for the new field object and choose Properties.

9. Click the Format tab and change the Caption property to Date Submitted.

Change the Tab Order for Fields

After you add controls to a form, you may need to change the tab order.

1. Choose View ➤ Tab Order.

2. Under Section, choose Form Header or Form Footer, if you are reordering the controls in one of these sections instead of in the Detail area.

3. Click Auto Order to order the fields automatically from left to right and top to bottom.

4. Click OK or the Close button for the Tab Order dialog box.

TIP TIP TIP TIP TIP TIP TIP TIP TIP TIP TIP TIP TIP TIP TIP TIP TIP TIP TIP TIP TIP TIP TIP TIP
You can also select fields on the Tab order list and drag them up or down.

Add Text to a Form

If you want to add text to a form, you can either use the Label tool or duplicate an existing label object and adjust it as needed. Both of these methods for placing a label are described next.

Use the Label Tool

This example shows how to add text to a form header using the Label tool:

1. Choose View ➤ Form Header/Footer from the menu, if the form header is not already visible. Then drag the bottom border of the Form Header area down to make more room for the label, if needed.

2. Click the Toolbox button, if the Toolbox isn't already open.

3. Click the Label tool in the Toolbox.

4. In the Design view window, point to the upper-left corner of the place where you the text to appear and drag a rectangle. You'll see a blinking cursor in a white box.

5. Type in the text and press Enter. Figure 6.5 shows the Weekly Records form with a label added to the form header.

SKILL
6

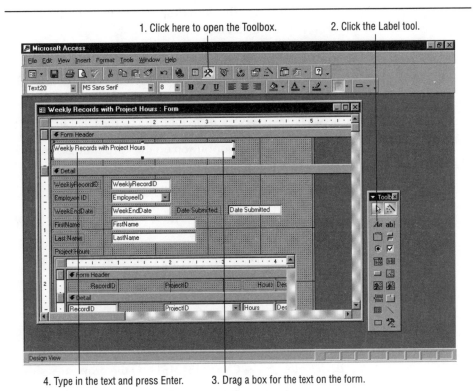

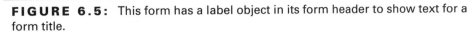

FIGURE 6.5: This form has a label object in its form header to show text for a form title.

Change a Label's Style

Once you've entered some text in a label, you'll probably want to change its style to make it more visible on the form. There's more than one way to change a label's style:

- Open the properties sheet for the label and change the properties on the Format tab.

- Right-click the label and use the Fill/Back Color, Font/Fore Color, and Special Effect options on the shortcut menu.

- Use the tools on the Formatting (Form/Report) toolbar.

This example uses the Formatting (Form/Report) toolbar to change the label shown in Figure 6.5:

1. Select the label.

2. Choose a font from the Font drop-down menu on the Formatting (Form/Report) toolbar.

3. Use the Font Size drop-down menu to change the text's size.

4. Click the Bold, Italic, Underline, Align Left, Center, and Align Right buttons as needed.

5. Choose Format ➤ Size ➤ To Fit to make the label fit its text.

6. Use the Fill/Back Color button on the Formatting (Form/Report) toolbar to change the background color for the label.

7. Use the Font/Fore Color button to change the color of the text itself.

8. If you want to add a border, choose one with a number from the Line/Border Width drop-down list.

9. Change the border color with the Line/Border Color tool.

10. If you want to give the label a shadow or use another effect, use the Special Effect button.

Figure 6.6 shows a label on the Weekly Records with Names form with these properties:

Back Color	Cyan (13421619 on the properties sheet)
Special Effect	Shadowed
Border Style	Solid

Border Width	3 pt.
Fore Color	Navy Blue (8388608 on the properties sheet)
Font Name	Futura Bk BT
Font Size	12
Font Weight	Bold

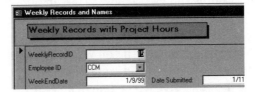

FIGURE 6.6: This label is the same one shown in Figure 6.5 after its properties were changed with the Formatting (Form/Report) toolbar buttons.

Copy a Label

If you already have a label on a form that's similar to a new one you want to add, you can copy the old one and then change it as needed. To do this:

SKILL
6

1. Click the label you want to copy to select it.

2. Choose Edit ➤ Duplicate from the menu.

3. When the new label appears, drag it to wherever it needs to be placed.

4. Click once inside the label to edit its contents, or double-click the label to overwrite whatever is already there.

Use Option Groups and Option Buttons

If you want to limit a field's values to a set of predefined entries that correspond to numbered codes, you can use a special kind of control called an *option group*. An option group consists of a group of labeled buttons that you can click to make a choice. Behind the scenes, Access assigns a code like 1 or 2 to the field the option group is tied to, depending on the button you click. For example, you could use an option group with buttons called Cash, Check, and Credit Card to store values of 1, 2, or 3 in a field called Payment Type.

Create an Option Group

This example shows you how to use an option group for a field called Type Of Time. The choices in the option group are Regular, Vacation, Sick Time, and Leave. When you click one of these options, Access stores a value of 1, 2, 3, or 4 in the Type Of Time field. (If you want to go through the following steps yourself, add a field called Type Of Time to the Weekly Records table. Assign the Text type to the field and give it a Length of at least 1.)

1. Open the Toolbox if it's not visible.

2. Click the Control Wizards button in the Toolbox if it's not dimmed.

3. Click the Option Group button in the Toolbox.

4. Open the Field List if it's not already open.

5. Drag the Type Of Time field from the field list to the spot on the form where you want the option group to appear.

6. In the first step of the Option Group Wizard, enter the labels for the options you want to show on the form and click Next.

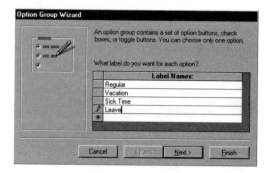

7. Select a default value for the field from the drop-down list in the next step, or change the setting to "No, I don't want a default" before moving to the next step.

8. Click Next in the step that asks what values you want to store in the field for each option choice. (Make a note of which values belong to which options if you will need to formulate queries later using this field.)

9. Click Next in the step that asks for the field in which you want to store the option group value. (You dragged Type Of Time from the field list to create the option group, so it should already be set to the right field.)

10. Choose a control type (option buttons, check boxes, or toggle buttons) and select a style in the next step. Then click Next.

11. Change the title for the option group and click Finish.

The final result of this procedure is shown in Figure 6.7. If you click Regular in the option group, a value of 1 is stored in the Type Of Time field.

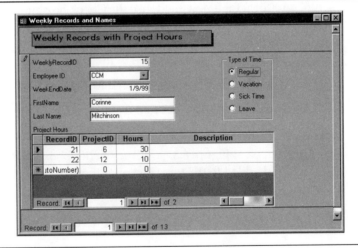

SKILL
6

FIGURE 6.7: This option group lets you click to make a choice; behind the scenes, Access stores a number code of 1, 2, 3, or 4 in the Type Of Time field.

Add an Option Button

If you need to add another choice to an option group, follow these steps:

1. Make sure the Toolbox is visible.

2. Click the Option Button tool in the Toolbox.

3. Point to the spot in the option group where the upper-left corner of the new button should appear.

4. Click to create the button. (The option group will expand automatically to accommodate the additional button.)

5. Click the text following the new button (Option*n*), type a label for the new choice, and press Enter.

Show a Field as a Check Box

The Form Wizard automatically creates a check box for any Yes/No fields you tell it to include on a form. When you click the box, it toggles a check mark on or off and changes the field value to True (on) or False (off). If you need to add a check box to a form for a new field, use the Check Box button in the Toolbox:

1. Open the Toolbox if it's not already open.

2. Click the Check Box button in the Toolbox.

3. Open the Field List, if you need to.

4. Drag the Yes/No field to the place you want the check box to appear on the form.

If you look at Figure 6.8, you'll see a check box for a Yes/No field called Reviewed added to the form just after the WeeklyRecordID field.

Use Combo Boxes and List Boxes

If you want to have a field appear as a drop-down list on a form, you need to create what's called a *combo box*. Another kind of value list you can use is called a *list box*. Both of these types of lists can be added to a form and tied to a field to make data entry easier.

What's the Difference?

The main difference between combo boxes and list boxes is their appearance. Figure 6.9 shows both a combo box and a list box for the EmployeeID field. As you can see, the list box takes more room than the combo box. It appears as a scrollable list of all the values it includes, with the selected value highlighted. In contrast, a combo box shows only its current value. You have to click the drop-down arrow for the combo box to show its list of values.

3. Open the Field List.   1. Open the Toolbox.

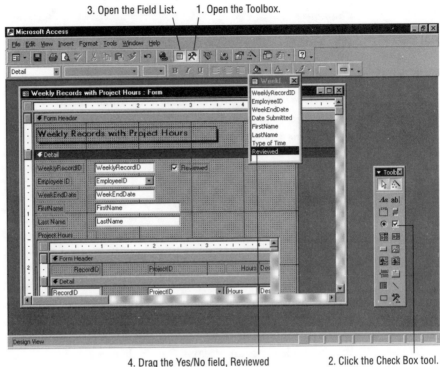

4. Drag the Yes/No field, Reviewed
in this example, to the form.

2. Click the Check Box tool.

FIGURE 6.8: The Yes/No field called Reviewed is shown as a check box on
this form.

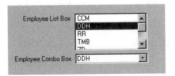

FIGURE 6.9: A list box and a combo box for the EmployeeID field

Besides the obvious visual variances, combo boxes and list boxes have another
difference. A list box always limits the values that can be entered in a field to the
values on the list. With a combo box, you have the option to either use the list to
limit field values or not. Check Table 6.1 for a quick summary of how combo
boxes and list boxes compare.

TABLE 6.1: Comparison of Combo Boxes and List Boxes

Characteristic	Combo Box	List Box
The list of values stays visible.	No	Yes
The list of values is a drop-down list.	Yes	No
Values not on the list can be entered in a field.	Optionally	No
You can type the first letter(s) to choose a value from the list.	Yes	Yes
You can specify the values for the list.	Yes	Yes
Values for the list can come from a table or a query.	Yes	Yes

Add a Combo Box

If you decide a combo box is what you need, follow these steps to add one for a field on a form. This example shows how to create a combo box for the Type Of Time field on the sample "Weekly Records with Project Hours" form. The values for the combo box are entered in the Combo Box Wizard instead of coming from a table. (If you want to follow along with this example with your own database, make sure the Type Of Time field in the Weekly Records table is long enough to hold all the possible values the combo box will include: Regular, Vacation, Sick Time, and Leave. For the last example, this field only needed to be one character long.)

1. Start from the Form Design view window and make sure the Toolbox and the Field List are open.

2. Click the Control Wizards button if it's not already dimmed.

3. Click the Combo Box button in the Toolbox.

4. To start the Combo Box Wizard, drag the field for the combo box from the Field List to the form. (The place you click should be the upper-left corner of the part of the combo box that shows the values; leave room for the label to the left.)

5. In the first step of the Combo Box Wizard, click I Will Type In The Values That I Want and click Next.

6. Change the number of columns, if you need to, and enter the values for the combo box like this before you click Next:

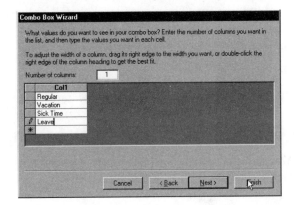

7. In the next step, click Store That Value In This Field and choose Type Of Time from the drop-down list of field names. Then click Next.

8. Enter a name like **Type Of Time** in the last step and click Finish.

9. Adjust the size of the combo box label and text object (the area where the values are displayed) if you need to.

When you switch to Form view, you'll see a combo box with a drop-down arrow. Just click the combo box's drop-down arrow to see a list of choices for the Type Of Time field:

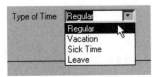

Add a List Box

The steps for adding a list box to a form are almost exactly the same as those for a combo box:

1. Make sure the Toolbox and the Field List are open.

2. Click the Command Wizards button if it's not already dimmed.

3. Click the List Box button in the Toolbox.

4. To start the List Box Wizard, drag the field for the list box from the Field List to the form. (The place you click will be the upper-left corner of the part of the list box that shows the values; leave room for the label to the left.)

5. In the first step of the List Box Wizard, select the source of values for the list and click Next.

6. Follow through the rest of the wizard's steps.

Use a Combo Box or a List Box to Find a Record

You can use a combo box or a list box to find a record instead of for data entry. When you choose a value from the list, Access finds the record that matches the value you selected.

1. Start the Combo Box Wizard or List Box Wizard as described in the last two examples.

2. In the first step of the wizard, click Find A Record On My Form. . . before you move to the next step.

3. Follow through the rest of the wizard's steps.

TIP TIP TIP TIP TIP TIP TIP TIP TIP TIP TIP TIP TIP TIP TIP TIP TIP TIP TIP TIP TIP TIP TIP TIP

When you name the list box or combo box that's used to find records, choose a name that makes it clear that the box acts as a finder, rather than as a data-entry box.

Use Pictures, Lines, and Boxes in a Form

Most of the objects you've worked with so far have been used to show field values or field labels. You can also add graphic elements like pictures, lines, and boxes to forms to make them more attractive and to point out key areas. Figure 6.10 shows the Weekly Records form after adding a picture, a line, and a box to its design.

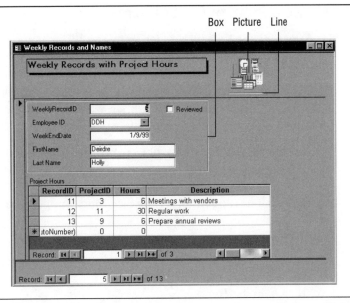

Box   Picture   Line

FIGURE 6.10: This form includes a picture, a line, and a box. All these elements were added with tools from the Toolbox.

Add a Picture

To add a picture to a form, use the Image tool like this:

1. Open the Toolbox.

2. Click the Image button in the Toolbox.

3. Drag an area on the form to show the picture. When you release the mouse, an Insert Picture dialog box will open.

4. Select a graphic file for the picture and click OK.

TIP TIP TIP TIP TIP TIP TIP TIP TIP TIP TIP TIP TIP TIP TIP TIP TIP TIP TIP TIP TIP TIP TIP TIP TIP

If you'd like to "borrow" one of the graphics that Database Wizard includes in it switchboards, browse `C:\Program Files\Microsoft Office\Office\Bitmaps\dbwiz`. **You can also find graphic files in** `C:\Program Files\Microsoft Office\Bitmaps\Styles` **and in** `C:\Windows`.

Make a Picture Fit Its Frame

After you choose a picture for an image object, it may not be completely visible. Whether you can see the picture in its entirety depends on the size of the graphic image and the size of the frame you are displaying it in. There are two ways to fix this problem. You can either adjust the size of the graphic image in a program like Paint, or you can change the properties of the image object. Follow these steps to tell Access to shrink the picture to fit its frame:

1. Right-click the image object and choose Properties from the shortcut menu.

2. Click the Format tab.

3. Change the setting for the Size Mode property to Zoom.

Add a Line

To place a line on a form:

1. Open the Toolbox.

2. Click the Line tool.

3. Click in the Design view window where you want the line to start.

4. Drag to the other end of the line and release the mouse.

Line Formatting Tips

There are several tricks you can use to change the appearance of a line:

- Lines have their own properties. You can change a line's width or give it a special effect using the properties sheet or buttons on the Formatting (Form/Report) toolbar.

- If you want to align a line with another object, select both objects and use Format ➤ Align.

- To make a line the same width as another object, select the line and the object. Use Format ➤ Size and then choose To Widest or another choice, depending on whether you need to make the line longer or shorter.

- To create a double line, create one line, select it, and choose Edit ➤ Duplicate.

- To change a line's width without having to handle a tight maneuver with the mouse, change the line's Width property using the properties sheet.

If you have trouble clicking a line to select it, use the Object drop-down box on the Formatting (Form/Report) toolbar and look for objects that start with *Line* followed by a number.

Add a Box

It's easy to add a box to a form:

1. Open the Toolbox.

2. Click the Rectangle button in the Toolbox.

3. Click in the Design view window where you want one of the corners of the box to appear.

4. Drag to the opposite corner of the box and release the mouse.

Spiff Up a Box

Boxes have their own properties that you can change to give them a special look.

- Use the Fill/Back Color button on the Formatting (Form/Report) toolbar to change a box's background color.

- Use the Line/Border Color button on the Formatting (Form/Report) toolbar to change the color of a box's border.

- Use the Line/Border Width button to change the thickness of a box's border.

- Use the Special Effect button to give a box a shadow or some other special look.

You can also use the properties sheet for a box to change its colors, size, border style, and so on.

Use a Tab Control

The properties sheet you've used to change the characteristics of design objects is an example of a *tabbed object*. It has pages with tabs you click to change the options you are working with. You can create your own *tab controls* to show multiple views of data on the same form.

SKILL 6

Add a Tab Control to a Form

Now you'll see how to add a tab control to the "Weekly Records with Project Hours" form. This set of steps will show the fields from the Weekly Records table and the subform for the Project Hours table on separate tab control pages.

1. Open the "Weekly Records with Project Hours" form in Design view.

2. Make a clear space on the form to place the tab control. For this example, drag a line around the field objects above the Project Hours subform to select them. Then click Cut on the toolbar to place them on the Clipboard. (You can skip this step if you are adding the tab control to a blank form.) Drag the bottom border for the form down and then the subform itself to make more room for the tab control.

3. Click the Tab Control button in the Toolbox.

4. Click in the Design view window and drag to create the empty tab control.

Add Objects to a Tab

Once you create a tab control, you can place objects on its pages in the usual way. Drag fields from the Field List, use the Toolbox to create new objects, or cut and paste objects from another location. The next set of steps shows how to paste objects from other parts of the "Weekly Record with Projects Hours" form to its new tab control:

1. Double-click the first tab's label to open its properties sheet and change its Caption property to whatever should appear on the tab. Use Weekly Record Details for this example.

2. Click the tab of the first page to select the first page and then click Paste on the toolbar to copy the fields objects that were cut to the Clipboard in the last set of steps.

3. Drag the properties sheet out of the way, if you need to, and click the tab for the second page. Then change its Caption property to Project Hours.

4. Click the Project Hours subform (which should now be under the new tab control in the Design view window) and cut it to the Clipboard.

5. Click the tab for the second page of the tab control to select it.

6. Click Paste on the toolbar to place the Project Hours subform on the second page of the tab control.

7. Click the first page again, select the EmployeeID and WeekEndDate fields, and cut them to the Clipboard.

8. Click the second tab control page and click Paste to copy the EmployeeID and WeekEndDate fields. (It's important to know whose records you are viewing without having to switch back and forth between the pages of the tab control.)

9. Move and resize the EmployeeID and WeekEndDate fields as needed to show them above the subform.

The end result of these steps is shown in Figures 6.11 and 6.12. The first page of the tab control displays fields from Weekly Records while the second shows the Project Hours records for each EmployeeID and WeekEndDate combination. (See Skill 5, "Use AutoForms and the Form Wizard," and the "Include a Subform" section later in this chapter for instructions on creating subforms to show records from a related table.)

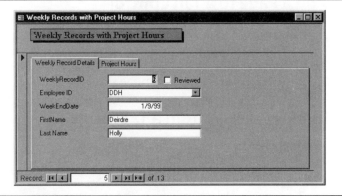

SKILL 6

FIGURE 6.11: A tab control is used on this form to show Weekly Records details and related records from Project Hours on separate pages.

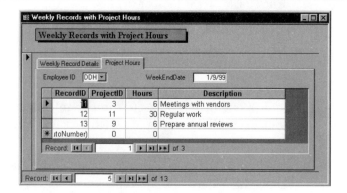

FIGURE 6.12: The second page of the tab control shown in Figure 6.11

Change the Number of Tabs

When you add a tab control to a form, Access includes two pages on the control.

Add a Page to a Tab Control

If you need to add more pages:

1. Right-click anywhere on the tab control.

2. Choose Insert Page from the shortcut menu.

Remove a Page from a Tab Control

If you need to get rid of a tab control page:

1. Right-click the tab for the page you want to delete.

2. Choose Delete Page from the shortcut menu.

Include a Subform

A *subform* can be included in a form to show records from another table or query. There's more than one way to add a subform to a form:

- Use the Subform/Subreport tool in the Toolbox.

- Drag a form from the Database window to the Design view window.

- Drag a table from the Database window.

You already saw how to create a subform by dragging a table in Skill 5. The technique for dragging a form is basically the same. Go through the following example of using the Subform/Subreport tool to see how it works.

Use the Subform/Subreport Tool

Start with this simple Employees form:

Then add a subform to show related records from the Weekly Records table.

1. Open the Employees form in Design view.

2. Drag the lower-right corner of the Design view window to make it larger.

3. Drag the lower-right corner of the form itself (the area with the grid) to make it large enough to hold the new subform.

4. Open the Toolbox.

5. Make sure the Control Wizards button on the toolbar is already pushed. (Its background should be dimmed.)

6. Click the Subform/Subreport tool.

7. Point to the Design view window and drag to create the area for the subform. This will also start the Subform/Subreport Wizard.

8. Click Next to create a subform from a table or query.

9. Choose Weekly Records from the Tables And Queries drop-down list.

10. Move the WeekEndDate, Date Submitted, Type Of Time, and Reviewed fields from the Available Fields list to the Selected Fields list. Then click Next. (Don't worry if you don't have the last few fields in your Weekly Records table; they were added in this chapter for other examples.)

11. Leave Choose From A List selected, leave Show Weekly Records For Each Record In Employees Using Employee highlighted, and click Next. (If you don't see this option on the list, click Define My Own and choose EmployeeID from the drop-down lists for both Form/Report Fields and Subform/ Subreport Fields.)

12. Enter a different name for the subform, if you like, and click Finish.

Figure 6.13 shows the Employees form with the subform for Weekly Records added. The subform automatically shows only the Weekly Records for whatever employee is being viewed in the main part of the form.

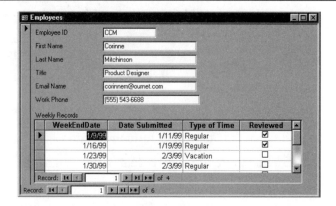

FIGURE 6.13: A subform to show related records from the Weekly Records table was added to this form using the Subform/Subreport tool in the Toolbox.

Edit a Subform

Access lets you edit a subform from the Design view window for the master form. To do this:

1. Click anywhere off the subform to make sure it's not selected.

2. Double-click the subform. A separate Form Design view window will open for the subform.

3. Make your changes to the subform.

4. Close the Form Design view window for the subform.

5. Click Yes when Access asks if you want to save your changes.

Specify the Linking Fields, If Needed

If you end up seeing more records than you should in a subform, check to see if it is properly linked to the master form.

1. Open the main form in Design view.

2. Right-click the subform and choose Properties, if the properties sheet is not already open. If it is open, click the subform once to select it and show its properties.

3. Click the Data tab.

4. Check the Link Child Fields and Link Master Fields settings. To change them, click either line and click the ellipsis to open the Subform Field Linker dialog box.

5. Select the linking fields from the drop-downs for Master Fields and Child Fields. You can select more than one pair of linking fields.

6. Click OK to return to the Design view window.

Other Controls You Can Include on a Form

SKILL
6

If you read through the last several examples, you are able to work with all the basic controls you will need to design most forms. Access includes another set of controls, called *ActiveX controls*, that provide special functions like showing spreadsheet data on a form. To access these controls, open the Toolbox and click the More Controls button. You'll see an extensive menu of other controls that you can include on a form. For more information on these controls, use the Office Assistant to look for Help topics on "ActiveX controls."

Change the Record Source for a Form

The table or query for a form is called the form's *record source*. There may be times when you want to use a form with a different table or query than the one it was originally designed for. You can switch the record source for a form pretty easily:

1. Open the form in Design view.

2. Double-click the form selector to open the properties sheet for the form.

3. Click the Data tab.

4. Click the Record Source line and choose a different table or query from the drop-down list.

5. Use File ➢ Save As to give the changed form a new name, if you want to save the old version.

WARNING WARNING WARNING WARNING WARNING WARNING WARNING WARNING

If you change the record source to a table or query with a different set of fields, you will end up with error messages in the unmatched field objects when you view the form. Either delete the unneeded fields from the form, or assign new fields to them by changing their Control Source property.

Create Your Own Form Template

When you create a new form by selecting Design view in the New Form dialog box, Access uses a *form template* called Normal. The form template determines whether or not the new form will have headers and footers, the size of the form sections, and the properties of controls like field objects and labels. It also uses whatever background may be a part of the template form.

Create a Template

To create your own template, all you have to do is design a form with the characteristics you want to see in new forms. You can use one of the Form Wizard's creations or come up with one of your own. This form was created by using the Form Wizard and selecting the Ricepaper style. It has no headers or footers and is called Employees On Ricepaper:

Put the Template to Use

After you decide on a form to use for a template, you have to tell Access about it.

1. Choose Tools ➢ Options from the menu.

2. Click the Forms/Reports tab.

3. In the box under Form Template, enter the name of the form you want to use for the template as shown in Figure 6.14.

NOTE NOTE NOTE NOTE NOTE NOTE NOTE NOTE NOTE NOTE NOTE NOTE NOTE NOTE NOTE

If you want to use a form template in another database, use File ➢ Save As to copy the form from the other database to the open one.

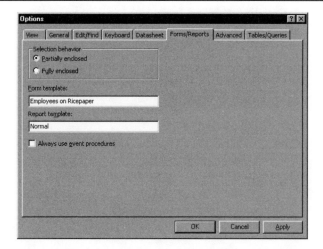

SKILL 6

FIGURE 6.14: The Employees On Ricepaper form is specified as the template for new forms in this Options dialog box.

Are You Experienced?

Now you can...

- ☑ Identify and utilize the elements of the Form Design view window
- ☑ Change the layout of a form
- ☑ Do basic maneuvers like move, resize, and align form objects
- ☑ Add fields and text to a form
- ☑ Include option groups, check boxes, combo boxes, and list boxes on a form
- ☑ Add pictures, lines, and boxes to a form
- ☑ Create a tabbed form
- ☑ Add and edit a subform
- ☑ Change the record source for a form
- ☑ Create and use your own form template

Find Data with Filters and Queries

- ➔ **Know the difference between filters and queries**
- ➔ **Create filters to view selected records**
- ➔ **Filter records using multiple fields and values**
- ➔ **Sort records with a filter**
- ➔ **Remove and save filters**
- ➔ **Find records with a query**
- ➔ **Query linked tables**
- ➔ **Make a table with a query**
- ➔ **Find duplicate and unmatched records with a query**

In Skill 4, "Enter, View, Find, and Sort Data," you saw how to search for records with the Find command. When you use Find, you enter the value you want Access to look for and then view any matching records one at a time.

The Find command won't work, however, if you need to formulate a search that checks for values in more than one field. It also won't limit the records you see in a datasheet or form to those that satisfy the search. For this type of job, you need to use a filter or a query. A *filter* shows you records in a datasheet or a form that matches whatever conditions you specify. A *query* is similar to a filter, but it is more flexible. You can formulate a query using related tables and then save the query to use it later. Figure 7.1 shows a table called Projects before and after it was filtered to show only the records with Tal Blackburn in the Project Manager field.

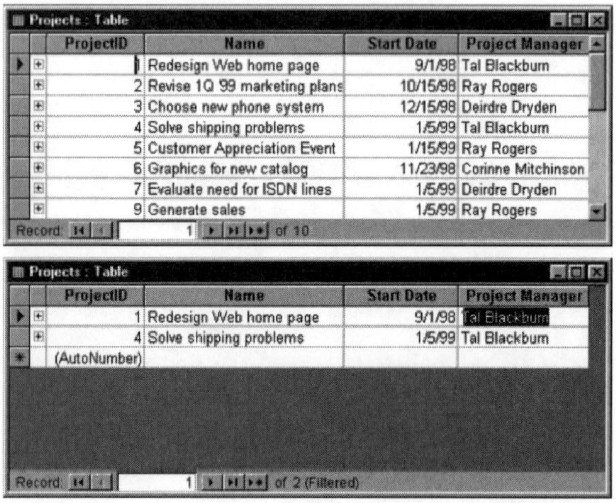

FIGURE 7.1: The Projects table before and after it was filtered to show the records for one manager only

When a view is filtered, you can edit the records just as if all the records were displayed. For queries that show you selected records from a table, you can also edit records in the resulting view.

The Difference between Filters and Queries

Both filters and queries can be used to find records, but there are differences in how you set them up and how they work. In a nutshell:

Use a filter to quickly limit the records you are already viewing in a datasheet or a form to those that match some criteria you specify.

Use a query to view selected fields and records from one or more tables; then save the query to open it later or use it as the basis of a form or a report.

Table 7.1 shows these differences in a little more detail.

TABLE 7.1: Differences between Filters and Queries

You Can. . .	With a Filter	With a Query
Change the set of records you are currently viewing in a Datasheet or Form view	Yes	No
Save the view of selected records as a separate database object	No	Yes
Create a form or report based on a subset of records	No	Yes
Choose the fields you want to see	No	Yes
Include fields from related tables in a view	No	Yes

In this chapter, first you'll look at the many ways Access lets you filter records. Then you'll find out how to create queries to find records.

**SKILL
7**

NOTE NOTE NOTE NOTE NOTE NOTE NOTE NOTE NOTE NOTE NOTE NOTE NOTE NOTE NOTE

Queries that find data like the ones described in this skill are called *select queries*. Other types of queries, called *action queries*, can be used to do things like delete records from a table, make global edits, and calculate summary information like totals and averages. Skill 8, "Master Advanced Queries," explains how to formulate these special purpose queries.

Filter Records Using One Field and One Value

If you want to find records that match a value in just one field, you can use any of these techniques:

- Filter By Selection lets you select a value in a datasheet or form and click a button to view any matching records.

- Filter Excluding Selection looks for values other than what you enter.

- Filter For shows up on the shortcut menu for any field; you just type the value you want to find.

- Filter By Form shows you a blank record where you can either enter the value you want to find or choose it from a drop-down list.

You could also create an Advanced Filter/Sort, but that would be like using a hammer on a thumbtack. The advanced filter option is discussed later, when you'll see how to filter records using criteria in more than one field. The next few section stick to simple examples that look for matches in one field only.

 NOTE NOTE NOTE NOTE NOTE NOTE NOTE NOTE NOTE NOTE NOTE NOTE NOTE NOTE NOTE

As you work through the examples, click Remove Filter on the toolbar if you need to remove a filter before applying a new one. You can check the bottom of a Datasheet view or Form view to see if you are looking at a filtered view. *(Filtered)* will appear just after the total number of records shown in the view.

Filter by Selection

With this technique, all you have to do is select the value you want to use and click a button. This example shows how to filter the Projects table to show the projects managed by Tal Blackburn:

1. Open the Projects table.

2. Find any occurrence of *Tal Blackburn* in the Project Manager field and select it or just click it:

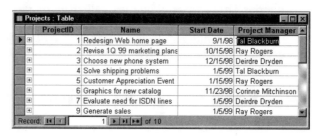

3. Click Filter By Selection on the Table Datasheet or Form view toolbar. You'll see a filtered Datasheet view window like this:

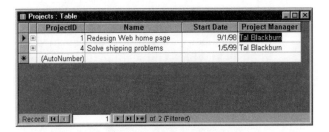

> **TIP TIP TIP TIP TIP TIP TIP TIP TIP TIP TIP TIP TIP TIP TIP TIP TIP TIP TIP TIP TIP TIP TIP TIP TIP**
> **After you select a value for a filter, you might prefer to right-click the field it's in and choose Filter By Selection instead of moving the mouse up to the toolbar.**

Filter Excluding Selection

Instead of filtering for a value, you can tell Access to show all the records that *don't* match a value you select:

1. In a Datasheet view window or a Form view window, select the value you don't want to see in the filtered view.

2. Right-click and choose Filter Excluding Selection.

Figure 7.2 shows the Projects table after selecting Tal Blackburn in the Project Manager field and using the Filter Excluding Selection command.

SKILL
7

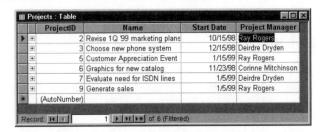

FIGURE 7.2: The Projects table after applying a filter to exclude all records with Tal Blackburn in the Project Manager field

Filter For

If you are working with a large number of records and it's not convenient to find a value to use Filter By Selection, try Filter For instead:

1. In a Datasheet view window or a Form view window, right-click anywhere in the field where you want to use the filter, except in its header. (If you click the field header, you'll get the wrong shortcut menu.)

2. Type a value in the box following Filter For:

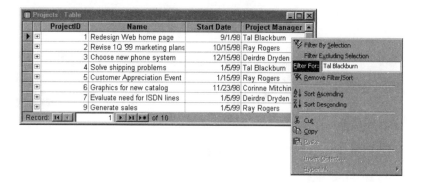

3. Press Enter to see the filtered view.

TIP TIP TIP TIP TIP TIP TIP TIP TIP TIP TIP TIP TIP TIP TIP TIP TIP TIP TIP TIP TIP TIP TIP

You can use wildcards in the Filter For text box or in the Filter By Form dialog box described in the next section. See Skill 4 for details on wildcards. You are also free to use Visual Basic expressions. For example, use Date() to see records with today's date in the filter field, or <= Date() + 90 to view records through the next 90 days.

Filter by Form

Filter By Form is another option for filtering a view using one or more fields. With this option, you can choose your filtering value from a drop-down list of all possible values for a field.

1. In a Datasheet view window or a Form view window, click Filter By Form on the toolbar. You'll see a window like this if you're working in Datasheet view.

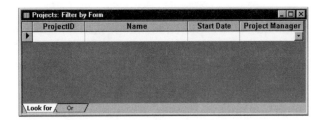

2. If you already applied a filter in the open view, you will see values in one or more of the form's fields. Delete any values that should not be part of the filter you are creating.

3. Click the filter field to see a drop-down menu of values like this list for the Project Manager field:

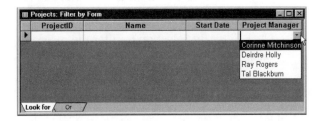

4. Make your selection from the list of values.

5. Click Apply Filter on the Filter/Sort toolbar that is visible when the Filter By Form window is open.

Filter Using Multiple Fields and Values

In the last few examples, you saw how to create filters with just one value applied to one field. You can actually create a filter using more than one field or even with multiple criteria applied to the same field.

AND Filters

If you want to see records that all meet more than one criteria, you need to formulate an *AND filter*. A filter that shows records from the Projects table where Tal Blackburn is the manager and the projects started on 1/5/99 is an example of an

AND filter. The next section discusses how to create this filter using each of the techniques you explored for single field/single value queries.

Filter by Selection

To create an AND filter using Filter By Selection, you have to apply a separate filter for each condition. Here's an example of how you would create an AND filter for the Projects table this way:

1. Open the Projects table.

2. Find a record that has *1/5/99* in the Start Date field and click that field.

3. Click Filter By Selection on the toolbar. You should see the records for all projects that started on 1/5/99.

4. Find a record in the filtered view that has *Tal Blackburn* in the Project Manager field. Then click anywhere on that field.

5. Click Filter By Selection to filter the records again so you only see the records for Tal that started on 1/5/99.

Filter by Form with Multiple Fields

With Filter By Form, you can create an AND filter without having to apply each criterion separately. You get to work in a window that looks like a blank form or an empty Datasheet view. In this window, you can enter criteria for multiple fields all at the same time. The following example finds the same records found in the last example using Filter By Form instead of Filter By Selection:

1. With the Projects table open, click Filter By Form.

2. Select *1/5/99* from the drop-down list for the Start Date field.

3. Select *Tal Blackburn* from the list of values for the Project Manager field. This Filter By Form window shows both criteria entered:

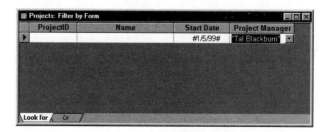

4. Click Apply Filter on the Filter/Sort toolbar to see a filtered view like this:

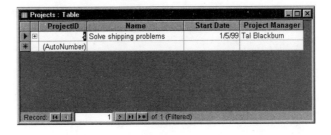

Filter For Input with a Complex Expression

Filter For is another quick and easy way to create an AND filter, if you don't mind doing a little typing:

1. Open the Projects table.

2. Right-click the Start Date field.

3. In the Filter For box, type **1/5/99 and [Project Manager] = Tal Blackburn**.

4. Press Enter to apply the filter. You should see the same filtered view shown in the last example.

TIP TIP TIP TIP TIP TIP TIP TIP TIP TIP TIP TIP TIP TIP TIP TIP TIP TIP TIP TIP TIP TIP TIP TIP TIP

You can use Filter For to find a range of values. To see projects started in the last quarter of 1998, enter *between 10/1/98 and 12/31/98* as the Filter For expression.

SKILL 7

OR Filters

An *OR filter* looks for records that match one condition or another. If you want to see project records managed by Tal Blackburn *or* those projects that started on 1/5/99, you can use Filter By Form or Filter For. (An Advanced Filter/Sort will also work, but that option is discussed later in this chapter.)

Filter by Form for One Condition or Another

The Filter By Form window has a special tab at its bottom border that you use to formulate OR filters. Let's look for either Tal Blackburn's projects or those that begin on 1/5/99:

1. Open the Projects table and click Filter By Form on the toolbar.

2. Choose 1/5/99 from the drop-down list for Start Date.

3. Click the Or tab at the bottom left of the Filter By Form window. You'll see another blank form.

4. Choose Tal Blackburn from the list of values for Project Manager.

5. Click Apply Filter on the toolbar.

After applying this OR filter, you'll see a mixed view of records for both Tal Blackburn and any other projects that begin on 1/5/99. Figure 7.3 shows a filtered view of the Projects table.

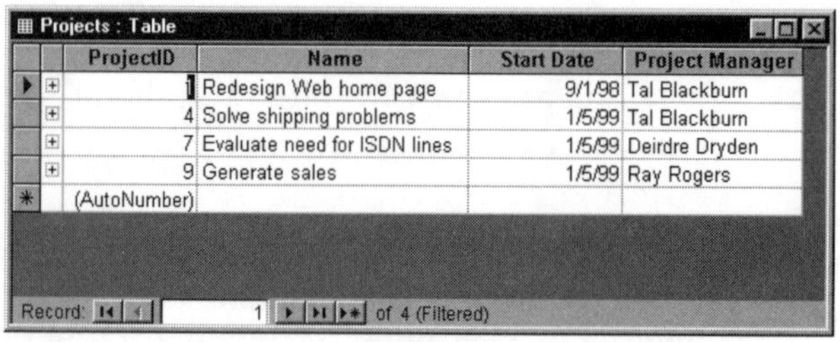

FIGURE 7.3: This filtered view of the Projects table shows records where either Tal Blackburn is the manager *or* the project starts on 1/5/99.

Filter for Input Using One Condition or Another

To use Filter For Input to create an OR filter, all you have to do is use the keyword *or* in the Filter For expression:

1. Open the Projects table.

2. Right-click the Start Date field.

3. In the Filter For box, enter **1/5/99 or [Project Manager] = Tal Blackburn**.

4. Press Enter to apply the filter.

Formulate an Advanced Filter

For AND or OR filters, you might want to jump directly to the option that lets you set up *advanced filters*. An Advanced Filter/Sort lets you combine conditions and fields freely for a filter. You can also use this feature to sort a filtered view or set up multifield sorts. (In Skill 4 you saw how to sort a Datasheet view window using just one field at a time.)

Open the Advanced Filter/Sort Window

To create an advanced filter or sort, you have to open a filter-editing window:

1. Open the Datasheet or Form view you want to filter.

2. Choose Records ➤ Filter ➤ Advanced Filter/Sort from the menu.

You'll see the filter window shown in Figure 7.4. Don't worry if you don't see anything in the columns in the bottom half of the window. It will show criteria already entered only if you previously applied a filter to the open view or saved a filter the last time the view was open.

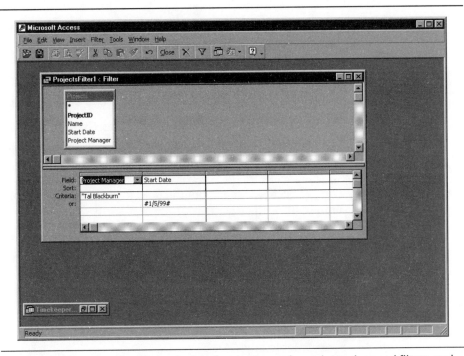

FIGURE 7.4: The filter window is where you formulate advanced filters and sorts. It shows the criteria for the last filter you used or saved.

Clear the Filter Window Grid

To clear the grid in the filter window of any old conditions, click Clear Grid on the Filter/Sort toolbar. The field list in the top part of the filter window will remain visible, but any conditions in the grid will disappear.

Enter Filter Conditions

To enter a condition in the filter window, first you enter a field name in the grid in the bottom half of the window. There are several ways to do this:

- Double-click a field name on the list in the top half of the window.
- Type a name in the Field row.
- Drag a field name from the list in the top of the window.
- Choose a field name from the drop-down list for the Field row.

Next, enter a value in the Criteria row for the field. For an OR filter, you enter an additional condition in the Or row for whatever field it applies to. The next two examples show all of this works.

Create an AND Filter

For this example, let's create a filter that shows records from the Projects table where the Project Manager is Deirdre Holly *and* the Start Date is 1/5/99:

1. Open a filter window for the Projects table as described earlier.

2. Drag Start Date from the field list in the top half of the filter window to the Field row in the first column of the grid.

3. Type **1/5/99** in the Criteria row of the same column.

4. Drag Project Manager from the field list to the Field row of the second column in the grid.

5. Enter **Deirdre*** in the Criteria row of the second column.

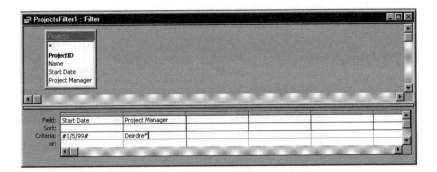

6. Click Apply Filter to view the filtered records:

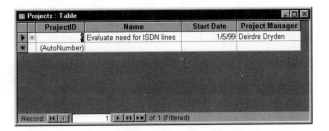

NOTE NOTE NOTE NOTE NOTE NOTE NOTE NOTE NOTE NOTE NOTE NOTE NOTE NOTE NOTE

Access will automatically change some of the values you enter in the Criteria or Or rows of the filter window grid. The # signs are placed around date values like the *1/5/99* in the last example to tell Access that the value is a date and not a mathematical expression. Similarly, Like and ""s are added to text values like *Deirdre** to show the value is to be used as a pattern match.

SKILL
7

Create an OR Filter

You can use similar steps to those listed in the last example to create an OR filter that looks for projects that begin on 1/5/99 *or* those that are managed by Deirdre Holly. Follow carefully: The only difference is where you place the criterion for the second field in the grid.

1. Click the filter window or use the Window menu command to return to the filter window. (Don't close the Projects table window or you'll end up closing the filter window, too.)

2. Follow steps 1–4 in the previous example.

3. Enter **Deirdre*** on the line labeled Or in the grid column for Project Manager:

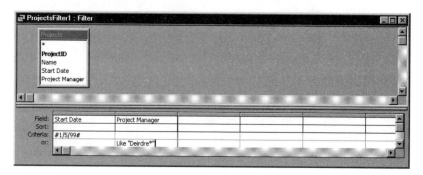

4. Click Apply Filter to view the filtered records:

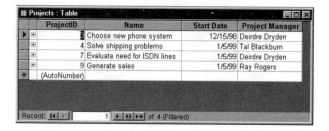

Sort Records with an Advanced Filter

You've probably already figured out how to sort records in an advanced filter. All you have to do is select Ascending or Descending from the drop-down list for Sort in the column for the field you want to sort by.

Sort on More than One Field

If you want to sort on more than one field, drag the column for the first sort field so it is the leftmost column in the filter grid. Then drag the rest of the sort fields into their respective positions (second, third, and so on).

To move a column in the filter grid:

1. Click the gray bar above the field name to select the field.

2. Point to the gray bar again and hold down the mouse key. You should see a zig-zaggy rectangle appear at the bottom of the pointer:

3. Drag the selected field to its new position.

Figure 7.5 shows the Projects table filtered to show records managed by Deirdre Holly and those projects that start on 1/5/99, as in the last example. The difference is that the records in the Datasheet view window are now sorted in descending order by Project Manager (first names), and then in ascending order by Start Date. The sort conditions are shown in the filter grid in the same figure. Note that the Project Manager field was dragged to the first column in the filter grid.

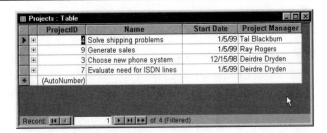

FIGURE 7.5: This filtered view of the Projects table is sorted first by Project Manager in descending order, and then in ascending order by Start Date.

Apply, Remove, or Save a Filter

Once you formulate a filter, you have to *apply* it to see the records it selects. Then you can toggle between a filtered view and all the records in the underlying table. When you are finished with a filter, you can remove it or save it with a table's properties. You also have the option of saving the filter as a query.

Apply a Filter

As you've seen in some of the previous examples, you click Apply Filter on the toolbar to see a filtered view. Access will apply the filter you are creating in either the Filter By Form or Filter window. Or, if you are not in one of these windows, it will apply the last filter you created or saved for the view.

Remove a Filter

To remove a filter, click Remove Filter on the toolbar. This button looks just like Apply Filter, except that its background resembles a checkerboard, and the button looks like it is pushed in.

Save a Filter

You can't save a filter as a separate object in a database, but there are other ways to preserve your work.

Save a Filter in Datasheet View

If you save your changes when you close a Datasheet view window, Access will remember the last filter you applied. Next time you open the same table, you can click Apply Filter to see the same set of filtered records. You don't have to re-create the filter.

If you choose not to save your changes when you close a Datasheet view window, Access will use the last filter saved with the table, if there is one. The Apply Filter button will be dimmed if there is no filter for Access to recall.

Use a Filter Saved with a Form

When you close a Form view window, the last filter you used automatically gets saved with the form. As in Datasheet view, the next time you open the form and click Apply Filter, the saved filter is applied.

If you create a form using a table that has a saved filter, the form *inherits* the filter. The form won't show the filtered records when it's opened, but it will when you click Apply Filter.

Activate a Filter Inherited by a Report

When you preview a report in Access, there are no tools available to set up and apply a filter. However, just as with forms, a report can inherit a filter from the table it is based on. To activate an inherited filter in a report:

1. Open the report in Design view.

2. Select Report from the Object drop-down list on the Formatting toolbar and click Properties on the toolbar.

3. Click the Data tab.

4. Double-click the line for Filter On to change it to Yes.

5. Without leaving the Data tab, reselect the table or query specified as the Record Source for the report. You'll see the inherited filter show up on the Filter line.

When you print or preview the report after going through the above steps, it will show only the filtered records. Next time you open the report, you may have to repeat this process if you want to see a filtered view again, even if you saved your changes to the report design.

Find Records with a Select Query

Now that you've dabbled with filters, it's time to experiment with *queries*. Queries are different from filters in these ways:

SKILL
7

- A query can be saved as a Database object.

- You don't have to be in an open Datasheet or Form view window to create a query.

- A query can include fields from more than one table.

- You can create a form or a report using a query, instead of a table.

- Special purpose queries can be used to do calculations, summarize information, append records from one table to another, delete records from a table, or do global edits.

This chapter focuses on *select queries*. With a select query, you choose the fields and records you want to see from one or more tables, and then run the query to see the result in Datasheet view.

NOTE NOTE NOTE NOTE NOTE NOTE NOTE NOTE NOTE NOTE NOTE NOTE NOTE NOTE
For information on working with *action queries*, see Skill 8.

Create a Query with One Table

To start, here's a simple example that creates a query to show selected fields and records from one table. It queries the Employees table in the Timekeeper database for those people who were hired in 1998, and then tells Access to show the First-Name, LastName, and Date Of Hire fields when the query is run.

1. In the Database window, click the Queries tab.

2. Click New to open the New Query dialog box:

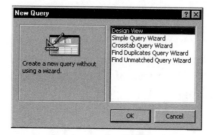

3. Double-click Design View to open the Show Table dialog box:

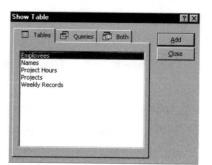

4. Select the Employees table, click Add, and then Close. You'll see a query window like this:

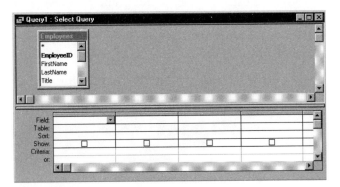

NOTE NOTE NOTE NOTE NOTE NOTE NOTE NOTE NOTE NOTE NOTE NOTE NOTE NOTE NOTE

There's a Simple Query Wizard option in the New Query dialog box that lets you choose the table(s) and fields for a query. It wasn't used for this example because it doesn't prompt you for any record selection criteria.

Choose Fields to See

Once you add a table to the Query window, the next step is to add fields to the query grid:

SKILL
7

1. Drag FirstName from the field list in the top half of the Query window to the Field row in the first column of the grid.

2. Drag the LastName field to the Field row in the second column of the grid.

3. Drag the Date Of Hire field to the Field row in the third column of the grid. (Use the vertical scroll bar on the field list to bring the Date Of Hire field into view first.)

TIP TIP TIP TIP TIP TIP TIP TIP TIP TIP TIP TIP TIP TIP TIP TIP TIP TIP TIP TIP TIP TIP TIP

Instead of dragging a field from the list in the top half of the Query window, you can click near the right border of the Field row to get a drop-down list of fields to choose from. Alternatively, you can double-click a field name on the list to move it to the grid.

Enter Criteria to Select Records

You could run the query at this point to show the FirstName, LastName, and Date Of Hire fields for all the records in the Employees table. Because you only want to see records for people hired in 1998, you need to add some criteria to the query grid:

1. In the Criteria row for the Date Of Hire column, enter ***98**. The Query window should look like this:

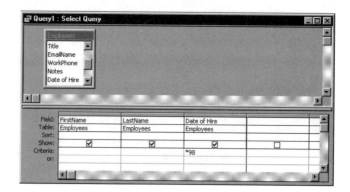

We are using a wildcard here to select all the records that show when people were hired in 1998. There are other ways to select the same records. See the example in "Look for a Range of Values" a little later in this chapter.

Choose a Sort Order

To sort a query by a particular field, choose Ascending or Descending from the drop-down list for the field's Sort row in the query grid. To create a more complicated sort, see "Sort on More Than Field" earlier in this chapter.

Run a Query

Click Run on the toolbar to see the results of a query in Datasheet view. The result of the query you've been working on is shown here:

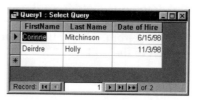

You can also click the View button on the toolbar to switch to Datasheet view from the Query Design view window.

Switch Back to Query Design View

After you run a query and land in a Datasheet view window, you can easily switch back to Design view. Just click the Design View button on the toolbar.

Look for Special Criteria

If you are using a constant value to select records in a query, all you have to do is type the value in the Criteria row of the query grid. You can also:

- Look for records with blank values

- Find records that satisfy a range of values

- Use expressions with Visual Basic functions like Date()

Following are a few quick examples of query criteria here. For more information, use the Office Assistant to look for help on "Expressions." You'll see several different topics you can explore.

Look for Blanks (or Not)

To select records that are blank in a certain field, enter **null** in the Criteria row of the query grid. Access will change the entry to "Is Null" before it runs the query. This query finds records for employees who don't have anything in the Last Review field:

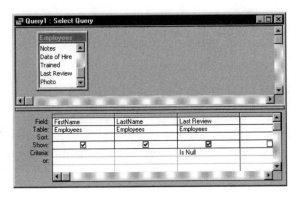

If you need to see records that are not blank in a certain field, use **not null** as the query criteria.

Use a Yes/No Field to Select Records

To find records that are blank in a Yes/No field, enter **No** or **False** in the Criteria row of the query grid. This query finds records for people who have not been trained:

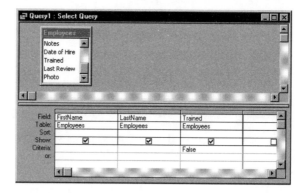

If you are looking for records that are checked in a Yes/No field, use **Yes** or **True** as the query criteria.

Look for a Range of Values

In your query to find employees hired in 1998, you used ***98** as criteria for the Date Of Hire field. You could have used **>=1/1/98** and **<=12/31/98** or **between 1/1/98 and 12/31/98** to select the same records.

NOTE NOTE NOTE NOTE NOTE NOTE NOTE NOTE NOTE NOTE NOTE NOTE NOTE NOTE NOTE
Access changes date values like 1/1/98 to #1/1/98# in the Query window.

Use Functions to Find Records

Access allows you to use Visual Basic functions like Date() as criteria in a query. In fact, you can combine functions with mathematical operators, constant values, and field references. Table 7.2 shows some examples of functions used in query expressions and the values they find.

TABLE 7.2: Examples of Functions Used as Query Criteria

This Expression. . .	Finds Values Like This. . .
>=Date() - 180 and <=Date()	Dates in the last 180 days
Len([Phone]) = 8	555-1234[1]
Left([Phone],3) = "415"	415-555-1234
Year([Date of Hire]) = 1998	12/17/98

1. This expression will find 555-1234 if the - is stored with the numbers in the field.

Use Wildcards to Find Records

Wildcards like * and ? are perfectly valid elements of query criteria. For example, you can use *???* in the FirstName field of a query to find records for *Ray* and *Zoe*.

NOTE NOTE NOTE NOTE NOTE NOTE NOTE NOTE NOTE NOTE NOTE NOTE NOTE NOTE NOTE

To see more wildcard tricks, see Skill 4.

AND versus OR Queries

Select queries can include multiple criteria to find records. When you want to find records that meet more than one criterion, you need to formulate an AND query. To find records that match on condition in a set of criteria, use an OR query.

SKILL
7

Create an AND Query

An AND query looks for records that satisfy multiple criteria. If you enter criteria for more than one field on the same line in a query, you create an AND query. For example, if you want to find all employees hired in 1998 who have already been trained, you could use an AND query that looks like the following window.

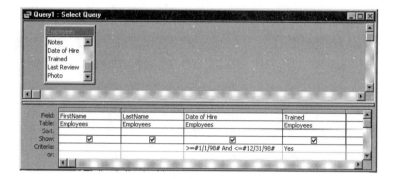

Note that if you need to use more than one criterion in the same field, as in the Date Of Hire field above, separate the criteria with the word *and*.

Create an OR Query

An OR query selects records that satisfy one criterion or another. To create an OR query, enter each criterion on a separate line of the query grid. This query shows records for employees hired in 1997 or 1998:

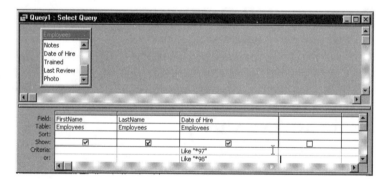

Save and Change Queries

Unlike filters, queries can be saved as objects unto themselves in a database. Once a query is saved, you can run it from the Database window or open it in Design view. A saved select query can also be used to create a form or report that shows selected data from one table or related tables.

Save a Query

To save a query:

1. Close the query window from either Design view or Datasheet view. (You'll be in Datasheet view if you ran the query.)

2. Choose Yes when Access asks you if you want to save your changes and enter a name for the query.

Change a Query

After you create a query, you are free to change it:

1. In the Database window, click the Queries tab.

2. Highlight the name of the query you want to change.

3. Click Design.

You can also right-click a query name and choose Design from the shortcut menu that pops up.

NOTE NOTE NOTE NOTE NOTE NOTE NOTE NOTE NOTE NOTE NOTE NOTE NOTE NOTE NOTE

Be sure to use File ≻ Save As after you make changes to a query if you want to keep the old version as it was.

SKILL
7

Query Linked Tables

One of the best things about queries is that you can view fields from related tables together. Follow these steps to create a query that shows fields from four tables: Weekly Records, Employees, Project Hours, and Projects:

1. In the Database window, click the Queries tab.

2. Click New.

3. Double-click Design View in the New Query dialog box.

4. Select Weekly Records and click Add.

5. Repeat the last step for Employees, Project Hours, and Projects.

6. Click Close.

Figure 7.6 shows the Query window with all four tables added. As you can see in the figure, Access automatically linked the tables using information from the Relationships window. (Remember, Access created relationships for you when you used the Lookup Wizard in Table Design view.)

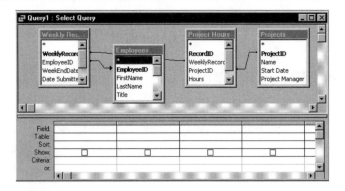

FIGURE 7.6: This Query window includes four tables that were linked automatically by Access.

TIP TIP TIP TIP TIP TIP TIP TIP TIP TIP TIP TIP TIP TIP TIP TIP TIP TIP TIP TIP TIP TIP TIP

You can hold down the Ctrl key while you select tables in the Show Table dialog box. When you click Add, all the tables will be added to the Query window at once in alphabetical order. If you want to control the order of the tables in the Query window to keep their linking lines neat, add tables individually.

Link Tables in a Query

If you need to link tables in a query yourself, drag from one linking field to another. Access will draw a line that shows the link.

Add Tables to an Open Query Window

If you want to add tables to a Query window you're already working in, click the Show Table button on the toolbar. Then use the Add button as described above and Close to return to Design view.

Select Fields for a Multi-Table Query

The process for selecting fields for a multi-table query is the same as that for a single-table query. You can drag fields from the field lists in the top of the Query window to the query grid, select fields from the drop-down lists for the Field row in each column, or double-click names on the field list.

Figure 7.7 shows the query from Figure 7.6 with fields from each table added to the query grid. When this query is run, it displays a Datasheet view window like the one in Figure 7.8.

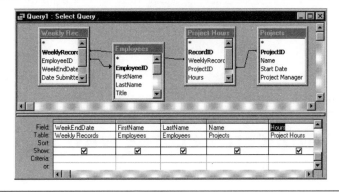

FIGURE 7.7: This query has fields from four tables added to its grid.

Field from the Weekly Records table   Field from the Projects table

WeekEndDate	FirstName	Last Name	Name	Hours
1/9/99	Deirdre	Holly	Choose new phone system	6
1/9/99	Deirdre	Holly	Administrative work	30
1/9/99	Deirdre	Holly	Generate sales	6
1/9/99	Corinne	Mitchinson	Graphics for new catalog	30
1/16/99	Corinne	Mitchinson	Graphics for new catalog	40
1/16/99	Corinne	Mitchinson	Administrative work	2
1/23/99	Corinne	Mitchinson	Generate sales	32
1/30/99	Corinne	Mitchinson	Graphics for new catalog	36
1/16/99	Deirdre	Holly	Choose new phone system	6
1/16/99	Deirdre	Holly	Customer Appreciation Event	12
1/23/99	Deirdre	Holly	Revise 1Q 99 marketing plans	24
1/23/99	Deirdre	Holly	Supervisory work	20
1/9/99	Tal	Blackburn	Redesign Web home page	50

Record: 1 of 8

Fields from the Employees table   Field from the Project Hours table

FIGURE 7.8: This Datasheet view window was created by running the query in Figure 7.7.

Make a Table from a Query

When you run a select query, Access shows a Datasheet view window that draws its data from the table(s) included in the query. If you edit the window, you end up changing the data in the underlying table(s).

There may be times when you want to create a new table from a query, so you don't end up changing the original tables. To do this:

1. Create a select query as described earlier or open a query in Design view.

2. Choose Query ➢ Make Table Query from the menu.

3. Enter a name for the new table and click OK.

4. Click Run on the toolbar.

5. Choose Yes to create the new table. (If the table already exists, you will be asked whether it's OK to delete it first.)

Find Duplicate Records with a Query

Access has a wizard that can help you find duplicate records in a table. It asks you which field(s) to check for duplicate values and shows the query results in a Datasheet view window. These steps check for duplicate FirstName and Last-Name combinations in the Employees table:

1. Click the Queries tab in the Database window.

2. Click New.

3. Double-click Find Duplicates Query Wizard in the New Query dialog box.

4. Highlight Employees and click Next.

5. Move FirstName and LastName from the Available Fields list to the Duplicate-value Fields list. Then click Next.

6. Add any other fields you want to see in the query result to the Additional Query Fields list. Click Next.

7. Change the query name, if you need to, and click Finish.

Figure 7.9 shows what the wizard produces after going through these steps. Note that in the resulting Datasheet view window, the FirstName and LastName fields are duplicated even though the other fields have unique values.

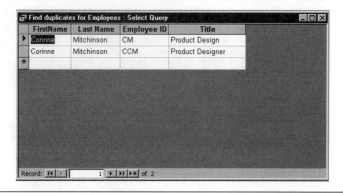

FIGURE 7.9: This Datasheet view window shows duplicate FirstName/Last-Name combinations found by the Find Duplicates Query Wizard.

Find Unmatched Records with a Query

The Find Unmatched Query Wizard finds records in one table that don't have matching values in one or more fields in another table. This example shows how to use the wizard to display records for people in the Employees table who don't have any records in the Weekly Records table:

1. Click the Queries tab in the Database window.

2. Click New.

3. Double-click Find Unmatched Query Wizard in the New Query dialog box.

4. Highlight Employees and click Next.

5. Highlight Weekly Records and click Next.

6. Click EmployeeID on each field list, if they are not already highlighted, then click the < = > button. Click Next.

7. Move each field you want to see in the final result from Employees to the Selected Fields list. Click Next.

8. Rename the query, if you need to, and click Finish.

The Datasheet view window in Figure 7.10 shows all the people in Employees without records in the Weekly Records table. You can check the Weekly Records table in the same figure to verify the Wizard's work.

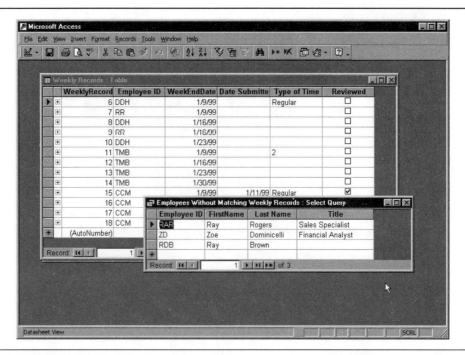

FIGURE 7.10: This Datasheet view window shows the records for people in Employees who don't have matching entries in the Weekly Records table.

Now that you understand how to use filters and select queries to find records, you can move on to the special purpose queries described in Skill 8.

Are You Experienced?

Now you can...

- ☑ Tell the difference between filters and queries
- ☑ Create filters to view selected records
- ☑ Filter records using multiple fields and values
- ☑ Formulate and work with advanced filters
- ☑ Sort records with a filter
- ☑ Remove and save filters
- ☑ Find records with a query
- ☑ Save and change queries
- ☑ Query linked tables
- ☑ Make a table with a query
- ☑ Find duplicate and unmatched records with a query

SKILL
7

Master Advanced Queries

- ➔ **Add records from one table to another**
- ➔ **Update records with a query**
- ➔ **Delete records with a query**
- ➔ **Create calculated fields with a query**
- ➔ **Summarize data with a query**
- ➔ **Use the Crosstab Wizard**
- ➔ **Have a query wait for criteria**

In Skill 7, "Find Data with Filters and Queries," you created views of selected information from one or more tables with queries. The type of query you used is called a *select query* for obvious reasons. This chapter explores Append, Update, Delete, and Crosstab queries. These are called *action* queries. You'll also create calculated fields with a query, summarize data with a query, and see how to make a query wait while you enter record selection criteria.

Add Records from One Table to Another

It's easy to append records from one table to another using an *Append query*. The tables don't need to have the same number of fields or the same field names. If the tables do have matching field names, however, it's quicker to formulate an Append query because Access will automatically know which fields to send data into.

In this example, you'll append records from the Employees table into another table called PhoneBook. These tables have the fields listed in Table 8.1. When you create the query, you'll see that Access knows where to append the name information, as there are FirstName and LastName fields in both tables. You will have to tell Access where to place the work phone number field, though, because these fields have different names in the two tables.

TABLE 8.1: Fields in the Employees and PhoneBook Tables

Fields in Employees	Fields in PhoneBook
EmployeeID	
FirstName	FirstName
LastName	LastName
HomePhone	
Title	
EmailName	
WorkPhone	WorkNumber
Fax	
Notes	
Date of Hire	
Trained	
Last Review	
Photo	

Follow these steps to create an Append query:

1. In the Database window, click the Queries button and click New.

2. In the New Query dialog box, leave Design View highlighted and click OK.

3. Highlight Employees, click Add, and then click Close in the Show Table dialog box.

4. Choose Query ➤ Append Query from the menu.

5. Choose PhoneBook from the drop-down list for Table Name and click OK.

6. Drag FirstName from the field list in the top half of the query window to the Field row in the first column of the query grid. Or you can double-click FirstName to move it to the grid.

7. Drag LastName from the field list to the second column of the query grid.

8. Drag WorkPhone from the field list to the third column of the query grid.

9. In the WorkPhone column, click the Append To row and select Work-Number from the drop-down list of fields from the PhoneBook table. The query window will look like this:

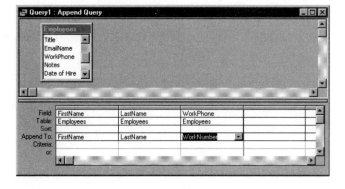

SKILL 8

10. Click Run on the toolbar and choose Yes to add the records from Employees to PhoneBook.

If you check the PhoneBook table shown in Figure 8.1, you'll see that the phone numbers in the new records don't have dashes. This is because the input mask for the WorkPhone field in Employees shows parentheses and dashes as phone numbers are entered, but doesn't store them with the numbers. This problem will be fixed later in this chapter in "Use Functions to Format Data."

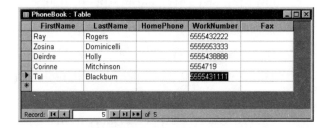

FIGURE 8.1: These records in the PhoneBook table were appended from information in the Employees table using an Append query.

TIP TIP TIP TIP TIP TIP TIP TIP TIP TIP TIP TIP TIP TIP TIP TIP TIP TIP ꜛIP TIP TIP TIP TIP TIP

You can select the records that get appended from one table to another by using the Criteria row of an Append query.

Update Records with a Query

You can use an *Update query* to make global changes to a table instead of using Edit ➢ Replace to change one record at a time. Update queries are quite flexible. They can:

- Do global search and replaces
- Use Visual Basic functions to do complex updates
- Update one table against another

Do a Global Search and Replace

The simplest type of Update query looks for a value and replaces it with another. This query changes all instances of *Deirdre Holly* in the Project Manager field of the Projects table to *Deirdre Dryden*. (To start this query, you'll use a shortcut that bypasses the Show Table dialog box.)

1. In the Database window, click the Tables button and highlight Projects.

2. Click the New Object drop-down button on the toolbar and select Query. (If the Query icon is already shown on the New Object button, you can just click it and skip opening the button's drop-down menu.)

3. Click OK in the New Query dialog box to open a Query Design view window with the Projects table already added.

4. Choose Query ➤ Update Query from the menu.

5. Drag Project Manager from the field list to the first column of the query grid.

6. Enter **Deirdre Dryden** in the Update To row of the Project Manager column.

7. Enter **Deirdre Holly** in the Criteria row of the Project Manager column. The Query window should now look like this:

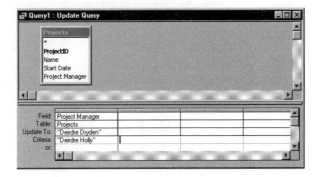

8. Click Run on the toolbar and choose Yes to change the records for Deirdre in the Projects table.

Use Functions to Format Data

Go back to those records you appended to the PhoneBook table earlier in this chapter to see how you can reformat data using an Update query. The problem is that the phone numbers in the new records have no parentheses or dashes. Instead of values like *(555)555-1234*, the WorkNumber field has values that look like *5555551234*.

Use an Update query to add the formatting characters to the phone numbers. Note that the query checks the length of the value in the WorkNumber field to make sure you don't end up adding parentheses to numbers without area codes. You would need to run a second Update query to add dashes alone to phone numbers without area codes.

1. In the Database window, click the Tables button and highlight PhoneBook.

2. Click the New Object drop-down button on the toolbar and select Query.

3. Click OK in the New Query dialog box to open a Query Design view window that already includes the PhoneBook table.

4. Choose Query ➤ Update Query from the menu.

5. Drag WorkNumber from the field list to the first column of the query grid.

6. In the Update To row of the WorkNumber column, enter **"(" + Left([WorkNumber],3) + ")" + Mid([WorkNumber],4,3) + "-" + Right([WorkNumber],4)**.

7. Enter **Len([WorkNumber]) = 10** in the Criteria row of the WorkNumber column so the query looks like this:

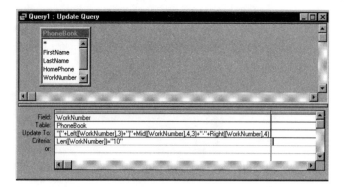

8. Click Run on the toolbar and choose Yes to change the phone numbers.

If you open the PhoneBook table now, it will look like Figure 8.2. Note that only the numbers with area codes were changed because you used criterion to check the field length before adding the parentheses and dash. To format the numbers that don't have area codes, make these changes to the Update query and run it again:

- Enter **Left([WorkNumber],3) + "-" + Right([WorkNumber],4)** in the Update To line for the WorkNumber column.

- Use **Len([WorkNumber]) = 7** for the query Criteria.

FirstName	LastName	HomePhone	WorkNumber	Fax
Ray	Rogers		(555)543-2222	
Zosina	Dominicelli		(555)555-3333	
Deirdre	Holly		(555)543-8888	
Corinne	Mitchinson		5554719	
Tal	Blackburn		(555)543-1111	

FIGURE 8.2: The parentheses and dashes in the WorkNumber field were added using an Update query.

Update One Table against Another

You can update fields in one table using matching field values in a joined table. This example shows how to change the EmailName field in the Employees table to the values found in the EmailAddress field in the EmailAddresses table. The update is possible because both the Employees and EmailAddresses tables have an EmployeeID field that can be used to join the tables.

1. In the Database window, click the Queries button and click New.

2. Click OK to select Design View in the New Query dialog box.

3. In the Show Table dialog box, hold down Ctrl while you click Employees and then EmailAddresses. Click Add and Close to go to the Query Design view window.

4. Choose Tools ➢ Update Query from the menu.

5. Drag EmailName from the field list for Employees to the first column of the query grid.

6. In the Update To row of the same column, enter **EmailAddresses .EmailAddress**.

7. Click Run and then choose Yes to update the e-mail addresses.

Figure 8.3 shows this Update query ready to run. If you look closely, you can see that Access adds square brackets ([ ]) around the table name and field name in the Update To row.

SKILL
8

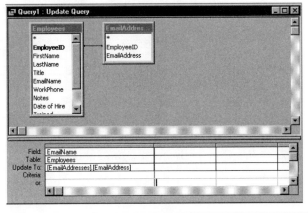

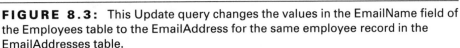
FIGURE 8.3: This Update query changes the values in the EmailName field of the Employees table to the EmailAddress for the same employee record in the EmailAddresses table.

Delete Records with a Query

While you're editing a table in Datasheet view or Form view, you can delete individual records or a contiguous group of selected records. This works fine in some cases, but is not very efficient when you want to get rid of a set of records, like the orders for a particular year or test scores below a certain number. For this kind of job, it's best to use a *Delete query*.

Delete Records That Match Criteria You Enter

Here's an example of a Delete query that removes all records from the Projects table with Start Dates in 1998:

1. In the Database window, click the Tables button and highlight Projects.

2. Click the New Objects drop-down button on the toolbar and select Query.

3. Click OK to select Design View in the New Query dialog box.

4. Choose Query ➤ Delete Query from the menu.

5. Drag Start Date from the field list to the first column of the query grid.

6. Enter *98 in the Criteria row of the same column:

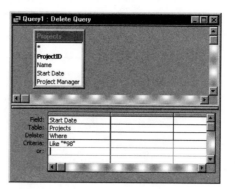

7. Click Run on the toolbar, and choose Yes to delete the records.

Delete Records That Match Those in Another Table

If you want to delete records from one table that have matches in another table, a Delete query can do the job nicely. These steps delete the records in the Email-Addresses table that have matching EmployeeIDs in the Employee table:

1. In the Database window, click the Tables button and highlight Email-Addresses.

2. Click the New Object drop-down button on the toolbar and select Query.

3. Click OK in the New Query dialog box to select Design View.

4. When the Query window opens, click Show Table on the toolbar, highlight Employees, click Add, and then Close. Access should automatically link the tables using the EmployeeID field.

5. Choose Query ➢ Delete Query from the menu.

6. Drag the asterisk from the field list for EmailAddresses to the first column of the query grid. The word *From* will appear in the Delete row of the query:

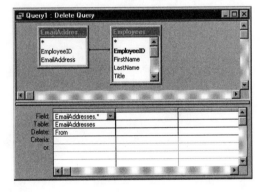

7. Click Run and choose Yes to delete the records.

Create Calculated Fields with a Query

When you create a select query, you can add your own fields to the query grid to show calculated values. For example, you could create a field called Extended

Price that calculates Quantity * Price, when Quantity and Price are fields in the table being queried. All you do is enter the new field name followed by a colon and the expression for the field in a blank column of the query grid.

Here's an example of a query on the Project Hours table that shows a calculated field called Person Days. The new field shows the result of dividing the Hours field by eight.

1. Click the Tables button in the Database window and highlight Project Hours.

2. Click the New Object drop-down button on the toolbar and select Query.

3. Click OK to select Design View in the New Query dialog box.

4. Drag the asterisk from the field list to the first column of the query grid. This tells Access to show all the fields in Project Hours when the query is run.

5. Click in the Field row of the second column of the query grid.

6. Enter **Person Days: [Hours]/8** so the query looks like this:

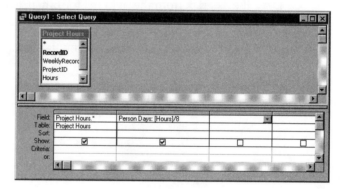

7. Click Run to show the Datasheet view window with the new calculated field.

Figure 8.4 shows the Datasheet window from this query. As you can see, the last field in the view is called Person Days, as entered in the query grid, and shows the values in the Hours field divided by eight.

NOTE NOTE NOTE NOTE NOTE NOTE NOTE NOTE NOTE NOTE NOTE NOTE NOTE NOTE NOTE
If you want to summarize data, use a Totals query as described in the next section instead of creating new calculated fields.

RecordID	WeeklyRecordID	ProjectID	Hours	Description	Person Days
11	6	3	6	Meetings with vendors	0.75
12	6	0	30	Regular work	3.75
13	6	0	6	Prepare annual review	0.75
14	7	2	10	Send out 2nd draft for	1.25
15	7	5	4	Get committee heads	0.5
16	7	0	28	Sales calls	3.5
17	9	2	14	Revise marketing plan	1.75
18	0	5	10	Detailed plan for Custc	1.25
19	0	0	20	Sales calls	2.5
20	0	0	1	Meet with boss	0.125
(AutoNumber)	0	0	0		

Record: [◄] [◄] [1] [►] [►I] [►*] of 10

FIGURE 8.4: The Person Days field in this Datasheet view window was created by running a query on the Project Hours table with a calculated field that divides Hours by eight.

Summarize Data with a Query

With a *Totals query*, you can summarize records to calculate the sum, average, minimum, maximum, or other summary values for a field. You can use the Simple Query Wizard, or you can do it yourself. With either technique, there's an option to show summary data for groups of records. For example, instead of just showing the total of the Hours field for all records in the Project Hours table, you could total the hours by project.

In this section, you'll find out how to:

- Summarize a table using the Simple Query Wizard

- Summarize data yourself by creating a Totals query in the Query Design view window

Summarize Records with the Simple Query Wizard

The Simple Query Wizard wasn't used in Skill 7, "Find Data with Filters and Queries," because it doesn't allow you to enter criteria for selecting records. It isn't totally useless though. Besides allowing you to choose fields from related tables to create a Datasheet view, the Simple Query Wizard can also show summary information instead of detail records.

SKILL
▼8

Here's how to get a total of the Hours fields in the Project Hours tables, broken down by ProjectID, using the wizard:

1. Click the Queries button in the Database window and click New.

2. Double-click Simple Query Wizard in the New Query dialog box.

3. Choose "Table: Project Hours" from the Tables/Queries drop-down menu in the wizard's first step.

4. Click ProjectID and then the > button to move the field to the Selected Fields list. You need this field to group the summary records. Repeat this for the Hours field (the field you will sum) and click Next.

5. Click Summary and then Summary Options.

6. Click the Sum button for the Hours field:

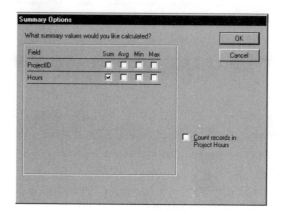

7. Click OK and then click Next.

8. Change the query name to something like **Hours by Project** and click Finish. You'll see a Datasheet view window with two fields, ProjectID and Sum of Hours:

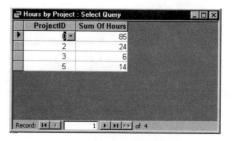

To make the query result more descriptive, add the Name field from the Projects table to the query:

1. With the Query Datasheet view window still open, click the View button to go into Design view.

2. Make the Query window larger, if necessary, to see the query grid.

3. Click Show Table, select Projects, click Add, and then click Close.

4. Drag Name from the field list for Projects to the third column of the query grid:

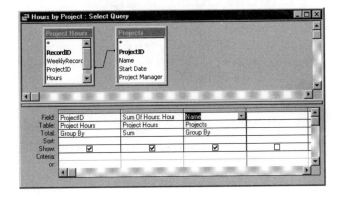

5. Right-click the line that joins the tables in the top half of the Query window, choose Join Properties, select "3: Include ALL Records from 'Project Hours'...," and click OK. (This tells Access to show a record from Project Hours, even if there is no matching record in the Projects table.)

6. Click Run on the toolbar to show a Datasheet view window with project names:

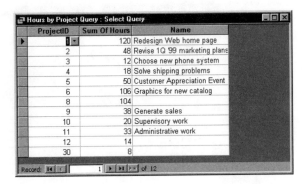

SKILL
8

The Name field in some of the records is blank because there is no record with a matching ProjectID in the Projects table.

If you don't see the Summary Options dialog box after you click Next in step 4 of the previous example, it's because you didn't select any number or currency fields in step one of the Simple Query Wizard. In the Summary Options dialog box, Access lets you calculate the sum, average, minimum, or maximum values for number or currency values only.

Create a Totals Query Yourself

You can create the same summary information shown in the previous section by going straight to Query Design view and using a Totals query. This example shows you how to calculate the total hours by project without the help of the Simple Query Wizard:

1. Click the Tables button in the Database window and highlight Project Hours.

2. Select Query from the New Object button drop-down button on the toolbar.

3. Click OK to choose Design View in the New Query window.

4. Click Totals on the Query Design toolbar.

5. Drag ProjectID from the field list to the first column of the query grid. It should automatically have Group By in its Total row.

6. Drag Hours to the second column.

7. Click the Total row in the Hours column and select Sum from the drop-down menu that appears:

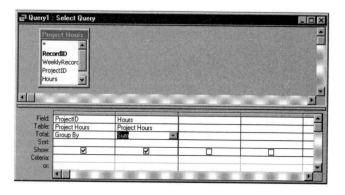

8. Click Run on the toolbar to open a Datasheet view window that shows the total hours for each ProjectID in the Project Hours table.

TIP TIP TIP TIP TIP TIP TIP TIP TIP TIP TIP TIP TIP TIP TIP TIP TIP TIP TIP TIP TIP TIP TIP

To group by additional fields, just drag them to the query grid and make sure their Total row is set to Group By. Access will calculate the total for each combination of the Group By field values.

Use Other Summary Operators

To calculate a value other than a sum:

- In the Query Design view window, choose one of the other options for the Total row: Avg, Min, Max, Count, StDev, Var, First, or Last.

- If you are using the Simple Query Wizard, check the boxes for Avg, Min, or Max as needed in the Summary Options dialog box. (This box is shown in "Summarize Records with the Simple Query Wizard" earlier in this chapter.)

Summarize Data with the Crosstab Wizard

There's another wizard in the New Query dialog box you haven't yet explored: the *Crosstab Wizard*. The Crosstab Wizard summarizes the data in a table or a query after grouping it by two or more fields and presents the results in a tabular fashion called a *crosstab*. A crosstab shows the values from up to three fields in the underlying table or query in its first column. These values are referred to as the *row headings* for the crosstab. The headings for the remaining columns are taken from the values in another field in the table or query being crosstabulated.

It's a lot easier to understand what a crosstab does if you see an example. If you look at Figure 8.5, you'll see a crosstab that shows the total number of hours worked by week and by employee. The row headings, shown in the first three columns of the crosstab, are taken from the EmployeeID, FirstName, and Last-Name fields in the query the crosstab is based on. The next column, Total Of Hours, shows the total number of hours in the query for each EmployeeID/ FirstName/LastName combination. The remaining fields, starting with 1/9/99, take their values from the WeekEndDate field in the crosstab's query. The other

Skill 8

cells in the crosstab (the ones at the intersection of each date and employee) show the sum of the hours for each EmployeeID/WeekEndDate combination.

NOTE NOTE NOTE NOTE NOTE NOTE NOTE NOTE NOTE NOTE NOTE NOTE NOTE NOTE NOTE NOTE NOTE

Besides showing sums, crosstabs can show several other types of summary values including averages, counts, maximum and minimum values, first and last values, standard deviation, and variance. Also, Date fields can be summarized by year, quarter, month, date, or date/time.

Row headings are from the
EmployeeID and name fields

Column headings are from
the WeekEndDate field

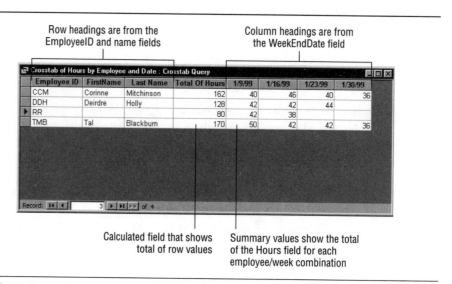

Calculated field that shows
total of row values

Summary values show the total
of the Hours field for each
employee/week combination

FIGURE 8.5: This crosstab shows the total number of hours worked by week and employee.

Create a Query for the Wizard to Use

If you want to crosstabulate data from related tables, you'll have to formulate a query before you start the Crosstab Wizard. The information in the crosstab in Figure 8.5 is drawn from three tables: Employees, Weekly Records, and Project Hours. The query that joins them is shown in the following dialog box.

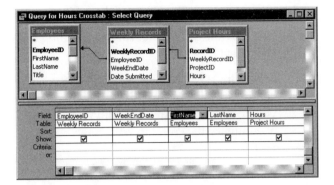

Start the Crosstab Wizard

Once you have a query that includes all the fields you need for the crosstab, you can start the wizard. This example creates the crosstab in Figure 8.5:

1. In the Database window, click the Queries button and click New.

2. Double-click Crosstab Query Wizard.

3. In the first step of the wizard, select Queries, highlight the query for the crosstab, and click Next.

4. The second step asks you to select the row headings. Add EmployeeID, FirstName, and LastName to the Selected Fields list so the dialog box appears like this before you click Next:

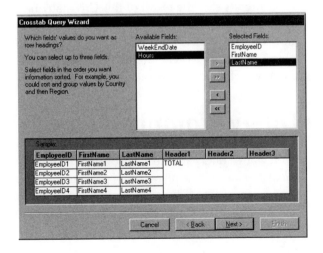

SKILL
8

5. Highlight WeekEndDate for the column headings and click Next.

6. Choose Date as the interval for grouping the WeekEndDate values and click Next.

7. Select Hours on the Fields list, and then highlight Sum on the Functions list before you click Next. The sample in the dialog box will reflect the fields you've chosen for row and column headings, and it will indicate what type of summary the crosstab will show:

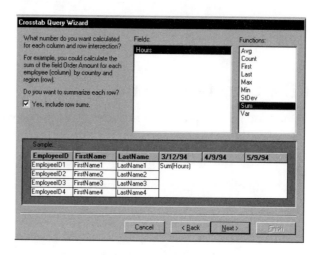

8. Change the Crosstab query name and click Finish.

You already saw the result of this Crosstab query in Figure 8.5. If you click the View button while viewing the crosstab to switch to Design view, you'll see a query like the one in Figure 8.6. This is the query the wizard creates for you behind the scenes to generate the crosstab. The Crosstab row in the query tells Access which fields to use for the various crosstab elements.

Have a Query Prompt You for Criteria

If you want a query to select a group of records you choose on the fly, you can use a *parameter query*. When you run a parameter query, Access waits for you to enter a value for the query criteria. To create a parameter query, you enter a prompt in the Criteria row of any field you want to supply a value for at run time.

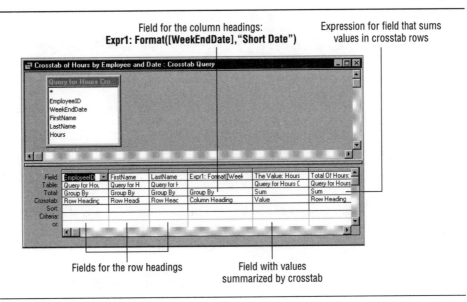

FIGURE 8.6: This query generates the crosstab shown in Figure 8.5.

This query prompts you to enter a ProjectID when it is run:

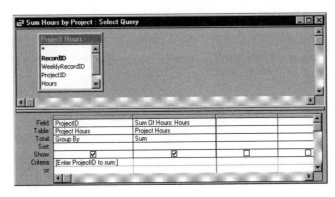

If you look at the Criteria row for the ProjectID field, you'll see *[Enter ProjectID to sum:]*. Access sees the [ ] and knows that their contents should be used as a prompt for query criteria. When you run this query, you see a prompt like the one shown in the following dialog box.

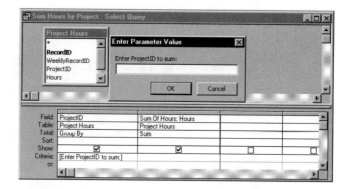

After you enter a value and press Enter, Access will add the criteria you entered to the query and run it as usual. This Datasheet view window is generated if you enter **1** in response to the query prompt:

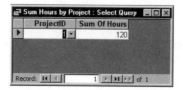

TIP TIP TIP TIP TIP TIP TIP TIP TIP TIP TIP TIP TIP TIP TIP TIP TIP TIP TIP TIP TIP TIP TIP

Create a report based on a parameter query if you want to choose report records on the fly.

Are You Experienced?

Now you can...

- ☑ Append records from one table to another
- ☑ Update records with a query
- ☑ Delete records with a query
- ☑ Create calculated fields with a query
- ☑ Summarize data with a query
- ☑ Use the Crosstab Wizard
- ☑ Have a query prompt you for criteria

**SKILL
8**

Create and Customize Reports

- ➔ **Create an AutoReport**
- ➔ **Use the Label Wizard**
- ➔ **Use the Report Wizard**
- ➔ **Preview a report**
- ➔ **Print a report**
- ➔ **Work in the Report Design view window**
- ➔ **Sort and group report records**
- ➔ **Add calculated and summary fields to a report**
- ➔ **Report on selected records**

In this chapter, you'll find out how to create "instant" reports and labels with Access. You'll also learn how to use the Report Design view window to customize the reports that Access creates with AutoReport and the wizards. The Report Design view window shares many of the features of the Form Design view window, so it won't be covered in detail. Instead, this chapter focuses on the tools that are unique to report design.

Options for Creating a New Report

You have several options for creating a new report with Access:

- AutoReports
- The Report Wizard, which works for single- or multi-table reports
- The Label Wizard
- The Chart Wizard
- The Report Design view window

This chapter gives a quick look at the first three tools on this list before you start working with the Report Design view window. The Chart Wizard is not discussed until Skill 10, "Create and Customize Charts."

AutoReports

AutoReport is the quickest way to create a report for a table or query with Access. It's even faster than using a wizard. All you have to do is supply the name of a table or query and optionally select the type of AutoReport you want, columnar or tabular. Access then creates a report for you that includes all the fields in the table or query you select.

TIP TIP TIP TIP TIP TIP TIP TIP TIP TIP TIP TIP TIP TIP TIP TIP TIP TIP TIP TIP TIP TIP TIP TIP TIP

You can use an AutoReport as the basis for a quick multi-table report. First create an AutoReport for the master table of the report. Then open the Auto-Report in Design view and drag the name of the table with the detail records from the Database window to it.

Columnar AutoReports

A *columnar AutoReport* shows the records from a table or a query with the fields arranged in columns. The report being previewed in Figure 9.1 is a columnar AutoReport for the Projects table. As you can see, the design is functional, but could benefit from some detail work in the Report Design view window.

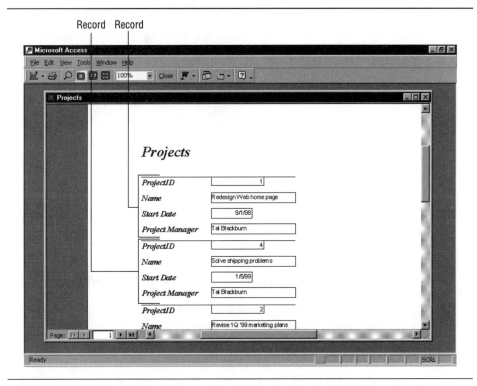

FIGURE 9.1: This report was created for the Projects table by choosing "AutoReport: Columnar" in the New Report dialog box.

SKILL
9

Create a Columnar AutoReport with the Last Style You Used

The style for an AutoReport created from the New Report dialog box comes from the last style you used with the Report Wizard or with AutoFormat. If you haven't yet chosen a style in one of these ways, an AutoReport will have the default Normal style.

To create a columnar AutoReport with the last style you used:

1. Click the Reports button in the Database window.

2. Click New to open the New Report dialog box:

3. Select a table or query for the report using the drop-down list in the bottom of the New Report dialog box.

4. Double-click "AutoReport: Columnar."

5. When you close the report window, choose Yes and enter a name to save the new report.

Create an AutoReport with the Normal Style

If you don't mind getting a report that has the plain Normal style, you can take a shortcut and create a columnar AutoReport this way:

1. Select a table or query in the Database window.

2. Choose AutoReport from the New Object drop-down button on the toolbar, or choose Insert ➤ AutoReport from the menu.

NOTE NOTE NOTE NOTE NOTE NOTE NOTE NOTE NOTE NOTE NOTE NOTE NOTE NOTE NOTE

As you can see, a report with the Normal style is pretty bare. It doesn't even include a title. To dress it up, you would have to open it in the Report Design view window and add whatever frills you like. Later in this skill, you'll find out how to open a report in Design view and add elements like text, graphics, and hyperlinks.

Here's an example of a columnar AutoReport created with the Normal style:

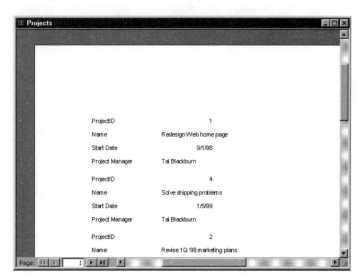

Tabular AutoReports

A *tabular AutoReport* shows records in a tabular listing, as illustrated in Figure 9.2. In this layout, all the fields in a table or query are arranged in columns and each record is shown as a row. The final result is similar to what you see when you open a table or query in Datasheet view.

Create a Tabular AutoReport

To create a tabular AutoReport:

1. Click the Reports button in the Database window.

2. Click New.

3. Select a table or query for the report using the drop-down list in the bottom of the New Report dialog box.

4. Double-click "AutoReport: Tabular."

5. When you close the report window, choose Yes and enter a name to save the new report.

SKILL
9

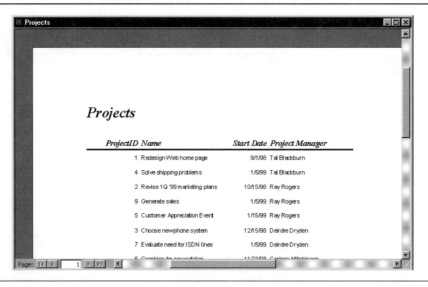

FIGURE 9.2: This tabular AutoReport was created for the Projects table.

TIP TIP TIP TIP TIP TIP TIP TIP TIP TIP TIP TIP TIP TIP TIP TIP TIP TIP TIP TIP TIP TIP TIP

If you don't like the style of the tabular AutoReport you end up with, open the report in Design view and use AutoFormat to give it a new look. AutoFormat works the same for a report as for a form. See Skill 6 for details on AutoFormat.

Tabular AutoReports for Tables with Many Fields

A tabular AutoReport works well for a table or query with a small number of fields. If you are working with more fields than can fit on a page, though, you will end up with a mess. Access will squeeze and squish fields and their headings to show all of them on the page. You will end up having to do a lot of resizing and rearranging in the Report Design view window to make the report presentable.

To avoid this, when you're working with a wide table it's best to decide on the fields you need for a tabular report before you use AutoReport. Then, design a query that selects those fields and create an AutoReport for the query. Or skip AutoReport altogether and go directly to the Report Wizard. The Report Wizard, as you'll see later in this skill, lets you choose fields from one or more tables at the beginning of the report design process.

The Label Wizard

The Label Wizard creates report designs that can be used to print labels to fit standard forms like Avery, EXPE, Herma, and Zweckform. It also gives you the option to set up your own label specifications if you're not working with ones that match a ready-made format. Here's how to get it started:

1. In the Database window, select the Reports button and click New.

2. Choose a table or query for the labels.

3. Double-click Label Wizard to open the first wizard step:

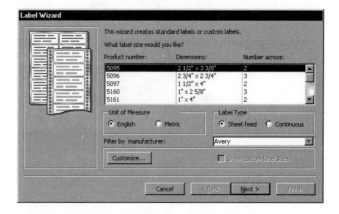

Select a Label Format and Font

In its first Label Wizard dialog box, you are prompted to choose the type of label you want to print.

1. If necessary, change the Unit Of Measure to Metric.

2. Use the Filter By Manufacturer drop-down list to choose the type of label you are using (Avery, EXPE, Herma, Tab1, Tab2, or Zweckform). Then use the tabular list under Product Number to select the right label size. Or, if you want to use a label you designed yourself and saved earlier, click Show Custom Label Sizes to change what's shown on the list before you make a choice. (See the next section for instructions on creating a custom label.)

SKILL
9

3. Check the Label Type option to make sure it's set properly to Sheet Feed or Continuous.

4. Click Next to move to the next step where you choose a style for the labels.

Create Your Own Label Format

If you need to specify your own label dimensions:

1. In the first step of the Label Wizard, click the Customize button and then click New to open the following window:

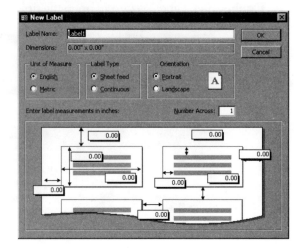

2. After Label Name, enter a name for the new label format.

3. Select the proper settings for Unit Of Measure, Label Type, and Orientation.

4. In the boxes with zeros in the bottom half of the window, enter the measurements for the labels, margins, and spaces between label columns and rows.

5. For Number Across, enter the number of columns of labels on a page.

6. Click OK to return to the New Label Size window. Then click Close to go back to step 1 of the Label Wizard.

7. Click Next to go to the next wizard step.

Choose the Text Style for the Labels

In the second step of the Label Wizard, you can change the font, font size, font weight, text color, and text style (normal, italic, or underline) of the labels. This step may appear to be strictly cosmetic, but it's actually pretty important. You want to make sure the font size is small enough for all the fields to fit completely on the label. The dialog box for this step shows a sample with the font characteristics you select to help you make the right choices:

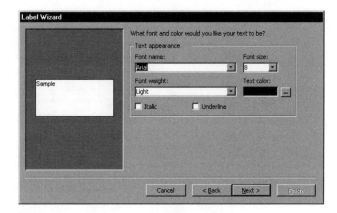

1. Choose a font name and size. You can check the box on the left side of the dialog box to see how your choices look.

2. Change the font weight and text color, if you like.

3. Check Italic and/or Underline if you want to apply these properties to the label text.

4. When you're finished, click Next to move on to the step where you lay out the fields for each label.

Arrange the Label Fields

In this step, you arrange fields in the Prototype Label box to create a label layout. You can include spaces and punctuation, or even literal text, in the sample label. The following steps show how to use a typical set of address fields, along with a comma and a few spaces, to create the label shown in a moment.

1. Double-click FirstName on the Available Fields list to move it to the prototype label.

2. Tap the spacebar.

3. Double-click LastName.

4. Press Enter to create a new line in the Prototype Label box.

5. Double-click Address on the Available Fields list and press Enter.

6. Double-click City, type a comma and a space, double-click State, tap the spacebar twice, and double-click Zip. The Prototype Label should look like this:

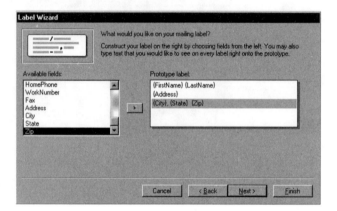

7. Click Next.

Sort and Name the Labels

In the next wizard step, you can sort the labels by one or more fields:

1. In turn, double-click each field on the Available Fields list that you want to sort by.

2. Click Next.

3. Change the name for the label report design, if you need to, and click Finish.

   After the Label Wizard finishes its work, Access will show the label report in a Report Preview window like the one shown in Figure 9.3. For information on using the Preview window and printing, see "Preview a Report" and "Print a Report" later in this chapter.

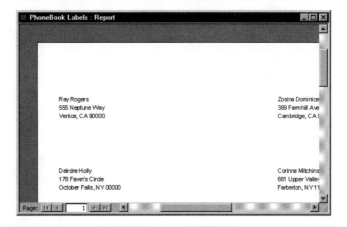

FIGURE 9.3: The Label Wizard created this report design to print Avery 5162 labels for records in a table called PhoneBook.

The Report Wizard

It takes more work to create a report with the Report Wizard than with Auto-Report, but you have a lot more control over what the final result looks like. With the Report Wizard, you can:

- Choose fields from one or more tables and queries

- Decide whether you want the report records grouped

- Sort the report by up to four fields

- Optionally show summary values and even hide the underlying detail records

- Choose a layout for report records (Stepped, Block, Outline, and so on) and the report orientation (portrait or landscape)

- Select a style (Bold, Casual, Compact, and so on)

SKILL
9

The examples in this section use the Report Wizard to create a single-table report, a multi-table report, and a *summary report*. Summary reports can show information like the average value of a number type field, the sum of a field's values, and the count of records in a report.

A Single-Table Report

This example creates a tabular report for the Project Hours table that also shows the total number of hours worked for each project:

1. Select the Project Hours table in the Database window.

2. Select Report from the New Object drop-down menu on the toolbar.

3. Double-click Report Wizard.

4. In the first step, make sure Tables/Queries is set to "Table: Project Hours." Then highlight ProjectID and click the > button. Repeat this for the Hours and Description fields so the Selected Fields list looks like this before you click Next:

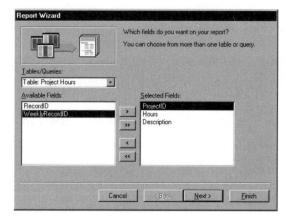

5. Double-click ProjectID in the next dialog box to group the report records by this field. Click Next after the dialog box looks like the one on the following page.

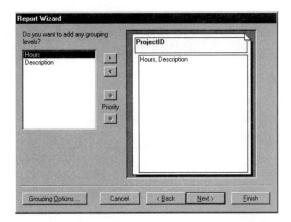

6. In the next step, click the Summary Options button. In the Summary Options dialog box, check the Sum box for the Hours field and then click OK. Click Next when you return to the Report Wizard without choosing any sort fields.

7. Choose a layout (Stepped, Outline, and so on) and change the Orientation to Landscape if you need to fit several fields across the page. Then click Next.

8. Pick a style and click Next.

9. In the last step, name the report and click Finish.

When the wizard finishes doing its thing, it will open the report in a Preview window like the one shown in Figure 9.4. As you can see in the figure, some of the formatting done by the wizard could use a bit of work. The object that shows the ProjectID is too wide and displays the value far to the right of its field label. Also, some of the space under the report title could be eliminated. You'll see how to make these and other adjustments in the section "Report Design View" later in this chapter.

A Multi-Table Report

This example creates a report like the one in the last example, but adds some fields from the Projects table (Name and Project Manager) to make the end result more descriptive:

1. In the Database window, click the Report button and click New.

2. Choose the Projects table from the drop-down list in the New Report dialog box.

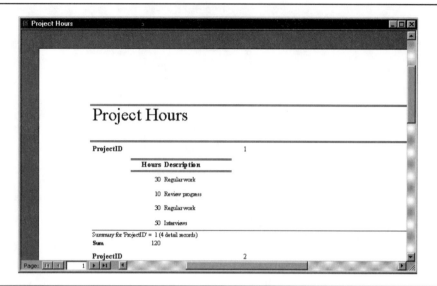

FIGURE 9.4: This report was created by the Report Wizard for the Project Hours table.

3. Double-click Report Wizard.

4. In the first step of the wizard, make sure Tables/Queries is set to "Table: Projects." Then move the ProjectID, Name, and Project Manager fields from the Available Fields list to the Selected Fields list.

5. Change the Tables/Queries selection to "Table: Project Hours."

6. Add the Hours and Description fields to the Selected Fields list:

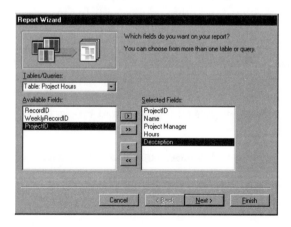

7. Click Next.

8. Under "How Do You Want To View Your Data?", highlight By Projects and click Next.

9. Click Next in the step that asks if you want to add any grouping levels.

10. Click the Summary Options button, check the Sum box for Hours, click OK, and click Next.

11. Choose a layout and a style in the next two steps.

12. Name the report and click Finish.

Figure 9.5 shows the result of this exercise. The Report Wizard automatically placed the fields from the Projects table—Name and Project Manager—in the header for each group of project records. It also created a group footer to show the total hours for each project.

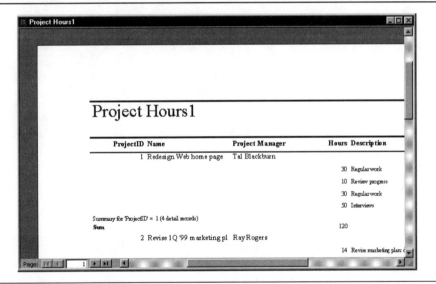

FIGURE 9.5: This report was created with the Report Wizard and shows fields from two tables: Projects and Project Hours.

A Summary Report without Details

It's easy to create a summary report with no detail records using the Report Wizard. The following steps make yet another version of the Project Hours report that shows only the total hours worked on each project:

1. Follow steps 1–9 from the last example.

2. For the next step, click the Summary Options button.

3. Check the Sum box for Hours.

4. Select Summary Only under Show so the Summary Options window looks like this:

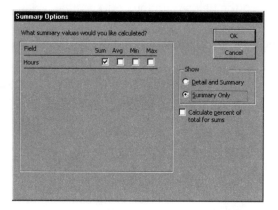

5. Click OK.

6. Proceed with the rest of the Report Wizard as described in the last example.

The resulting Project Hours summary report is shown in Figure 9.6. This report is a little difficult to read because some areas are crowded, but with just a few changes, it can be transformed into something more comprehensible. With the Preview window for the new report open, click the View button to go into Design view. Then use the techniques in Skill 6 to change the report so it looks more like this after you switch back to the Preview window.

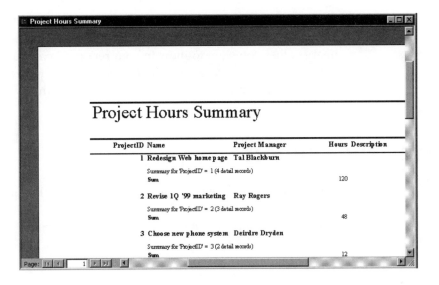

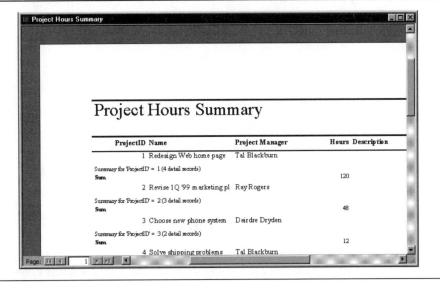

FIGURE 9.6: This summary report was created by selecting Summary Only in the Summary Options dialog box of the Report Wizard.

Sometimes it's easier to get a nice-looking summary report this way: Create a Totals query as described in Skill 8, "Master Advanced Queries," to calculate the summary values you want to show in your report. Then create a tabular Auto-Report for the query to get a quick report that you don't have to finesse. Or, if all you need are the numbers, just click the Print button while viewing the query in Datasheet view.

Preview a Report

All the reports you've created in this chapter with AutoReport and the Report Wizard have been shown in the Print Preview window. There are actually two ways to preview a report: *Print Preview* and *Layout Preview*.

Print Preview

When a report is shown in the Print Preview window, it appears almost exactly as it will when it is printed. Access runs any queries it needs for the report and does all the necessary math for calculated and summary fields.

To open a report in Print Preview, you can use any of these techniques:

- From the Database window, highlight the report's name and click Preview.

- In the Database window, right-click the report you want to view and choose Print Preview from the shortcut menu.

- From Report Design view, click Print Preview on the toolbar, or select Print Preview from the View drop-down menu.

- In the last step of the Report Wizard, click Finish without changing the open mode for the new report.

The Print Preview Toolbar

The Print Preview window has its own toolbar. Most of the buttons on the Print Preview toolbar are self-explanatory, but here are a few notes on what they do:

View   Takes you to Design view.

Print   Sends the report to the printer without opening the Print dialog box.

Zoom   Toggles between a 100% view and Fit.

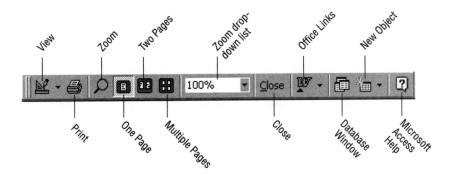

One Page   Shows one complete page of the report in the Preview window.

Two Pages   Shows two complete pages side by side.

Multiple Pages   Lets you choose whether to see 1 by 1, 1 by 2, 1 by 3, 2 by 1, 2 by 2, or 2 by 3 pages. (To make your selection, click the button and then drag over the choices in the box that appears.)

Zoom drop-down list   Offers menu choices that range from 200% down to 10% and Fit.

Close   Returns you to the last window you were in.

Office Links   Offers a drop-down list of choices for Publish It with MS Word and Analyze It with MS Excel.

Database Window   Brings you to the Database window without closing the Preview window.

New Object   Offers the same drop-down list that's available when you are in the Database window, with the AutoForm and AutoReport choices dimmed.

Microsoft Access Help   Opens the Office Assistant in whatever persona you have chosen for it (Clippit, The Dot, F1, The Genius, Mother Nature, and so on).

SKILL
9

TIP TIP TIP TIP TIP TIP TIP TIP TIP TIP TIP TIP TIP TIP TIP TIP TIP TIP TIP TIP TIP TIP TIP TIP

You can toggle between a full-page view (Fit) and 100% in the Preview window by clicking the report background.

Layout Preview

There's another view you can switch to from Report Design view: Layout Preview. In this mode, Access displays the report in a Preview window but doesn't do all the calculations that are necessary for Print Preview. This gives you a quick way to check your work as you design a report without having to wait for Access to do math or long queries.

To switch to Layout Preview:

1. Make sure you are in Design view for the report.

2. Choose Layout Preview from the View drop-down list on the Report Design toolbar.

NOTE NOTE NOTE NOTE NOTE NOTE NOTE NOTE NOTE NOTE NOTE NOTE NOTE NOTE NOTE
The Layout Preview window has the same toolbar as the Print Preview window.

TIP TIP TIP TIP TIP TIP TIP TIP TIP TIP TIP TIP TIP TIP TIP TIP TIP TIP TIP TIP TIP TIP
If you use Layout Preview frequently, you may want to add a button for it to the Report Design toolbar. See Skill 16, "Customize Access," for details on customizing toolbars.

Print a Report

There's more than one way to print a report from a Print Preview or Design view window:

- Click the Print button on the toolbar to send the report directly to the printer.

- Choose File ➣ Print from the menus to open the Print dialog box.

- Press Ctrl+P to open the Print dialog box.

TIP TIP TIP TIP TIP TIP TIP TIP TIP TIP TIP TIP TIP TIP TIP TIP TIP TIP TIP TIP TIP TIP
You can also print a report right from the Database window. Just highlight the report and click the Print button on the toolbar, press Ctrl+P, use File ➣ Print, or right-click the report and choose Print from the shortcut menu. Using the first or the last option bypasses the Print dialog box. If you want to change print settings, use File ➣ Print or Ctrl+P.

When to Use the Print Dialog Box

Unlike the Print button, which sends a report directly to the default printer, the Print dialog box gives you some choices about printing. It lets you:

- Change the printer the report will go to
- Open the properties dialog box for the selected printer
- Send the report to a `.prn` file you name
- Print a range of pages
- Print only the selected records for an open query or table
- Print more than one copy and optionally collate the report
- Open the Page Setup dialog box to change the report's margins and set the number of columns that are printed.

The Print dialog box is shown in Figure 9.7. Check the figure labels to find out what each part of the Print dialog box does. After you set up your printing options to your liking, click OK to print the report.

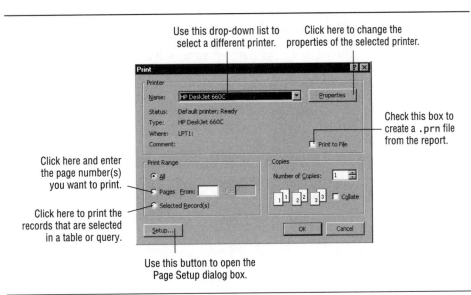

FIGURE 9.7: When you use File ➢ Print, Access opens the Print dialog box, where you can change how a report is printed.

NOTE NOTE NOTE NOTE NOTE NOTE NOTE NOTE NOTE NOTE NOTE NOTE NOTE NOTE
To change the default settings for a printer or to add printers to your system, choose Start ≻ Settings ≻ Printers from the Windows menu.

Report Design View

The Report Design view window is the place where you design reports from scratch or add your own touches to reports you create with the Report Wizard. The examples that come next don't do the former, since it's quite time-consuming. Instead, they start with AutoReports or ones produced by the Report Wizard and use the Report Design view window to improve them.

TIP TIP TIP TIP TIP TIP TIP TIP TIP TIP TIP TIP TIP TIP TIP TIP TIP TIP TIP TIP TIP TIP TIP TIP TIP
If you do want to take on the task of designing a report from scratch, select the Reports button in the Database window and double-click Create Report In Design View. If you are familiar with the material in Skill 6 and in the rest of this skill, you'll be able to add fields, text, graphics, and other objects to the blank Report Design view window that opens.

What You Already Know from Form Design

If you read Skill 6, or have spent time working in the Form Design view window, you already know a lot about Report Design view. You most likely can:

- Use tools such as the Formatting Toolbar, the Toolbox, the Field List, and properties sheets
- Enable the Control Wizards
- Customize the page layout, change the report size, switch the style with AutoFormat, add headers and footers, show a background graphic, and use page breaks
- Do basic maneuvers like move, resize, and align objects
- Add objects such as fields, text, and graphics to a design
- Use the Subform/Subreport Wizard
- Change the record source for a design
- Create a report template

If you need help doing any of these jobs in Report Design view, refer back to Skill 6. You'll have to translate *form* to *report* in some cases (for example, check the section on "Form Templates" to find out about report templates), but the instructions are the same whether you are in Form Design view or Report Design view.

The rest of this skill focuses on how to use the elements that are unique to Report Design view.

Open a Report in Design View

To open a report in Design view:

- From the Database window, select the report you want to change and click Design. Alternatively, right-click the report and choose Design from the shortcut menu.

- From a Preview window, click the Design View button on the toolbar.

Figure 9.8 shows a report called Project Hours Summary open in Report Design view. As you can see, there is a Report Design toolbar (which is discussed in more detail a little later in this chapter) and the Formatting (Form/Report) toolbar that you already know from working in Form Design view.

The Report Design View Toolbars

There are two toolbars in the Report Design view window: the Report Design toolbar and the Formatting toolbar. The Report Design toolbar looks like this:

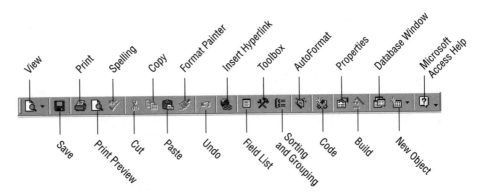

SKILL
9

The Report Design toolbar is just like the Form Design toolbar except for one additional button: Sorting And Grouping. You'll see how to use this button to organize a report into groups of records later in this skill.

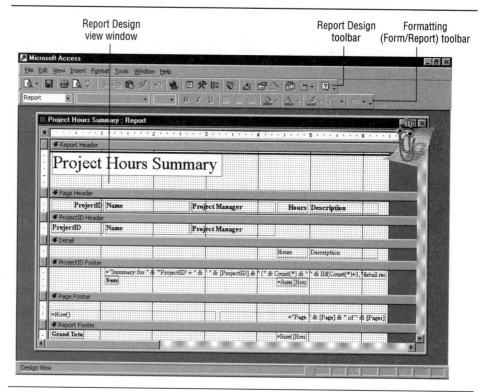

FIGURE 9.8: This report is open in Report Design view.

The Formatting (Form/Report) toolbar is exactly the same for both Form Design view and Report Design view. See Skill 6 for instructions on using all the buttons on the Formatting toolbar.

The Toolbox for Reports

The Toolbox for Report Design view is also the same one you see in Form Design view:

Skill 6 explains how to use each of the buttons in the Toolbox.

Report Sections

If you look at Figure 9.8, you'll notice that the Report Design window is divided into various sections. These sections are used to control where report elements, such as titles, group headers and footers, and detail records, appear on a report. A report may include these sections:

Report Header   The controls in this section appear at the beginning of a report.

Page Header   Anything in this section of a report appears at the beginning of each new page.

Group Header   A group header has the name of the field value it is based on. For example, in Figure 9.8 there is a header called ProjectID Header. A new group header appears when the group value changes.

Detail   This is where the detail records of a report appear. The Visible property of this section can be turned off to hide detail records from view, creating a quick summary report.

Group Footer   The controls in this section appear after the last record for a group.

Page Footer   Anything in this section appears at the bottom of each report page.

Report Footer   The contents of this section appear at the end of a report, before the last page footer.

Changing a Section's Properties

Each report section has its own properties. To change the features of a report section, right-click the background of the section and choose Properties. Click the line for whatever property you want to change. Then change the value by typing a new one or selecting one from the drop-down list, if there is one. As soon as you move off the property's line or the properties sheet, the change will take effect. Here are a few section properties you may want to change:

Visible   When this property is set to Yes, the section appears on the report. When set to No, the section is invisible when the report is run.

Height   This property sets the height of the section.

NOTE NOTE NOTE NOTE NOTE NOTE NOTE NOTE NOTE NOTE NOTE NOTE NOTE NOTE
A section can be resized by changing its Height property on the report's properties sheet or by dragging on its bottom border.

Sort and Group Report Records

The Sorting And Grouping button on the Report Design toolbar opens a dialog box that you can use to organize a report's records. You can simply sort records, or you can create groups with header and footer sections that show summary information.

Open the Sorting And Grouping Dialog Box

Let's group and sort the records shown in the AutoReport in Figure 9.9 so that they are arranged in separate groups for each state. Within each group, the records will be sorted by the LastName field.

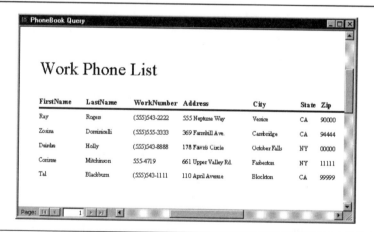

FIGURE 9.9: A tabular AutoReport with no sorts or groups added to organize the records

1. Open the report you want to sort in Design view.

2. Click the Sorting And Grouping button on the Report Design toolbar.

3. Click the first blank line under Field/Expression to show its drop-down arrow and select State from the list of fields.

4. In the bottom half of the dialog box, change the settings for Group Header and Group Footer to Yes. (This is what turns a sort into a group.)

5. Back in the top half of the dialog box, select LastName from the drop-down list for the second line under Field/Expression.

If you click back on the line for State, the Sorting And Grouping box will look like this:

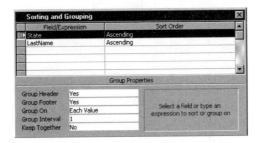

You won't actually add any controls to the group header and group footer that you see included in this example, but using these sections will ensure that there is space between the groups of records for each separate state. If you wanted to, you could place a control for the state name in the group header, and another control for the count of records for each group in the group footer.

Figure 9.10 shows the report as it appears in Print Preview after the group and sort are added. As you can see, there is a blank area above and below the group of records for each state. These areas are the group headers and the group footers. You can resize them by dragging on their bottom borders, and you can also place objects like text and fields in them. See the next main section, "Add Calculated and Summary Fields to a Report," for instructions on creating fields that show summary information like counts, totals, or averages.

Remove a Sort or a Group from a Report

To remove a sort or a group from a report design:

1. Open the report in Design view.

2. Click the Sorting And Grouping button on the Report Design toolbar.

3. Click the record selector for the sort or group you want to delete. (The record selector is the gray box to the left of each Field/Expression line.) Access will highlight the entire line.

4. Press Delete, and then choose Yes.

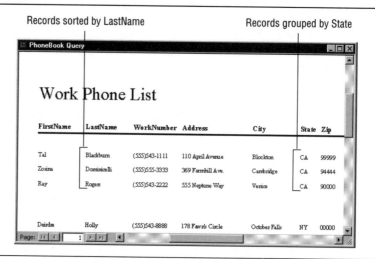

FIGURE 9.10: This AutoReport has its records grouped by the State field and sorted within each group by LastName.

NOTE NOTE NOTE NOTE NOTE NOTE NOTE NOTE NOTE NOTE NOTE NOTE NOTE NOTE NOTE
When you delete a group, its header and footer, along with any controls they include, are also deleted.

Add Calculated and Summary Fields to a Report

Earlier in this chapter, you saw how to use the Report Wizard to show summary information in a report. Now you'll go through the steps of setting up summary fields and calculated fields by hand, just in case you need to add one to a report after it's already done.

Define a Calculated Field

The report in Figure 9.11 is based on a query that calculates the total number of hours worked by project. The query has a Total line and looks like this:

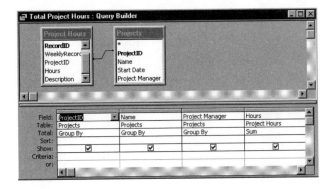

The datasheet that results when this query is run has the fields shown in the report in Figure 9.11: ProjectID, Name, Project Manager, and SumOfHours. Follow the steps below to open the report in Design view and add a calculated field, SumOfHours/8, to show the number of person days, too.

1. Open the report in Design view.

2. Resize some of the text and field objects and move them to make room for the new field at the end of the report.

3. Select the field object for SumOfHours and its label at the same time (hold down Shift while you click on each control), and then choose Edit ➢ Duplicate from the menu. (You can also use the Text Box button in the Toolbox to create a field object, but this way is quicker.)

4. Drag the new field and label to the place they should appear. Or, instead of dragging, press Ctrl while pressing the right arrow key to move the objects sideways without disturbing their vertical placement.

5. Change the text for the new label to PersonDays. (To edit the text, click the label twice and start typing when you see the I-beam. Don't double-click or you'll open the properties sheet for the label instead of going into edit mode.)

6. Remove any extra space created in the Page Header. Drag the bottom border of the Page Header up to shrink it.

SKILL
9

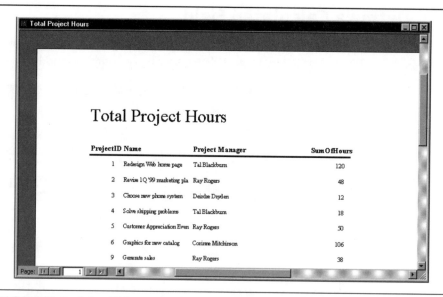

FIGURE 9.11: This report shows the total number of hours by Project. A calculated field called PersonDays will be added that is equal to SumOfHours/8.

7. Right-click the new field object (not its label) and choose Properties.

8. Click the Data tab and change the Control Source to **=[SumOfHours]/8**. The Properties Sheet should look like this:

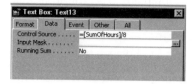

9. Make the line that runs horizontally across the report design under the labels longer so it underlines the new label, too.

When you preview the report, you'll see a new field like the one in Figure 9.12.

Calculated field that shows [SumOfHours]/8

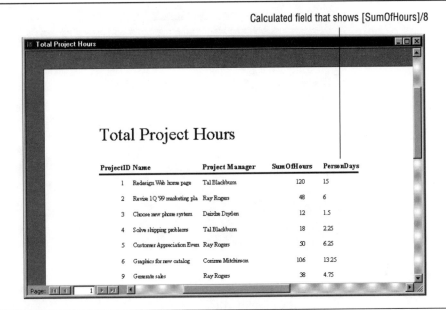

FIGURE 9.12: A calculated field was added to this report to show person hours by project.

Define a Summary Field

Next you'll add a summary field to the same report you used in the last example to show the average number of hours worked per project:

1. Open the report in Design view.

2. Drag the bottom border of the gray line labeled Report Footer to make some room in the report footer.

3. Click Toolbox on the toolbar, if the Toolbox isn't already open.

4. Click the Text Box tool and drag in the Report Footer to create a box to show the average.

5. Right-click the new control and choose Properties.

6. Click the Data tab and enter **=Avg([SumOfHours])** for the Control Source property. The properties sheet will look like the one on the following page.

**SKILL
9**

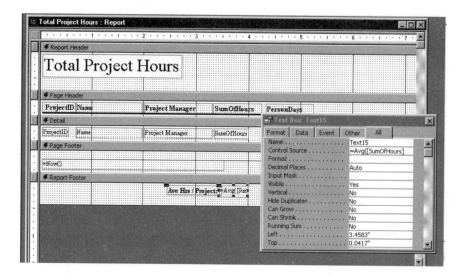

7. Click the label for the new field twice and edit it to read **Ave Hrs / Project**. Resize the label if you need to.

Figure 9.13 shows the report being previewed with the new summary field added.

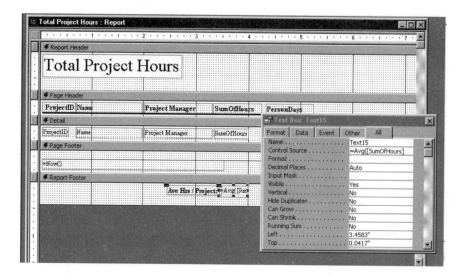

FIGURE 9.13: A summary field in the report footer of this report shows the average hours worked per project.

Create a Quick Summary Only Report

You've already seen how to create a summary report using the Report Wizard. However, the resulting report wasn't perfect. The group headers and footers were squished together somewhat, making the report hard to read. One workaround is to create a Totals query that calculates the summary information you want to see and use an AutoReport on the query. (This technique was used to create the report used in the last two examples.) Or, if you have a report that already includes summary fields in a group footer, you can just hide the detail area of the report with this trick:

1. Open the report in Design view.

2. Right-click the Detail area of the report and choose Properties from the shortcut menu.

3. Click the Format tab, if it's not already active.

4. Change the setting for Visible to No.

When you preview the report, the detail records will be hidden from view. All you'll see are the contents of the other report sections: the report header, the group headers and footers, and the report footer. Figure 9.14 shows the same report shown in Figure 9.5 after the Detail section was hidden this way. If you compare Figure 9.14 to the summary created with the Report Wizard in Figure 9.6, you'll see they are almost the same.

Report on Selected Records

If you want to report on selected records in a table, there are several ways to do it:

- Base a report on a query if you want to show records that always match the same criteria.

- Create a parameter query that prompts you for criteria if you want to change the records for the report on the fly.

- Open a table, apply a filter to it, and save it. Then create a report for the table. This method can be tricky, though. You may have to activate the filter in the report before it will work. See "Activate a Filter Inherited by a Report" in Skill 7 to find out how to activate the filter for a report permanently.

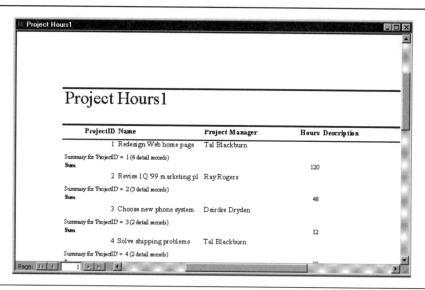

FIGURE 9.14: This summary report was created by hiding the Detail section of the report in Figure 9.5.

Base a Report on a Query

To base a report on a query, just select the query from the drop-down list in the New Report dialog box. Or, highlight the query in the Database window and select Report or AutoReport from the drop-down list for New Object on the toolbar. Skill 7 explains how to create queries.

Make a Report Prompt You for Record Selection Criteria

To have Access stop and prompt you for record selection criteria for a report, design a report that's based on a parameter query. At the end of Skill 8, you'll find instructions on how to create a parameter query.

Figure 9.15 shows the query for the report shown in Figures 9.12 and 9.13 with a parameter added that prompts you for a Project Manager. When you open the report this query is attached to, you see a window like this:

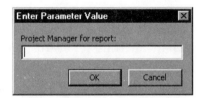

Access waits for you to enter the name of a Project Manager in this window.

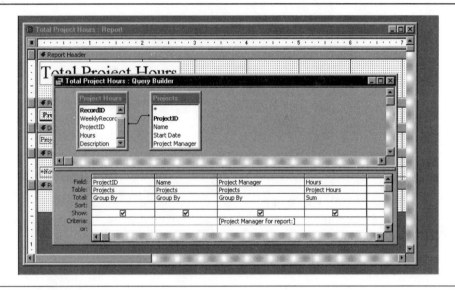

FIGURE 9.15: This query has a parameter entered as criteria for the Project Manager field. When the query is run, or a report based on the query, Access waits for you to enter a value.

After you enter a parameter value, Access will open the Total Project Hours report shown in Figure 9.13, but it will show only the projects belonging to the person you entered in the Parameter Value dialog box. Figure 9.16 shows the report after Tal Blackburn was entered as the Project Manager.

Include a Filter in a Report

When you create a report for a table that has a filter saved with it, the filter gets inherited by the report. The first time you use the report, Access will apply the filter to the report records. If you want to apply the filter every time you use the report, you'll have to change the report's properties. See "Activate a Filter Inherited by a Report" in Skill 7 for instructions on how to do this.

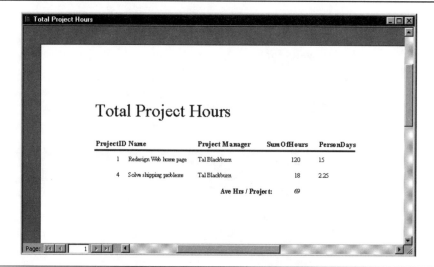

FIGURE 9.16: This report is based on the query shown in Figure 9.15. In this example, Tal Blackburn was entered in response to the prompt for a Project Manager.

Are You Experienced?

Now you can...

- ☑ Create an AutoReport
- ☑ Use the Label Wizard
- ☑ Create a report with the Report Wizard
- ☑ Preview a report
- ☑ Print a report
- ☑ Work in the Report Design view window
- ☑ Sort and group report records
- ☑ Add calculated and summary fields to a report
- ☑ Report on selected records

SKILL
9

Create and Customize Charts

- ➔ Choose the fields for a chart
- ➔ Use the Chart Wizard to create a pie chart
- ➔ Create a column chart
- ➔ Create a chart with multiple series of data
- ➔ Customize a chart
- ➔ Edit a chart
- ➔ Change the chart type
- ➔ Change titles and legends
- ➔ Choose labels, tick marks, colors, patterns, and scale
- ➔ Move and resize chart elements
- ➔ Link a chart to a record

In this chapter, you'll learn how to create pie charts (see Figure 10.1) as well as several other types of charts. Charts can be used to show the "big picture" of what's happening with all the data in a table or a query. A chart can also be set up to change the detail data it displays as you scroll through the records in a form. You'll use the Chart Wizard to create both of these types of charts and then learn how to customize them using the chart editing window.

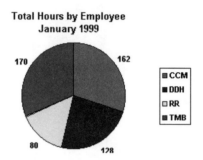

Total Hours by Employee January 1999

FIGURE 10.1: This pie chart shows the total number of hours worked by each employee in January 1999. The data for the chart comes from a query.

Get Ready to Chart

Before you can use the Chart Wizard, you need to have Microsoft Graph and the Access Advanced Wizards installed. An easy way to see if they are already on your system is to go ahead a bit in this chapter and follow the steps under "Use the Chart Wizard." Depending on how your copy of Access or Office is installed, you may get a message saying you need to install one or both components. If you installed these components with the Install On First Use option, Access can go ahead and do the install on the fly for you.

Start with a Form or Report

As you may have noticed, there is no separate button for "Charts" in the Database window. In Access, a chart is shown on a form or a report. There are two ways to add a chart to a form or report:

- Use the Chart Wizard to design a chart without leaving Access.

- Embed or link a chart you create with Microsoft Graph using the Unbound Object Frame tool.

This book doesn't cover embedding or linking charts; to do so, you have to know how to set up a chart in Microsoft Graph. Instead, this skill focuses on the Chart Wizard and launching Microsoft Graph automatically from Access to change chart properties.

Decide on Chart Fields

Before you start a chart, you need to decide on the fields you will use for various chart elements.

- For a pie chart, decide on a category field for each slice of the pie, and pick another field that contains the values to chart. For example, the chart in Figure 10.1 uses two fields: EmployeeID and Sum Of Hours.

- For a column chart or any other chart with two axes, choose the field for the x-axis categories, and another field for the y-axis values. You can optionally use a third field to categorize the y-axis values and create a graph that shows multiple *series*. A series is a subset of the data shown on a chart, grouped by the values in a field. For example, you could use EmployeeID for the x-axis, Sum Of Hours for the y-axis, and WeekEndDate to plot separate sets of y-axis values. In this example, each WeekEndDate value creates a separate series for the chart.

Don't get too hung up on this part. Talking about series and axes can be confusing unless you're looking at concrete examples. As you go through the Chart Wizard, the relationships between fields and chart elements should become clear.

Use the Chart Wizard

You can create a multitude of different charts with the Wizard: column charts, bar charts, area charts, line charts, and more. You'll begin your tour of the Chart Wizard by using it to create a pie chart like the one shown back in Figure 10.1. Then you'll use the Chart Wizard to display the same data as a column chart.

Create a Pie Chart

Before you start the Chart Wizard, you need to make sure the data you want to chart exists in a table or a query.

SKILL
10

If you'd like to find out more about queries, check Skill 7.

Choose a Table or Query for the Chart

The chart in Figure 10.1 is based on this query:

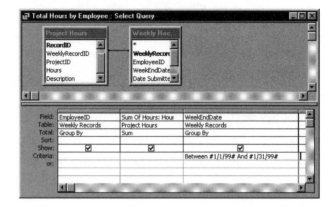

When you run the query, Access shows a datasheet with three fields:

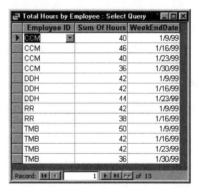

Here's how the fields correspond to the chart elements:

- The EmployeeID field is used for the pie slice categories.

- Sum Of Hours holds the values that are summed for each pie slice.

- WeekEndDate is used by the query to select the Project Hours records for January 1999 only. (You didn't have to include this field in the query; you could have just used it for criteria. By including it, though, you can use the same query later for a column chart with series that breaks the hours down by week as well as by employee.)

Start the Wizard

After you have the query with the fields you need, you can begin creating your chart.

1. In the Database window, click Forms and then New.

2. Click OK to select Design view. You don't have to select a table or a query because you are charting all the records in the query. You'll see an empty Design view window.

3. Choose Insert ➤ Chart from the menu.

4. In the Form Design view window, point to the upper-left corner of where you want the chart to appear and drag a box for the chart. When you release the mouse, the Chart Wizard will begin. Depending on your computer's resources, it may take a few seconds to show up.

5. Click Queries, select the query for the chart (Total Hours By Employee for this example), and click Next.

6. Move the first two fields, EmployeeID and Sum Of Hours, from the Available Fields list to the Fields For Chart list. Click Next.

7. Click Pie Chart, as shown here, and then click Next.

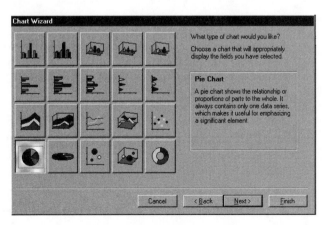

SKILL
10

8. Now it's time to specify how you want the fields charted. In this example, Access assumes that EmployeeID is used for the slice categories and that it should show the sum of the Sum Of Hours field in each slice:

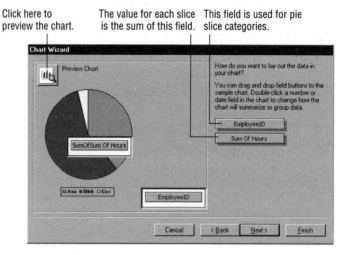

Because this is correct, click Next. (To check your work, you can click the Preview Chart button before you click Next.)

9. If the Chart Wizard asks you how it should link the chart to the form, change the setting for both Form Fields and Chart Fields to <No Field> and then click Next. If you don't see this question, ignore it and proceed to step 10.

10. Enter the title you want to appear on the chart and click Finish. Then click View on the Form Design toolbar to see the Wizard's handiwork.

TIP TIP TIP TIP TIP TIP TIP TIP TIP TIP TIP TIP TIP TIP TIP TIP TIP TIP TIP TIP TIP TIP TIP

Instead of inserting a chart object in an unbound form as described previously in steps 2 and 3, you can select a table or query and double-click Chart Wizard in the New Form dialog box. If you go this route, the Chart Wizard will skip the step where it asks you to select a table or query.

The chart in Figure 10.2 shows what you will see at this point. It is somewhat different from Figure 10.1; in Figure 10.2, there are no labels to show the pie slice values, and the title doesn't reflect the time frame for the chart. In the "Customize a Chart" section a little later in this chapter, you will see how to add these touches to the Chart Wizard's work:

• Edit the title to show the time frame for the chart.

- Change the colors for the pie's slices.
- Add labels that show the value of each slice.

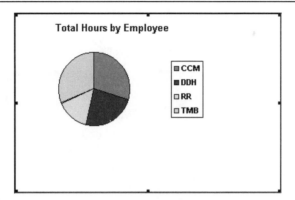

FIGURE 10.2: This pie chart was created with the Chart Wizard to show the total number of hours worked by employee.

TIP TIP TIP TIP TIP TIP TIP TIP TIP TIP TIP TIP TIP TIP TIP TIP TIP TIP TIP TIP TIP TIP TIP TIP TIP

A chart can show a summary value as an average instead of a total. In the dialog box described previously in step 8, double-click a field in the sample graph to open a Summarize dialog box, and choose Average or one of the other options.

Save a Chart

When you're finished viewing your chart:

1. Close the window for the form the chart appears in.

2. When Access asks whether you want to save your changes, choose Yes.

3. Enter a name for the form and click OK.

When you're ready to view the chart again, just open the form it's part of.

Create a Column Chart

Now it's time to chart the same data shown in Figures 10.1 and 10.2 using a *column chart*. This example shows just one series of data. There will be one column for each EmployeeID that shows the total of the Sum Of Hours field for that person.

1. Follow steps 1–6 as described in "Start the Wizard."

2. In the next step, leave Column Chart (the default selection) selected and click Next.

3. Access will guess that the EmployeeID field should be used for the x-axis and that it should sum the Sum Of Hours field for the y-axis:

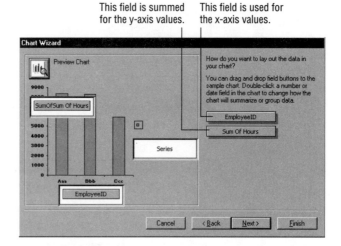

Click Next without changing anything in this step.

4. Change the chart's title if you need to, select No, Don't Display A Legend, and then click Finish.

Figure 10.3 shows the column chart you just created. Because there's just one series of data, the total hours for January 1999 as described by the chart's title, you don't need to include a legend.

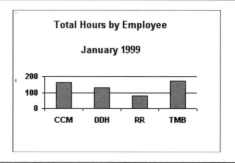

FIGURE 10.3: This column chart shows the same data charted in Figures 10.1 and 10.2.

A *legend* is a set of labels that describe the series of data in a column or bar chart, or the slices in a pie chart. To see an example of a legend, check Figure 10.1 or Figure 10.2. Both these figures include a legend that shows the employee for each pie slice.

The Chart Wizard will let you enter a two-line title in its last step. Enter the first line, press Ctrl+Enter, and enter the second line. You'll end up with a blank line between the two title lines that you may want to delete in Microsoft Graph. See "Change the Title and Legends" later in this chapter.

Create a Chart with Multiple Series

With some chart types, like columns and bars, you can include an additional field to divide the data into *series*. A series is just a subcategory used to further describe the chart values. For example, you can take the column chart shown in Figure 10.3 and break the column shown for each employee into separate pieces for each week.

To define the series, use the WeekEndDate field that's already part of the query you used for the other two examples. The Chart Wizard has several choices for summarizing a date field (Year, Month, Week, Day, and so on) but won't let you use the date value itself. (It shows a week # for Week, and Sun, Mon, and so on, for Day.) Follow the steps below to create the chart, then change its Row Source property to tell Access to create a different series for each unique week-ending date in the query records (1/9/99, 1/16/99, 1/23/99, and 1/30/99).

1.   Follow steps 1–6 as described in "Start the Wizard" with this change: Add the WeekEndDate field, along with EmployeeID and Sum Of Hours, to the Fields For Chart list in step 6. Click Next, leave Column Chart selected as the chart type, and click Next again.

2.   In the next step, Access will automatically use the WeekEndDate field for the series. You don't need to change the grouping for the series field yet. (If you do want to change the way the field values are grouped, double-click the field's name in this step and make your choice in the dialog box that appears before you close it.) Before you click Next, the Chart Wizard will look like it does in the following dialog box.

SKILL 10

This field is summed for the values in each series. This field is used for the x-axis values. This field defines the y-axis series.

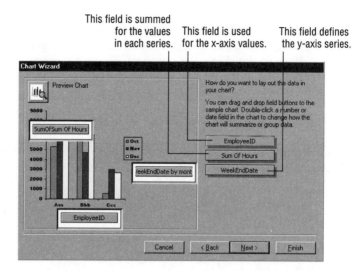

3. Change the chart title, let the wizard display a legend, and click Finish.

4. Before you click View to check the chart, right-click the chart object and choose Properties.

5. Click the Row Source line on the Data tab and click the ellipsis that appears at the end of the line. This will open an SQL Statement: Query Builder window so you can change how the WeekEndDate values are grouped.

6. Make the second column, the one for Expr1: Format[(WeekEndDate]. . ., wider so you can see the entire expression. Then change the *mmm* in the expression to *Short Date:*

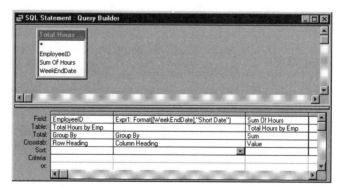

7. Next you need to tell Access not to bother grouping the data values by month, the default that is selected by the wizard. You'll make an additional change directly to the SQL statement for the query. To do this, click the drop-down arrow for the View button on the toolbar and choose SQL View.

8. In the SQL Statement window, delete everything after *Short Date)* except the semicolon (;), so the statement looks like this:

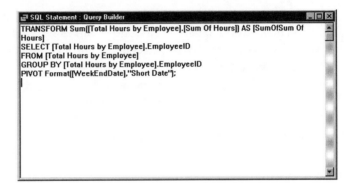

9. Close the SQL Statement window and choose Yes to save your change.

If you switch to Form view now, you'll see the chart shown in Figure 10.4. As you can see, there are up to four bars for each EmployeeID, one for each week the employee worked in January 1999.

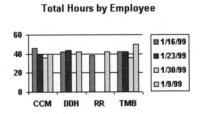

FIGURE 10.4: This column chart shows up to four series of values for each employee. The series represent the total hours worked during the weeks that end on the dates shown in the legend.

SKILL
10

TIP TIP TIP TIP TIP TIP TIP TIP TIP TIP TIP TIP TIP TIP TIP TIP TIP TIP TIP TIP TIP TIP TIP TIP

In the Chart Wizard step that asks you to assign fields to chart elements, you can drag fields around in the sample chart to change how the data is summarized.

Customize a Chart

After you create a chart using the wizard, you can change many of its elements (type, title, legend, labels, colors, and so on) using Microsoft Graph. All you have to do is double-click the chart object in the Form Design view window. Access hands control over to Microsoft Graph behind the scenes, and you find yourself in chart editing mode. It appears as if you are still working within Access, but you are really using the features of Microsoft Graph to make your changes. When you're finished, all you have to do is click off the chart object in the Form Design view window. Access resumes control and you can continue your work in Access as usual.

Edit a Chart

To open a chart for editing:

1. Open the form or report the chart is part of in Design view.

2. Double-click the chart object or right-click the chart object and choose Chart Object ➢ Edit from the shortcut menu.

Figure 10.5 shows the chart from Figure 10.2 open for editing. When you switch to chart editing mode, the Access window changes in these ways:

• The chart appears with a cross-hatched border around it to show that it is in editing mode.

• A form window labeled Datasheet appears that shows the data for the chart.

• The Form Design toolbar is replaced with the Standard Microsoft Graph toolbar.

• The Drawing toolbar appears along the bottom of the Access window.

Once you're in chart editing mode, you can follow these steps to change most chart elements:

1. Click the element to select it.

2. Right-click and choose Format to open a dialog box where you can change patterns, fonts, and sometimes other properties.

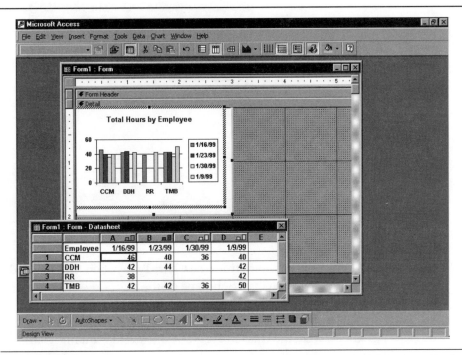

FIGURE 10.5: The chart from Figure 10.2 is shown here, ready to be edited.

Change the Chart Type

As you saw in the Chart Wizard, there are lots of different chart types: column, bar, line, pie, and more. In Microsoft Graph, there are even more to choose from. With 14 standard types that have their own subtypes and a whole other set of custom types, you can choose from dozens of different charts.

You are free to change a chart's type at any time. You may end up with strange results, depending on your choice and how many fields you are charting, but it's fun to experiment.

To change a chart's type, just click the Chart Type button on the toolbar and make a selection from the palette that pops up. Or, if you want to choose from more options:

1. Right-click anywhere on the chart's background and choose Chart Type to open the Chart Type dialog box.

SKILL
10

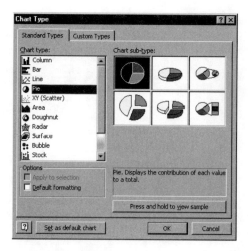

2. Make your choice from the Chart Type list on the Standard Types tab, and then select a Chart Sub-Type on the right side of the window.

3. Click OK to change the chart.

Here's what the chart in Figure 10.4 looks like after its chart type was changed to one of the Bar types:

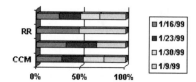

TIP TIP TIP TIP TIP TIP TIP TIP TIP TIP TIP TIP TIP TIP TIP TIP TIP TIP TIP TIP TIP TIP TIP
Use the button called Press And Hold To View Sample to do just that while you are still in the Chart Type dialog box. You won't see real data, but you'll get a good idea of whether the selected chart type will work for what you want to show.

Change the Title and Legends

Titles and legends are perhaps the most important part of any chart. Without meaningful text on a chart, the picture can be pretty useless. In chart editing mode, you can change the text for titles and legends, or make cosmetic modifications like changing colors and fonts.

Change a Title's Text

To edit the text in a title:

1. Click twice on the title. (Don't double-click; if you do, you'll open the Format Chart Title dialog box.)

2. Edit the text. Press Enter at the end of a line to add another line.

3. Click outside the title to leave text editing mode.

TIP TIP TIP TIP TIP TIP TIP TIP TIP TIP TIP TIP TIP TIP TIP TIP TIP TIP TIP TIP TIP TIP TIP
The text for a legend's labels comes from the field that defines the chart's series or pie chart categories. Edit the field values to change the labels if they are too lengthy.

Change a Title or Legend's Appearance

To change the pattern and color, border, font, alignment for titles, or placement of a legend:

1. Right-click the title or legend.

2. Choose Format Chart Title or Format Legend from the shortcut menu.

3. Make your changes in the Format dialog box.

4. Click OK to return to the chart design window.

TIP TIP TIP TIP TIP TIP TIP TIP TIP TIP TIP TIP TIP TIP TIP TIP TIP TIP TIP TIP TIP TIP TIP
You can also edit a title or change a label's placement in the Chart Options dialog box. Right-click the background of the chart and choose Chart Options to open this tool.

**SKILL
10**

TIP TIP TIP TIP TIP TIP TIP TIP TIP TIP TIP TIP TIP TIP TIP TIP TIP TIP TIP TIP TIP TIP TIP

Use the Legend button on the toolbar to toggle the legend on a chart in or out of view.

Show Data Labels

You can choose whether or not to show labels for the data in a chart. Access also lets you say whether actual values or percents should be displayed. To select data label options:

1. Right-click the background of the chart and choose Chart Options.

2. Click the Data Labels tab to show this window:

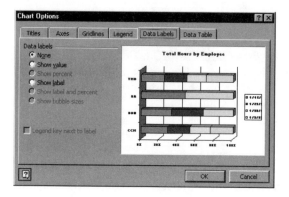

3. Make a selection under Data Labels (Show Value, Show Percent, and so on).

4. Click OK.

Change Tick Marks for an Axis

Tick marks are the little lines that mark off intervals along a chart's axes. With the Format Axis dialog box, you can choose the number of categories between tick marks and other settings. To change how tick marks are used on a chart with axes:

1. Point to the value axis or category axis, right-click, and choose Format Axis.

2. Click the tab for Scale.

3. Make your changes and click OK.

Choose Colors and Patterns

You can change the color, borders, or pattern of many chart elements.

1. Right-click the element you want to change and choose Format.

2. Click the Pattern tab to show this palette:

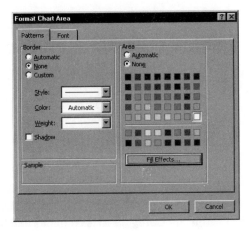

3. Select the color or border you want to use.

4. If you want to change the color gradient, the texture, pattern, or picture for the background of the selected object, use the Fill Effects button and click the Gradient, Texture, Pattern, or Picture tab. The Texture options are shown below. After you make your choice, click OK in this window to save your changes and return to the Format window.

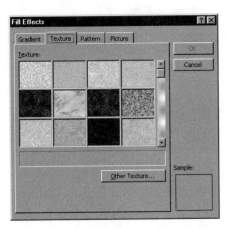

SKILL
10

5. When you're finished with the Format window, click OK.

TIP TIP TIP TIP TIP TIP TIP TIP TIP TIP TIP TIP TIP TIP TIP TIP TIP TIP TIP TIP TIP TIP

If you want to remove a fill pattern from a chart element, open the Format dialog box and select the None option under Area. Any fill pattern settings will be removed from the selected element.

Change a Chart's Gridlines and Scale

To change the color, style, and scale for gridlines:

1. Point to a gridline until you see Value Axis Major Gridlines or the appropriate label displayed in the floating bubble help.

2. Right-click and choose Format Gridlines.

3. Make your adjustments and click OK.

NOTE NOTE NOTE NOTE NOTE NOTE NOTE NOTE NOTE NOTE NOTE NOTE NOTE NOTE NOTE

The buttons for Category Axis Gridlines and Value Axis Gridlines can be clicked to toggle a chart's gridlines in or out of view.

Move and Resize Chart Elements

Sometimes you may need to move or resize parts of a chart. You might want to make room for a longer title or align things more nicely.

Move Part of a Chart

To move a chart element like a title or the plot area:

1. Click the element until it's selected (you'll see handles on its sides and corners).

2. Drag the element to the desired spot.

Resize a Chart Element

To change the size of part of a chart:

1. Click the element you want to resize to select it.

2. Drag one of the handles that appear around the selected element to change its size.

TIP TIP TIP TIP TIP TIP TIP TIP TIP TIP TIP TIP TIP TIP TIP TIP TIP TIP TIP TIP TIP TIP TIP TIP TIP

To see what part of a chart will be selected when you click, point to an area of the chart and wait a second. Microsoft Graph will show you floating help that describes the chart element under the pointer. For example, point just outside the circle for a pie chart to see Plot Area. Point a little farther away from the pie to see Chart Area.

Save Your Changes to a Chart

When you are finished customizing a chart, click anywhere outside the chart object. You will be returned to the normal Form Design view window. Then click the Save button on the Form Design toolbar to save your work.

Link a Chart to a Record

The charts you've created so far in this chapter have shown all the records from their underlying queries. If you prefer, you can limit the records shown in a chart so you only see the ones that correspond to the record you are viewing in a form or a report. For example, instead of showing data for all employees in a chart, you could present the data for one person only as you page through the records in a form for the Employees table.

To see how this works, create a series column chart, like the one in Figure 10.4, in a form called Employees With Hours. You'll tell the Chart Wizard to link the chart to a record in the form so you see the data for just one employee at a time.

1. Open a form for the Employees table in Design view, or make a new form for this table.

2. Make space for the chart.

3. Choose Insert ➢ Chart from the menu and drag a space for the chart in the Design view window.

4. When the Chart Wizard starts, choose the Total Hours By Employee query and click Next.

5. Add the EmployeeID, Sum Of Hours, and WeekEndDate fields to the Fields For Chart list and click Next.

**Skill
10**

6. Leave Column for the chart type and click Next.

7. Click Next in the dialog box where you lay out the chart data. (You can change the grouping for the series as described earlier in "Create a Chart with Multiple Series.")

8. In the next dialog box, leave Form Fields and Chart Fields both set to EmployeeID before you click Next:

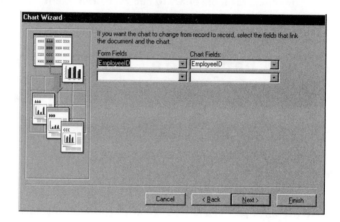

9. Change the chart title to something like **Total Hours By Week** and click Finish.

10. Change the SQL statement for the chart's query as outlined in the example "Create a Chart with Multiple Series."

Figure 10.6 shows the resulting chart displayed in the form for the Employees table. The chart has only one set of columns. Each series shows the hours worked during one week by the employee whose record is being viewed.

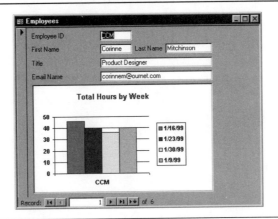

FIGURE 10.6: This chart is linked to the record shown in the form using the EmployeeID field.

Are You Experienced?

Now you can...

- ☑ Choose the fields for a chart
- ☑ Use the Chart Wizard to create a pie chart
- ☑ Create a column chart
- ☑ Create a chart with multiple series of data
- ☑ Customize and edit a chart
- ☑ Change the chart type
- ☑ Change titles and legends
- ☑ Choose labels, tick marks, colors, patterns, and scale
- ☑ Move and resize chart elements
- ☑ Link a chart to a record

SKILL
10

Import, Export, and Share Data

- → **Know when to import, link, or share data**
- → **Import data from another database**
- → **Import Excel data**
- → **Import text and HTML files with wizards**
- → **Link a table, a spreadsheet, or other type of file**
- → **Publish a table using Word**
- → **Merge data with a Word document**
- → **Analyze data with Excel**
- → **Export data to other file formats**

One of the best things about Access is the way it makes it easy to exchange information with other programs. You can import or link data from non-Access files, export Access information into several different kinds of files, or share Access data directly with programs like Excel, Word, and Publish. New with Access 2000, you also have the option to create an Access project (.adp file) and use it to work with tables stored on a Microsoft SQL server.

NOTE NOTE NOTE NOTE NOTE NOTE NOTE NOTE NOTE NOTE NOTE NOTE NOTE NOTE NOTE
See "Linking SQL Server Tables versus Using a Project" later in this skill for notes on when to link SQL tables to an Access database instead of creating a project.

When to Import, Link, or Share Data

With so many options for exchanging data, it might not be clear which one is best to use for your project. Here are some quick guidelines on how to make a choice:

Import data into Access tables if you don't need to share the information with anyone else.

Link data to an Access database if you need to share the information with someone who has to use it in its original format.

Share data with another program using OfficeLinks or OLE if the other program can handle Access data directly; this way you avoid the process of exporting the data to the other program's file format.

The sections that follow go through examples for each of these options.

Import Data

When you *import* data, Access reads a file outside of the database you are working in and creates a new table from it. There are several different kinds of files Access can import:

- Tables from other Access databases
- dBASE files
- FoxPro files
- Excel spreadsheets

- Text files (delimited or fixed length)

- HTML documents

- ODBC databases, such as tables on an SQL server

The process is similar for all these files. This book won't cover each type in detail, but some examples for common file formats follow.

Get Data from Another Database

To import a table or other type of object from an Access database:

1. Right-click the background of the Database window and choose Import, or use File ≻ Get External Data ≻ Import to open the Import dialog box:

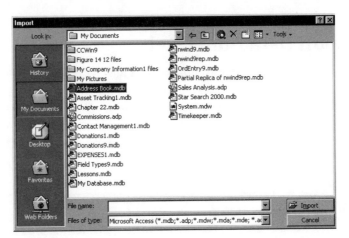

2. Choose a database and click Import. You'll see an Import Objects dialog box that resembles a Database window:

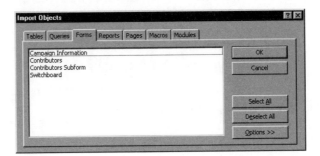

3. Click the tab for the type of object you want to import, and then click the desired item to select it.

4. Repeat step 3 for all the items you want to select. You don't have to hold down Ctrl to select multiple objects. (Or, click Select All to choose all the items in the window.) To deselect an object, if you need to, just click again.

5. Click OK to create the new object(s) in the open database.

TIP TIP TIP TIP TIP TIP TIP TIP TIP TIP TIP TIP TIP TIP TIP TIP TIP TIP TIP TIP TIP TIP TIP

The Options button in the Import Objects dialog box lets you indicate whether to import relationships, menus and toolbars, or import/export specifications. You can also choose whether tables should be imported with data or not, and if queries should come across as queries or tables.

Import Data from Excel

You can import Excel data into a new or existing Access table if the data falls neatly into rows and columns. The first row of data can hold column headers (Access can use these as field names) or values, but other information such as titles in the first row will cause problems during the import. Because of this, it's a good idea to check the worksheet before the import to make sure it's a suitable candidate for importing.

TIP TIP TIP TIP TIP TIP TIP TIP TIP TIP TIP TIP TIP TIP TIP TIP TIP TIP TIP TIP TIP TIP TIP

If the worksheet you want to import has headers and other information you don't need, first create a *named range* for the area of the spreadsheet with the useful data. Then import the named range in the first step of the Import Spreadsheet Wizard instead of the entire worksheet.

Use the Import Database Wizard to walk you through the import process. Once you're ready to import:

1. Right-click the background of the Database window and choose Import.

2. Change the Files Of Type setting to Microsoft Excel (*.xls).

3. Choose the spreadsheet with the data you need and click Import to open the Import Spreadsheet Wizard.

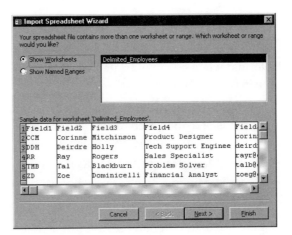

4. Select the worksheet or named range you want to import, if you have the option to do this, and click Next.

5. Check First Row Contains Column Headings if the first row in the table that's shown has field names instead of data. Then click Next.

6. Click Next again without changing anything to create a new table from the Excel data. (If you want to add the data to a table that already exists, first select In An Existing Table and choose a table. Then choose Finish in the last step.)

7. In the next step, you have the option to index fields or to leave them out of the import. For some fields, you can also change the field type. Highlight each field you want to work with in turn and select the options you want to use before you move on to the next step. If you don't need to create any indexes or make any other changes, just click Next.

8. This step is where you let Access create a primary key field (the default), choose a field for the primary key, or opt not to have a primary key field. After you make your choice, click Next.

 NOTE NOTE NOTE NOTE NOTE NOTE NOTE NOTE NOTE NOTE NOTE NOTE NOTE NOTE NOTE
See Skill 2, "Plan a Database," if you need to find out what key fields do.

9. Finally, name the new table and click Finish.

Import Text Files

Text files can be created by lots of programs, so they are often used as the interim file format when you move data from one program to another. Basically, they come in two flavors:

Delimited text files have separators such as commas or tabs between the fields of data in each record and often have quotes around text values. Each record appears on its own line.

Fixed-length text files also have one record on each line, but the field values line up in columns with spaces (rather than tabs) between the field values.

Figure 11.1 shows both these kinds of text files being viewed in Notepad. As you can see, the values in the fixed-length file appear in columns. In contrast, the values in the delimited file are not separated by spaces. Each value is surrounded by quotes and separated by commas.

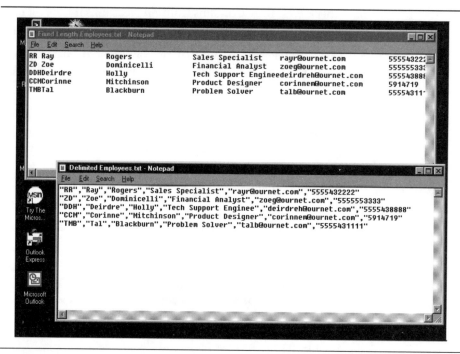

FIGURE 11.1: A delimited text file and a fixed-length text file open in Notepad. The same employee information is stored in both files.

NOTE NOTE NOTE NOTE NOTE NOTE NOTE NOTE NOTE NOTE NOTE NOTE NOTE NOTE NOTE

You don't have to know what kind of text file you're importing before you start the import process. Access has an Import Text Wizard (discussed below) that lets you view a file as you're importing it and suggests either delimited or fixed-length for the file type.

Here are the steps for importing a delimited text file:

1. Right-click the background of the Database window and choose Import.

2. In the Import dialog box, change Files Of Type to Text Files (*.txt;*.csv;*.tab;*.asc).

3. Select the file you want to use and click Import to start the Import Text Wizard:

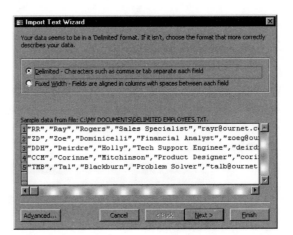

4. Leave the format set to Delimited and click Next.

5. If the default Comma is not OK, change the character used to separate fields. If the first row of data holds names that can be used as fields for the new table, check First Row Contains Field Names. Then click Next.

6. In the next step of the wizard, select In A New Table or In An Existing Table, depending on where you want the imported data to land. Then click Next.

7. If you chose to put the data in a new table, you can change the name and type of the fields being imported in the next step. You can also tell Access to index fields. To change these attributes for a field, click anywhere on the

field to select it. Then change the values under Field Options as needed. Click Next to continue.

8. Choose a key field, let Access add a key, or choose to have no key field at all. Then click Next.

9. Enter a name for the new table and click Finish.

TIP TIP TIP TIP TIP TIP TIP TIP TIP TIP TIP TIP TIP TIP TIP TIP TIP TIP TIP TIP TIP TIP TIP TIP TIP

If you will need to import the same type of file again, you can save your work setting up the import. Just click the Advanced button in any wizard step where it appears. Then click the Save As button and enter a name for your specification. You can load this information later by clicking the Specs button in the same window. You can also use the Import Specifications window to change the format of date and number values.

Import HTML Documents

You can take an HTML file and turn it into an Access table if it contains data that Access can recognize as records and fields. Figure 11.2 shows an HTML file being viewed with Internet Explorer. The data are organized in rows and columns that can easily be imported into an Access table.

FIGURE 11.2: This HTML file shows employee information in a tabular format when it's viewed with a Web browser.

Behind the scenes, the data for the Web page is stored in an HTML file, as shown in Figure 11.3. As you can see, the HTML file is full of codes that are used to format the data before it's displayed. When the HTML file is imported, Access strips out all the formatting codes and stores the remaining data in a table.

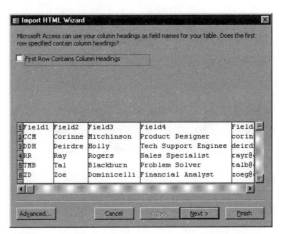

FIGURE 11.3: The HTML file shown in Figure 11.2 is viewed here with its formatting codes visible.

Here's how to import an HTML file into Access:

1. Right-click the background of the Database window and choose Import.
2. Change Files Of Type to HTML Documents (*.html;*.htm).
3. Select a file and choose Import. You'll see the first step of the Import HTML Wizard:

4. If applicable, check First Row Contains Column Headings, and then click Next.

5. Follow the rest of the wizard's prompts to import the data.

Other Import Options

As mentioned earlier, you can also import data from Exchange, Lotus 1-2-3, Paradox, dBASE, Outlook, and ODBC databases into Access. The process is similar to the one outlined in the last few examples. Start by right-clicking the Database window and choosing Import from the shortcut menu. Then choose the appropriate file from the Files Of Type drop-down list in the Import dialog box. If Access starts a wizard, follow its instructions. Otherwise, just enter a name for the new table of imported data when Access asks you to supply one.

Link Data

When you *link* a file to an Access database, you establish a link between the file and Access so you can use it directly. (In contrast, when you import a file, you end up creating a table that holds a copy of the imported data.) The process for linking a file to an Access database is similar to the one you used for importing. You won't see separate examples for several file types as you did with importing, because using the Link Table Wizard is pretty self-explanatory. Here's an example that shows how to link an Excel spreadsheet to a database:

1. Right-click the background of the Database window and choose Link Tables.

2. In the Link dialog box, change Files Of Type to Microsoft Excel (*.xls).

3. Select a file and click Link. You'll see a Link Spreadsheet Wizard dialog box similar to the Import Spreadsheet dialog box.

4. Select a worksheet or named range and click Next.

5. If necessary, click the box that says to use the first row as field names before you click Next again.

6. Enter a name for the linked table and click Finish. (This doesn't rename the linked file; it's just a reference to it.)

After you link a file to a database, it will appear on the Tables list in the Database window preceded by an arrow and an icon for its source program. Figure 11.4 shows a Database window with two linked tables: one from an Excel spreadsheet and another from an HTML file.

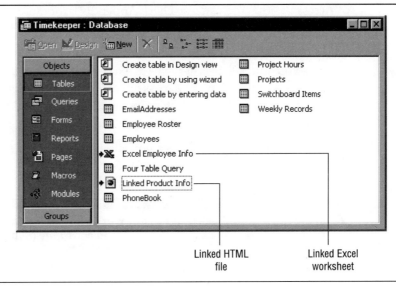

Linked HTML file   Linked Excel worksheet

FIGURE 11.4: There are two tables linked to this database: a worksheet in an Excel spreadsheet and an HTML file.

Remove a Link

To unlink a table from a database:

1. Go to the Database window.

2. Right-click the linked table you want to remove from the database.

3. Choose Delete from the shortcut menu.

4. Click Yes when Access asks if you really want to delete the link.

NOTE NOTE NOTE NOTE NOTE NOTE NOTE NOTE NOTE NOTE NOTE NOTE NOTE NOTE NOTE

When you delete a linked table from a database, the underlying file does not disappear. Only the link to the database is deleted, not the data file itself.

Linking SQL Server Tables versus Using a Project

If you are planning to use Access 2000 to work with tables on a Microsoft SQL server, you can link the tables as described just above or set up a project instead of a database. (The difference between projects and databases is outlined in Skill 1, "Access Basics." You can also check Appendix B for more information on projects.) Here are a few things to keep in mind as you decide which approach will work best for you:

- If you link SQL Server tables to a database, you can query them the same way you would query Access tables. To query tables in a project, you need to create *views*. Microsoft Office includes Client Visual Design Tools to help you with this task, but it's not as easy as using the Query Design view window.

- If you plan to use a project, you should probably be familiar with the basic skills required to work with SQL Server databases.

TIP TIP TIP TIP TIP TIP TIP TIP TIP TIP TIP TIP TIP TIP TIP TIP TIP TIP TIP TIP TIP TIP TIP TIP

If you need to find out more about working with SQL Server databases, you may want to reference *SQL Server 7 In Record Time* (Sybex, 1999).

Share Access Data with Other Programs

The best thing about Office 2000 is that you can *share* data between its various programs without importing and exporting files. For example, you can:

- Include an Access table, report, or other object in a Word document

- Merge data from an Access table or query into a Word document

- Analyze an Access table using Excel without first exporting the data to a spreadsheet yourself

These are only a few of the "tricks" you can perform using Access along with other parts of Office 2000. Following are some quick examples.

Publish an Access Object with Word

You can take a table, query, form, or report and plunk it right into a new Word document without leaving Access. Once the information from Access is inserted into Word, you are free to edit it or add other text. Try publishing an Access report called Work Phone List to see how it will appear in Word:

1. In the Database window, click the Reports button.

2. Highlight the report you want to include in a Word document.

3. If the Word icon is visible, click the OfficeLinks button on the toolbar, or choose Publish It With MS Word from the drop-down list for the button:

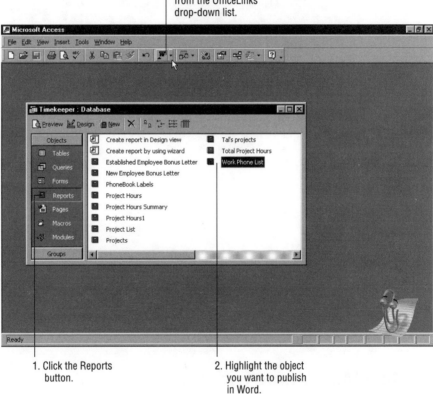

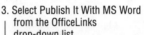

3. Select Publish It With MS Word from the OfficeLinks drop-down list.

1. Click the Reports button.

2. Highlight the object you want to publish in Word.

If you haven't published the selected object from Access before, Word will create a new `.rtf` file named after the object. If a file with this name already exists, you will be given a chance to overwrite the old file or supply a different name for the new file. After you select Publish It, Word will open a new document with the report inserted, as shown in Figure 11.5. You can edit the report in Word just as you would any other Word document.

The file that's created by Word is a Rich Text File (.rtf). If you want to work with a .doc file instead, Use File ➤ Save As while you're still in Word to save the file as a Word file (.doc).

When you're finished with Word, just close its window to return to Access.

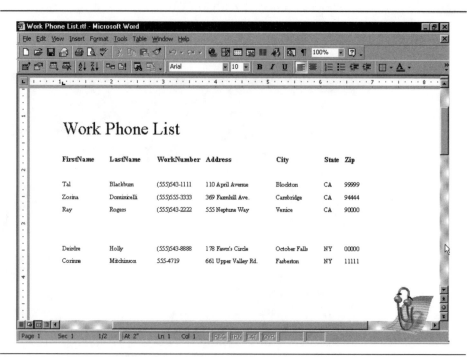

FIGURE 11.5: An Access report that has been published using Word

Do a Mail Merge with Word

If you have to do a mailing using Access data, it's usually easiest to create letters and envelopes in Word and *merge in* name and address fields from a table or a query. While you could create Access reports for the letters and envelopes, the job is much simpler in Word, especially if the document has lots of different font styles and sizes. There's a wizard to help you set up a merge, and you can use a new Word document or one you already created:

1. In the Database window, highlight the table or query containing the fields you want to merge into a Word document.

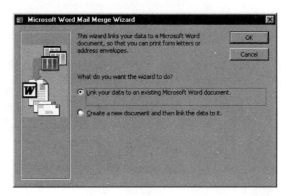

2. From the OfficeLinks drop-down list on the toolbar, select Merge It With MS Word to start the Word Mail Merge Wizard:

3. If you haven't already created an appropriate document, select "Create a New Document. . ."; otherwise, leave it set to "Link your data to an existing Microsoft Word document." Then click OK.

4. After a bit of a delay, you'll see a Word window open that contains a special Mail Merge toolbar like the one in Figure 11.6. Enter the text for the letter or envelope.

5. To insert a field, select it from the Insert Merge Field drop-down list.

6. When you are finished with the merge document, click View Merged Data on the Mail Merge toolbar to view it with the Access data inserted.

7. At this point, you can merge the document to a new document (with separate pages for each Access record) or merge it into the printer. Depending on what you want to do, click either the Merge To New Document button or the Merge To Printer button:

Merge to New Document

Merge to Printer

If you choose to merge to a new document, Word will open a new .doc file with the data from Access substituted for any merge fields you included. If you choose to print the merged document, it will go directly to the printer.

8. Close the Word window to return to Access.

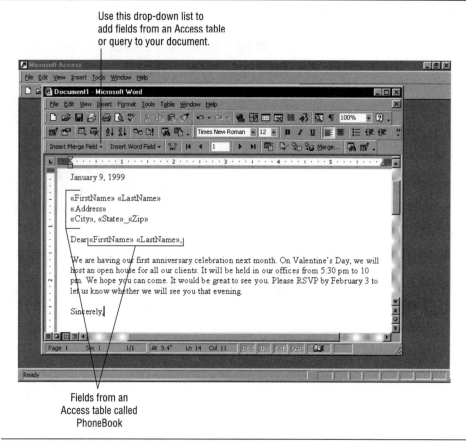

Use this drop-down list to
add fields from an Access table
or query to your document.

Fields from an
Access table called
PhoneBook

FIGURE 11.6: This Word window was opened with the Word Mail Merge Wizard and has a special Mail Merge toolbar.

Analyze a Table with Excel

Although it's possible to get summary information from Access tables using queries or reports, sometimes it's easier to do this type of work in Excel. With

OfficeLinks, you can export a table or a query to a spreadsheet and open it in Excel with one mouse click:

1. In the Database window, highlight the table or query you want to open in Excel.

2. Select Analyze It With MS Excel from the OfficeLinks drop-down list on the toolbar.

Excel will start and the data from the object you selected in Access will appear in a new spreadsheet. Any changes you make to the data while it's viewed in Excel will affect this new .xls file, but they will not change the original table or query.

Figure 11.7 shows an Access table called Project Hours being analyzed with Excel. As you can see, the table has been opened as a new spreadsheet called Project Hours.xls. If you click the Restore button for the Excel window, you'll see that Access is still open. To return to Access, just close Excel, click the Access window, or click the Access button on the Taskbar.

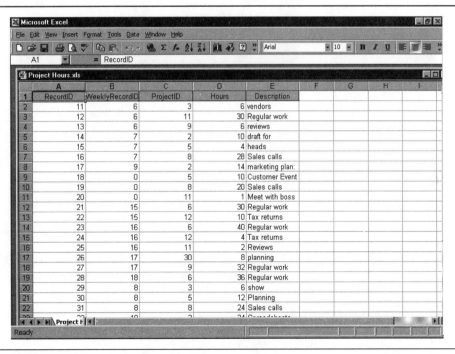

FIGURE 11.7: A table called Project Hours is opened as an .xls file in Excel after clicking Analyze It With MS Excel in Access.

Export Data

Just as you can import data into an Access database, you can also *export* data to different files, including other Access databases. To do so:

1. In the Database window, right-click the object you want to export and choose Export to open this dialog box:

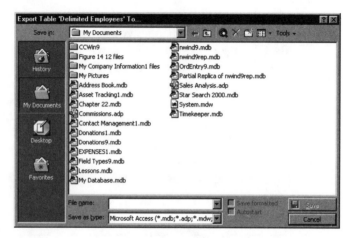

2. Change Save As Type to the type of file you want to export to.

3. Change the folder, if needed, and enter a name for the new file.

4. Click Save.

5. If you are exporting to an Access database, enter a name for the exported object in the Export dialog box, select Definition Only if you want to export an empty table, and click OK.

TIP TIP TIP TIP TIP TIP TIP TIP TIP TIP TIP TIP TIP TIP TIP TIP TIP TIP TIP TIP TIP TIP TIP
To export just some of the fields from a table, create a query with those fields. Then export the query instead of the table.

NOTE NOTE NOTE NOTE NOTE NOTE NOTE NOTE NOTE NOTE NOTE NOTE NOTE NOTE

You can export Access data directly to HTML files or create data access pages to get more control over the final result. See Skill 13, "Create Web Pages with Access," for instructions on how to create Web pages using both these techniques.

Are You Experienced?

Now you can...

- ☑ Know when to import, link, or share data
- ☑ Import data from another database
- ☑ Import Excel data, text files, and HTML files
- ☑ Link tables from another database
- ☑ Link spreadsheets and other types of files
- ☑ Publish a table using Word
- ☑ Merge data with a Word document
- ☑ Analyze data with Excel
- ☑ Export data to other file formats

Database Housekeeping

- Keep a database tidy
- Use descriptions for database objects
- Repair a database
- Protect a database
- Optimize database performance
- Analyze a database
- Document a database

After you've worked with a database a while, the Database window can get pretty cluttered. Some objects might not be needed anymore, others might need better names, and you might not even remember what some objects do. In this skill, you'll find out how to keep a database tidy by deleting unneeded objects and adding descriptions to others. You'll also see how to repair and protect databases, optimize database performance, and create documentation using tools that are part of Access.

Keep a Database Tidy

Most people don't enjoy housekeeping, but they do it anyway for the peace of mind it brings. It's easier to find things and takes less time to get things done in an orderly space. This is as true for databases as it is for houses and offices. Access 2000 has tools you can use to:

- Delete, rename, or copy database objects
- Show object descriptions in the Database window
- Repair a damaged database, or compact one that has accumulated dead space

TIP TIP TIP TIP TIP TIP TIP TIP TIP TIP TIP TIP TIP TIP TIP TIP TIP TIP TIP TIP TIP TIP TIP
Before you delete or rename objects in a complex database, you may want to make a backup copy of the file using Windows Explorer.

Delete Objects

The Database window can get quite messy as you add more and more objects to a database. Figure 12.1 shows the Forms tab of the Database window for the Time-keeper database. As you can see, there are several objects that look like they may no longer be needed, judging from their names. We can straighten up this mess by deleting the obsolete objects.

To delete a database object:

1. Open the object to see if it's something you no longer need. If you aren't sure, check the Warning below for steps you can take to prevent a disaster.

2. Right-click the object in the Database window and choose Delete.

3. When Access asks you to confirm the deletion, choose Yes.

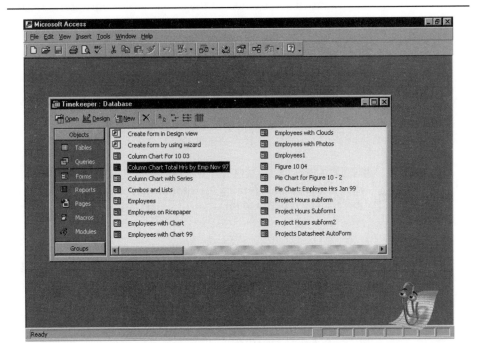

FIGURE 12.1: This Database window has objects that can be deleted to make it easier to use.

WARNING WARNING WARNING WARNING WARNING WARNING WARNING WARNING

To avoid problems that can arise when an object is deleted or renamed, open each query, form, and report you use and make a note of the tables and queries involved in each. For a query, just check the Query Design view window. For forms and reports, go into Design view and check the Record Source property on the properties sheet.

Rename Objects

You can always rename a database object to make it easier to recognize. Be careful, though. If you rename an object that's part of another object (perhaps a form, a report, or a macro), you'll have to make additional changes to update the reference to the old object name.

To rename an object:

1. Right-click the object in the Database window and choose Rename. The name will appear highlighted in a box like this:

2. Start typing to overwrite the entire name, or click where you want to edit.

3. Press Enter to complete the change.

WARNING WARNING WARNING WARNING WARNING WARNING WARNING WARNING

See the previous Warning for information on checking for references to objects before you rename them.

Copy Objects

When you're creating a new object that's similar to one that already exists, it's easier to copy the existing one and then do some modification. This is usually quicker than starting a new object from scratch.

To copy a database object:

1. In the Database window, click the object to select it.

2. Click the Copy button on the toolbar, or press Ctrl+C.

3. Click the Paste button on the toolbar (or press Ctrl+V) to open a Paste As dialog box:

4. Enter the name for the copied object and select OK.

Use Descriptions

If you find it difficult to remember what various database objects are used for, don't despair. You can add descriptions to objects and display them in the Database window.

SKILL
12

Add a Description to an Object

To add a description to a database object:

1. In the Database window, right-click the object and choose Properties, or select the object and click Properties on the toolbar. A Properties dialog box will open:

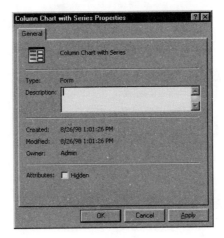

2. Type whatever you like in the Description box.

3. Click OK.

View Descriptions in the Database Window

You may need to change the way objects are displayed in the Database window to make any descriptions you've added visible. To do this:

1. Right-click the background of the Database window.

2. Choose View ➤ Details.

Access will show the Database window with columns for Name, Description, Modified, Created, and Type, as shown in Figure 12.2. You can drag the border at the right side of a column header to change the column width, or you can use the scroll bar at the bottom of the Database window to change the columns that are currently displayed.

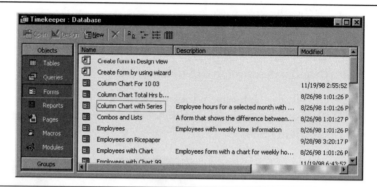

FIGURE 12.2: After choosing View ➤ Details from the shortcut menu, this Database window includes a Description column.

Repair a Database

A database can become damaged due to a power failure or some other circumstance that causes the information stored in your computer to become garbled. Thankfully, Access has a built-in utility you can use to repair a database after this happens. As long as the database isn't too far gone, you'll probably be able to recover your database successfully.

Repair the Open Database

If for some reason you need to repair the open database, choose Tools ➤ Database Utilities ➤ Compact And Repair Database from the menu. Access will rewrite the file and then reopen it for you.

Repair a Closed Database

If the database you want to repair isn't open:

1. Close any other database you might have open.

2. Choose Tools ➤ Database Utilities ➤ Compact And Repair Database from the menu.

3. In the Database To Compact From dialog box, select the database you want to fix.

4. Click Compact.

5. In the Compact Database Into dialog box, select the same database, or enter a new name in the File Name box.

6. Click Save. If you are replacing the existing file, choose Yes when Access asks if you are sure you want to overwrite the old file.

Use an MDE File to Protect a Database

If you create a database that will be used by someone else, you can protect its forms and reports, and any Visual Basic code you may have added, by saving the database as an MDE file. With an MDE file, you can open forms and reports to view and edit data, but you can't open these objects in Design view.

Create an MDE File from a Database

To create an MDE file:

1. From the menus, choose Tools ➢ Database Utilities ➢ Make MDE File.

2. In the Save MDE As dialog box, enter a name for the new MDE file. You can use the original database name, if you like, since it will have a different file extension, .mde.

3. Click Save.

NOTE NOTE NOTE NOTE NOTE NOTE NOTE NOTE NOTE NOTE NOTE NOTE NOTE NOTE NOTE
You can protect a project (.adp file) in the same way. Open the project and choose Tools ➢ Database Utilities ➢ Make ADE File to make a protected version of the project.

Open an MDE File

To open a database that's been saved as an MDE file:

1. Click the Open button on the toolbar, or choose File ➢ Open from the menu.

2. In the Open dialog box, leave the Files Of Type set to Data Files (…), or change it to MDE Files (*.mde).

3. Choose the MDE file you want to open.

4. Click Open.

The Database window for an MDE file looks just like its counterpart in the original MDB file, except that the Design and New buttons are dimmed for the Forms, Reports, Pages, and Modules tabs, as shown in Figure 12.3. The Run button for Modules is also dimmed.

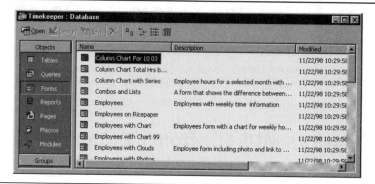

FIGURE 12.3: In the Database window for an MDE file, the Design and New toolbar buttons are dimmed for Forms, Reports, Pages, and Modules.

Optimize Database Performance

If you notice that it takes longer and longer for tasks like queries and sorts to complete in Access, you may want to try some things to optimize database performance. For example, within Access, you can compact a database to remove unused disk space. You can also use the Performance Analyzer tool; it gives suggestions on how database objects might be changed to improve performance and can even make some of the changes for you.

TIP TIP TIP TIP TIP TIP TIP TIP TIP TIP TIP TIP TIP TIP TIP TIP TIP TIP TIP TIP TIP TIP TIP TIP TIP

Access Help has lots of tips for improving database performance. Open the Office Assistant, enter "analyze," and click the topic called *Optimize Performance.* **You'll find quite a number of additional topics you can explore in the Help window.**

Compact a Database

As you work with a database, adding and deleting objects, it uses more and more disk space. Some of this space can be recovered by *compacting* the database; during this process, Access rewrites the database to disk, getting rid of unneeded space as it works. It also resets the next number for AutoNumber fields if the records at the end of the database have been deleted.

 NOTE NOTE NOTE NOTE NOTE NOTE NOTE NOTE NOTE NOTE NOTE NOTE NOTE NOTE NOTE

The process for compacting a database is the same as that for repairing a database.

Compact the Open Database

To compact a database you are working with, choose Tools ➤ Database Utilities ➤ Compact And Repair Database from the menu. Afterward, if you check the size of the database in the Open dialog box (assuming the Details view is activated), you should see that it is smaller.

Compact a Closed Database

To compact a database that's not open:

1. Close any other database you might have open.

2. Choose Tools ➤ Database Utilities ➤ Compact And Repair Database from the menu.

3. In the Database To Compact From dialog box, select the database you want to fix.

4. Click Compact.

5. In the Compact Database Into dialog box, select the same database, or enter a new name in the File Name box.

6. Click Save. If you are replacing the existing file, choose Yes when Access asks if you are sure you want to overwrite the old file.

Analyze Database Performance

The Performance Analyzer can give you suggestions on how to speed up a database, and it can implement some of these changes for you.

Start the Performance Analyzer

To analyze a database:

1. Open the database you want to check.

2. Choose Tools ➤ Analyze ➤ Performance from the menu to open a Performance Analyzer dialog box:

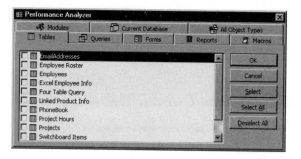

3. For each object you want to include in the analysis, check the box to the left of the item's icon and name. Use the Select All button to check all the items on a tab at once. You will have to repeat this procedure for each type of database object; alternatively, click the All tab to scroll through all the objects on one list.

4. To analyze the relationships that are defined in a database, click the Current Database tab and check Relationships. (VBA Project is another option you can select on this tab to check any code that's part of a database.)

5. Choose OK.

The Performance Analyzer will do its work and then open a dialog box like the one in Figure 12.4. Each suggestion is listed under Analysis Result and has an icon to show the category it falls into: Recommendation, Suggestion, or Idea. (The Fixed icon is used to mark an item after it has been changed.) At the bottom of the list in Figure 12.4, the Performance Analyzer is suggesting that the Weekly Records table be related to the Employees table. (This relationship was deleted before the Performance Analyzer was run just to see if it would catch this. It did!)

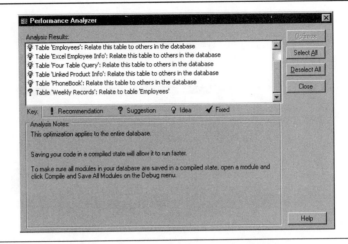

FIGURE 12.4: The Performance Analyzer presents its findings and categorizes them as Recommendations, Suggestions, Ideas, or Fixed.

Let the Performance Analyzer Make Changes

The Performance Wizard can take actions for the items it marks as Recommendations or Suggestions. To make a change:

1. Click any items you need to change. (Hold down Shift to select contiguous items; use Ctrl while you click to select multiple items anywhere on the list.)

2. Choose Optimize.

3. When you are finished with the Performance Analyzer, click Close.

After the Performance Analyzer makes the changes you request, it marks the items with the Fixed icon. If you look at the item Table 'Weekly Records': Relate To Table 'Employees' in Figure 12.5, you'll see it's marked as Fixed.

NOTE NOTE NOTE NOTE NOTE NOTE NOTE NOTE NOTE NOTE NOTE NOTE NOTE NOTE NOTE

The Optimize option is not available for Ideas. It only works for Recommendations and Suggestions.

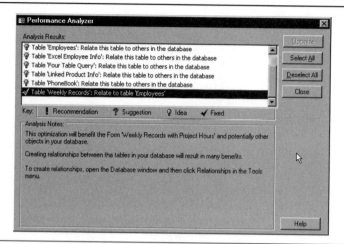

FIGURE 12.5: The Performance Analyzer marked the last item on the Analysis Results list as Fixed after it was optimized.

Document a Database

Access can create database documentation that includes table structures and field properties, form and report properties, SQL statements for queries, and other details.

Create the Documentation Report

To document the open database:

1. Choose Tools ➤ Analyze ➤ Documenter from the menu. You'll see a Documenter dialog box:

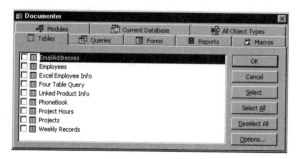

2. Check the boxes for the objects you want to document. (Click the All Object Types tab if you want to scroll through all the database objects on the same tab.)

3. If you want to check or change the items that are included in the documentation for the current tab's objects, click the Options button and change the items before you click OK:

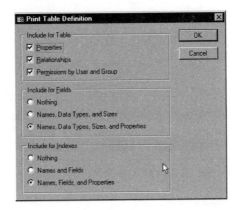

4. If you want to document database properties and relationships, click the Current Database tab and check Properties and Relationships.

5. Choose OK.

You'll see some messages displayed at the bottom of the Access window as the Documenter examines the selected database objects and writes up its findings. When the work is complete, a Preview window will open for a report called Object Definition like the one in Figure 12.6. In this example, the first page of the report documents the properties of the table called Employees. If you move to the last page of the report, you'll see information on the relationships defined for the database, as shown in Figure 12.7. The organization of your documentation will vary, depending on the options you choose in the Documenter dialog box.

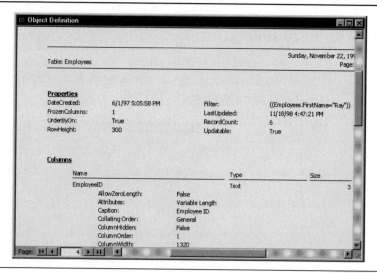

FIGURE 12.6: When the Documenter is finished working, it opens a report called Object Definition. The first page of this report shows information on the Employees table.

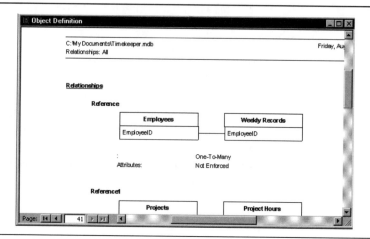

FIGURE 12.7: The last page of the Documenter report from Figure 12.6 presents information on the relationships in the Timekeeper database.

Print the Documentation

To print the Documenter's work, just click the Print button on the toolbar. Use the File ➤ Print command if you want to print selected pages, choose a different printer, or change printer properties.

In the next skill, "Create Web Pages with Access," you'll see how to export Access data to HTML files. You also learn about a new type of Access 2000 object: data access pages. These are special purpose Web pages that you can open from Access or Internet Explorer 5. With an active Internet connection and Office 2000, you can use data access pages to browse Access data on the Web.

SKILL **12**

Are You Experienced?

Now you can...

- ☑ **Keep a database tidy**
- ☑ **Use descriptions for database objects**
- ☑ **Repair a database**
- ☑ **Protect a database**
- ☑ **Optimize database performance**
- ☑ **Analyze a database**
- ☑ **Document a database**

Create Web Pages with Access

- → **Export a document to HTML**
- → **Learn data access page basics**
- → **Create a page with the Page Wizard**
- → **Create a page on your own**
- → **Choose a theme for a page**
- → **Group records on a page**
- → **Use a PivotTable on a page**
- → **Browse a page**

You can publish your database information for use on the World Wide Web or an intranet right from Access 2000. This skill explains the different options available for doing this.

There are two ways to create World Wide Web pages from Access:

- Export a table, query, form, or report to an HTML file.

- Design a data access page that can be used to browse data from Access or with Internet Explorer.

Export a Document to HTML

If you read through Skill 11, you know that you can export information from Access tables and queries to other files, like text, spreadsheets, or HTML. *HTML* stands for *Hypertext Markup Language,* the system of coding used to format text files that are used as the source for Web pages. Figure 13.1 shows an HTML file called PhoneBook.html being viewed with Internet Explorer.

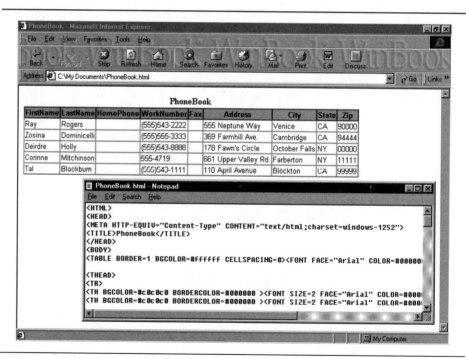

FIGURE 13.1: An HTML file called PhoneBook.html viewed with Internet Explorer. The Notepad window shows the same file with its HTML tags visible.

In the figure, a Notepad window shows the same file viewed as text with its HTML tags (codes) visible. The tags are recognized by Web page browsers like Internet Explorer and Netscape Navigator. The browser interprets the tags to determine how the data should be displayed.

The Web page shown in Figure 13.1 was created by exporting an Access table called PhoneBook to an HTML file. The information shown on the page is like a snapshot of the table as it was at the time the HTML file was created. To keep the PhoneBook Web page current, you would have to export the PhoneBook table to HTML every time the source data in the PhoneBook table changes.

The process of exporting to HTML is quite simple:

1. In the Database window, right-click the table or query you want to export and choose Export from the shortcut menu.

2. In the Export. . . dialog box, change the Save As Type to HTML Document (*.html; *.htm).

3. Change the filename, if you need to.

4. If you are exporting a table or a query, the Save Formatted box will be available. Check this option to create a page where the data is formatted similarly to its Datasheet view. This option also lets you specify an HTML template, and it enables the Autostart option.

5. Check Autostart (only available if Save Formatted is checked) if you want the HTML file to be shown in your default Web page browser after it's created.

6. Click Save.

7. If you chose Save Formatted and the HTML Output Options dialog box comes up, either enter an HTML Template or leave it blank. Then click OK.

Figure 13.2 shows the PhoneBook table viewed with Internet Explorer after it was exported to an HTML file. This is the same page shown in Figure 13.1 without the Notepad window that shows the HTML source code for the page. As you can see, the formatting for the page is fairly basic.

You aren't stuck with this plain look for a page, though. In the Page Design view window, you can choose from an extensive group of *themes* to apply a predefined look to a page. For example, Figure 13.3 shows the page in Figure 13.2 after the Citrus Punch theme was applied to it. You are free to use this feature with a page created by exporting to HTML. Follow the instructions outlined later in this skill to "Edit an Existing Page" and "Apply a Theme to a Page."

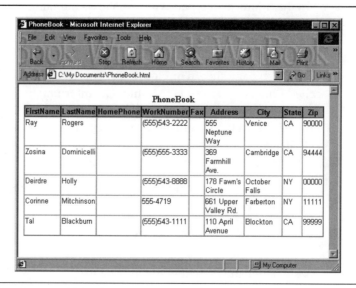

FIGURE 13.2: This Web page was created by exporting a table called PhoneBook from Access to HTML.

PhoneBook : Data Access Page									

PhoneBook

FirstName	LastName	HomePhone	WorkNumber	Fax	Address	City	State	Zip
Ray	Rogers		(555)543-2222		555 Neptune Way	Venice	CA	90000
Zosina	Dominicelli		(555)555-3333		369 Farmhill Ave.	Cambridge	CA	94444
Deirdre	Holly		(555)543 8888		178 Fawn's Circle	October Falls	NY	00000
Corinne	Mitchinson		555-4719		661 Upper Valley Rd.	Farberton	NY	11111
Tal	Blackburn		(555)543-1111		110 April Avenue	Blockton	CA	99999

FIGURE 13.3: This exported HTML file was opened in the Page Design view window and had the Citrus Punch theme applied to it.

Know Data Access Page Basics

If you want to browse the actual data in an Access database instead of viewing a snapshot like those created when you export to HTML, you can use a *data access page*. Data access pages, or simply *pages*, are a new type of object in Access 2000 that let you browse current data from tables or queries using a Web page.

Unlike other Access objects which are part of the database (.mdb file) they belong to, data access pages are stored in their own HTML files. These files can be opened with Access or Internet Explorer. If you're wondering why anyone would use a data access page instead of a form, the main reason is to be able to work with data from the Web or an intranet without starting Access. When you open a data access page from Internet Explorer, Office 2000 gets the data from Access (or wherever it resides, perhaps on a SQL server) and then displays it on the page.

SKILL
13

NOTE NOTE NOTE NOTE NOTE NOTE NOTE NOTE NOTE NOTE NOTE NOTE NOTE NOTE

In Access 97, the Publish To The Web Wizard and the Web Publishing Wizard were the tools you used to create Web pages and copy them to the Web. These Wizards have been replaced with the Page Wizard in Access 2000.

Before you start working with the Page Wizard and the Page Design view window, take a quick look at the types of data access pages you can design. Some pages are for viewing data only. Others allow you to edit data as well as view it.

Types of Data Access Pages

Pages can show data from just one table or multiple tables. They can also include controls to show objects like spreadsheets and hyperlinks. The kinds of objects you choose to place on a page determine the page's functionality—whether you can just view data or edit it, too, and if you can dynamically change the way data is summarized right from the page. In general, pages can be used for these functions:

- Data entry: Pages with one level of data let you view, enter, and edit data. There are some restrictions on a page that allows data entry. For example, you can't expand and collapse records to switch between summary and detail views.

- Interactive reporting: When you create a page with multiple levels of data (where multiple groups are defined), you can expand or collapse records to switch between seeing summary information only or viewing detail records as well. This is similar to using a report where records are grouped, but it is different in that you can change your view dynamically. In this respect, browsing a grouped data access page is more like using a datasheet that includes Subdatasheet views.

- Data analysis: By including objects like Office PivotTable lists, spreadsheets, or charts on a page, you create a page that lets you analyze data. Not only do you get to view summary information, but you can do things like drag and drop the rows and columns on a PivotTable list to interactively change what you see.

Next you'll see how to create all of these types of pages. For more information on this topic, open Microsoft Access Help and click the Show button if the Contents tab isn't visible. Then scroll down to the topic "Pages: Basics" and explore the subtopic called *Data access pages: What they are and how they work*.

Create a Page with the Page Wizard

Using the Page Wizard is the easiest way to get started with a data access page. You don't have to spend time learning how to use the Page Design view window. All you need to do is answer the questions asked by the Page Wizard. You can include fields from more than one table or query on a page; you then can optionally group them to create a page where you can expand or collapse the master record for each group to bring detail records in and out of view. The first of the following examples shows you how to create a simple page that allows data entry. The second example is for using the wizard to create a grouped page that lets you expand or collapse the information you browse.

Create a Page That Allows Data Entry

As mentioned earlier, if you create a data access page without any levels of grouping, you can use the page to edit and enter data, as well as for viewing information. This example shows you how to create a page like this that lets you work with data in the Employees table in the Timekeeper database.

1. In the Database window, click the Pages button. If you haven't created any pages for your database yet, the Database window will look like this:

2. To start the Page Wizard, double-click Create Data Access Page By Using Wizard. The first step of the Page Wizard is like the one for the Report Wizard or Form Wizard. For this example, use the Tables/Queries drop-down list to select Table: Employees. Then double-click fields on the Available Fields list to add them to the Selected Fields list. When you're finished selecting fields, click Next.

3. Click Next again to create an ungrouped page like the one shown in Figure 13.4.

4. The next window lets you select a sort order for the records that are shown on the page. Optionally select up to four fields, and then click Next to continue.

5. Enter a title for the new page and click Open The Page if you don't think you'll want to make changes to the design. If you want to select a theme for the visual elements on the page, check Do You Want To Apply A Theme To Your Page?, and then click Finish.

6. If you opted to apply a theme to the page in step 5, Access will open the Theme dialog box. Select a theme and click OK. (Not all of the themes on the list are instantly available. You may need to follow the instructions for installing themes, depending on your choice.)

After you click Finish and optionally choose a theme, Access will create the new page for you. If you chose to apply a theme, Access opens the page in Page Design view. If you did not choose a theme and you want to see what the page will look like when it's open, click the Page view button on the toolbar. Figure 13.4 shows the ungrouped page for the Employees table that results from following the steps listed above and applying the Spiral theme.

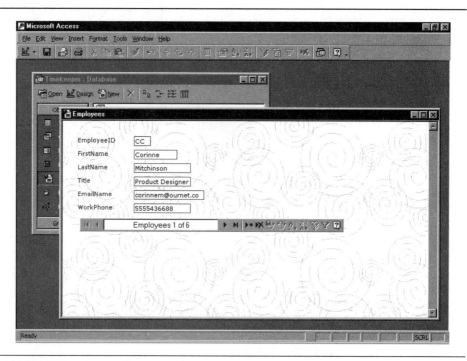

FIGURE 13.4: This page for the Employees table was created with the Page Wizard. It allows you to enter and edit data.

Create a Grouped Page with the Wizard

The next example uses the Page Wizard to create a grouped page that shows fields from the Employees, Weekly Records, and Project Hours tables in the Timekeeper database. The page can show just the Employee records, or the detailed information from the other tables at the same time.

1. Start the Page Wizard as described in the last example.

2. Use the Tables/Queries drop-down list to select the Employees table. Then add the EmployeeID and LastName and FirstName fields to the Selected Fields list. Change the Tables/Queries setting to Table: Weekly Records and add the WeekEndDate field to the Selected Fields list. Then set Tables/Queries

to Table: Project Hours and add the ProjectID, Hours, and Description fields to the Selected Fields list. Click Next when you are finished selecting fields.

3. This window is where you select the fields for grouping the records that will appear on the page. Click the EmployeeID field and then the > button so the diagram on the right side of the Page Wizard window looks like this:

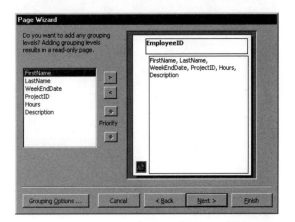

Click Next to continue after you add the group.

4. Select up to four fields for sorting the detail records shown on the page and click Next.

5. Enter a title for the new page. Click Open The Page, and then click Finish to create the page.

Figure 13.5 shows the page that results from following the above steps. As you can see in the figure, the EmployeeID field has a collapse button that you can use to hide the detailed information on the page. Note that because the page is grouped, you can't use it to change any of the data you see on the page.

TIP TIP TIP TIP TIP TIP TIP TIP TIP TIP TIP TIP TIP TIP TIP TIP TIP TIP TIP TIP TIP TIP TIP

The page in Figure 13.5 would look better if the FirstName and LastName fields from the Employees table appeared with the EmployeeID field near the top of the page. This type of change can be made in the Page Design view window. See "Edit an Existing Page" later in this skill for details.

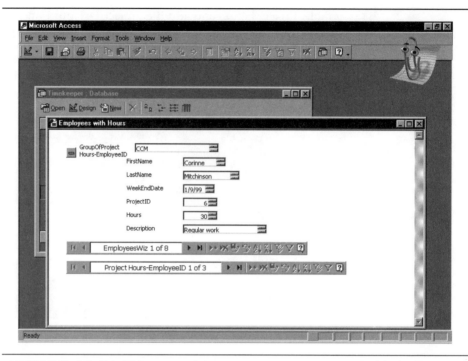

FIGURE 13.5: This grouped data access page was created with the Page Wizard. It doesn't allow editing of information, but it lets you change the level of detail you see.

Create a Page on Your Own

Working with the Page Wizard is definitely the quickest, easiest way to create a page, but you can also work on your own in the Page Design view window, if you prefer. To get to a new Page Design view window:

1. In the Database window, click the Pages button.

2. Double-click Create Data Access Page In Design View.

You'll see a window like the one shown in Figure 13.6. The Page Design view window is similar to the Form and Report Design view window, but not exactly the same. The toolbars have some buttons you won't find on those for forms and reports. Also, the way you work with objects in the Page Design view window is at times different from what you might expect. For example, you can't use Shift+click to select multiple objects at the same time. Instead, you have to move and resize objects one at a time.

Page Design view window   Page Design toolbar   Formatting (Page) toolbar

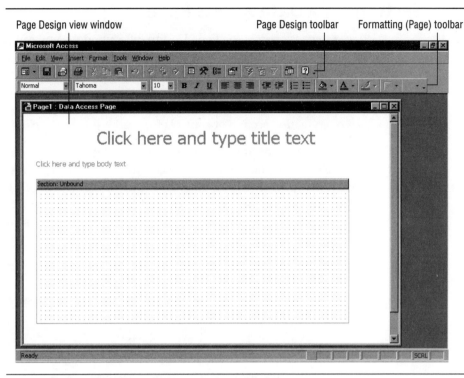

FIGURE 13.6: Create data access pages on your own or revise existing pages in the Page Design view window.

The Page Design Toolbar

The Page Design toolbar has many buttons that you'll recognize from working on forms and reports. It also has some unique buttons that are identified below. You'll find out how to use these special purpose buttons in the examples in the rest of this skill.

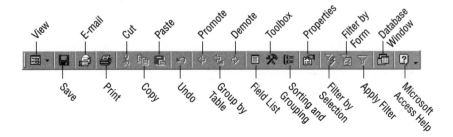

Sections of a Data Access Page

When a page is open in the Page Design view window, you can see that it is comprised of various sections. The page in Figure 13.7 has two sections besides the background:

- A group header for the Employees table
- A navigation section of controls for working with the page records

When you are working with a page that is not grouped, you'll see only one group header. That header holds the controls for the table or query data that is shown on the page. In Figure 13.7, the group header is labeled Header: Employees. In a grouped page, you would see additional headers with the names of the fields or expressions used to define the groups. A page can also include group footers to show summary information.

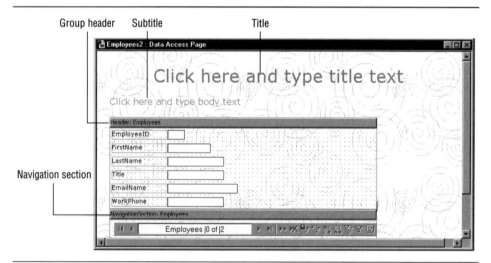

FIGURE 13.7: This page is open in Page Design view to show the different sections that are part of a page.

Working with Objects in the Page Design View Window

The way you work with objects in the Page Design view window is similar to what you do in the Form or Report Design view windows. However, there are some big differences to be aware of:

- You can only select one object at a time. Shift+clicking or dragging around a group of objects does not allow you to select multiple objects at once.

- Since you can't select more than one object at the same time, you have to size and align objects individually. There is an Alignment and Sizing toolbar you can use to align or size one object to another, but not an entire group of objects at once.

- The Undo option is not always available.

- To delete an object, right-click it and choose Cut. Alternatively, you can select an object and press Delete.

- Working with the background of a page is not the same as with forms and reports. Clicking does not change the insertion point. New objects are always added after the last object on the background.

Change the Default Title

When you open a new page or create a page with the Page Wizard, Access includes a default title: *Click here and type title text*. If you look back at Figure 13.7, you can see the text for this title near the top of the Page Design view window. To change the title, just click the default text and edit it. If you choose not to change the title, no title will be visible when you switch to Page view or open the page with Internet Explorer.

Each page also includes a place where you can enter additional text near the top: *Click here and type body text*. As with the title, you can edit this or leave it unchanged. If you don't edit it, it will not appear in Page view.

TIP TIP TIP TIP TIP TIP TIP TIP TIP TIP TIP TIP TIP TIP TIP TIP TIP TIP TIP TIP TIP TIP TIP

To remove the space that's allowed for the body text, click the line for *Click here and type body text* and press Backspace.

Add Data to a Page

When you're ready to add controls to show data on a page, click the Field List button on the Page Design toolbar. The Field List window that opens has two tabs:

- The Database tab is for adding tables, queries, or fields from the open database to the page you're working on.

- The Page tab shows you the fields that are already part of the page.

Add a Table to a Page

You can add the fields from a table or query to a page one at a time. Or, if you want to show all the fields from a table or query, you can take a shortcut and just drag the table or query name from the Field List to the Page Design view window. Access will prompt you to select a layout for the fields that are placed on the page.

Here's an example that shows what happens when you drag the Employees table onto a new page:

1. Click the Field List button to open the Field List window.

2. On the Database tab, click the Expand button (+) next to the Tables folder.

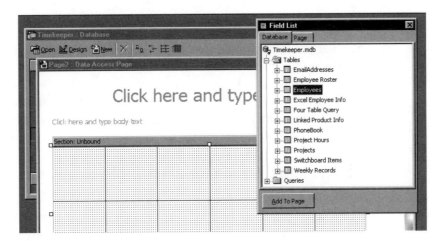

SKILL
13

3. Drag the icon for the Employees table to the area of the page labeled Section: Unbound. Before you drop the table, make sure the mouse is pointing to the place where you want to see the upper-left corner of the first box for data, not its label. When you release the mouse button, a Layout Wizard window will open:

4. To place the fields from the table as individual controls, as you saw in Figure 13.7, leave Individual Controls selected and click OK. (The other option, PivotTable List, is discussed later.)

The label for the main section on the page will now appear as Header: Employees. If you click the Page tab in the Field List window, you'll see that the Employees table is added to the list of objects for Page1 (or whatever the page is named).

Add a Field to a Page

You might not always want to drag an entire table or query to the Page Design view window. If you need to add an individual field to a page, open the Field List and click the Expand button for the table or query the field belongs to. Then drag the field to the page, or click the Add To Page button at the bottom of the Field List. If you use the latter technique, the field will be added after the last object in the Header section of the page.

Adding Fields from a Related Table to a Page

Fields from more than one table or query can be placed on the same page, as long as the tables can be related. You can create a relationship on the fly, but it's easiest to add fields from multiple tables when a relationship between the tables has already been defined. (See Skill 3 for information on relating tables.) When relationships are already in place, the Field List can display the tables that are related to other tables on the list.

This example shows how to add fields from the Weekly Records table to the page you already started for the Employees table.

1. Open the Field List if it's not already visible.

2. Click the Expand button for the Employees table if it hasn't been selected already. The first entry on the list should be a folder icon called Related Tables.

3. Under Employees, click the Expand button for Related Tables. The Field List will now look like this:

If you want to see how the tables are related, point with your mouse to the name for the Weekly Records table. The table name will be covered by a box that says *EmployeeID = EmployeeID*.

4. Click the Expand button for Weekly Records to show a list of that table's fields.

5. Select the field you want to add to the page. Then drag the field to the header area, or click the Add To Page button.

**SKILL
13**

NOTE NOTE NOTE NOTE NOTE NOTE NOTE NOTE NOTE NOTE NOTE NOTE NOTE NOTE NOTE

If you try to add a field from a table that is not related to the table the page is bound to, Access will open a New Relationship dialog box where you choose the fields that should be used to relate the tables.

Adding fields from a related table individually works fine when there is a one-to-one relationship between the records in the main table for the page and the related table. However, if you want to show a group of related records on the same page, see "Use a PivotTable List on a Page" later in this skill.

Choose a Theme for a Page

When you start a new page in an empty Page Design view window, you end with a plain white background and a simple style for any controls you add. You can make a page more interesting by changing the properties for individual controls one by one. (See Skill 6 for details on changing objects in the Design view window.) Or, you can bypass all the time it would take to do that and simply apply one of the themes that comes with Access. (As mentioned earlier, a theme is a predefined set of styles that you can apply to a page at any time.) You can choose from dozens of different themes to dress up a page with just a few mouse clicks.

To preview and apply a theme to a page:

1. In the Page Design view window, choose Format ➣ Theme from the menu.

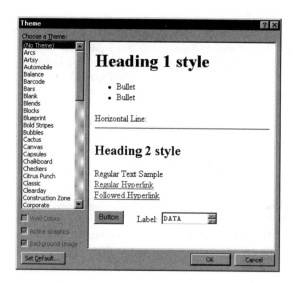

2. Under Choose A Theme, select the theme you want to preview or apply.

3. If you get a message that the selected theme is not available, follow the instructions for installing it. If you go through the installation, all the additional themes will be installed at the same time.

4. Optionally check or uncheck the boxes for Vivid Colors, Active Graphics, and Background Image in the bottom left corner of the screen. You can preview the effect of your choices before you apply them.

5. Click OK to apply the theme with any options you selected to the page.

6. Figure 13.8 shows a page for the Employees table after the Tvtoons theme with Vivid Colors was applied to it.

TIP TIP TIP TIP TIP TIP TIP TIP TIP TIP TIP TIP TIP TIP TIP TIP TIP TIP TIP TIP TIP TIP TIP TIP
To remove a theme from a page, choose Format ➢ Theme and select (No Theme) at the top of the list in the Theme dialog box. Then click OK.

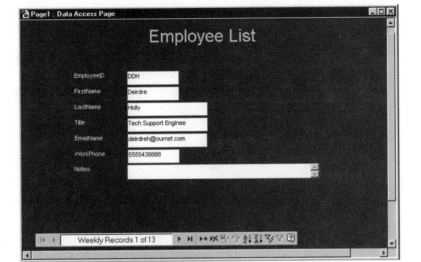

FIGURE 13.8: The Tvtoons theme with Vivid Colors was applied to this page.

Group Records on a Page

One of the unique things about data access pages is that you can *group* records and end up with a page where you can expand or collapse your view to see detail records as needed. Here's an example of how to create a grouped page that shows the records in the Project Hours table grouped by Project ID:

1. In the Database window, double-click Create Data Access Page In Design View.

2. When the new page opens, click the title and change it to Project Hours.

3. Click at the beginning of the line below where you can enter more text and press Backspace to remove the line altogether.

4. Click Field List on the toolbar.

5. Click the Expand button for Tables.

6. Click the Expand button for the Project Hours table.

7. In turn, select the ProjectID, Hours, and Description fields and click the Add To Page button to add these fields to the main section of the page. You should end up with a page that looks like this:

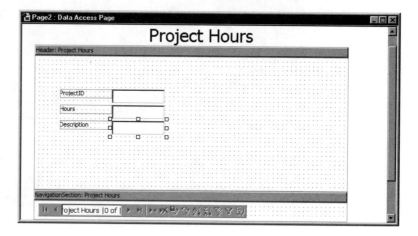

8. Click the ProjectID control to select it.

9. Click the Promote button on the Page Design toolbar. This tells Access to group the records by the selected field, ProjectID. You'll see a new header added to the page window labeled Header: Project Hours-ProjectID. The header will contain an Expand button and a control for the ProjectID field like this:

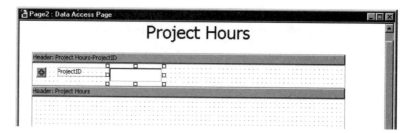

10. Drag the controls for Hours and Description in the header for Project Hours up to remove some of the empty space above them. Then click the Project Hours section to select it and drag the bottom border of the section up to make it smaller. The Page Design view window should now resemble the page shown in Figure 13.9.

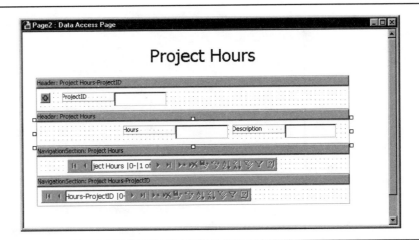

FIGURE 13.9: The ProjectID field on this page was promoted to create a new level of grouping for the page records.

If you switch to Page view, you'll now see a page like the one in Figure 13.10. The detail records for a project are hidden until you click the project's Expand button. Figure 13.11 shows the same page with the detail records for ProjectID 1 displayed.

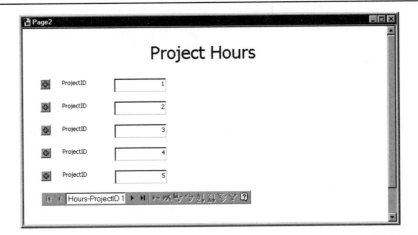

FIGURE 13.10: The page from Figure 13.9 shown in Page view rather than in Page Design view

SKILL
13

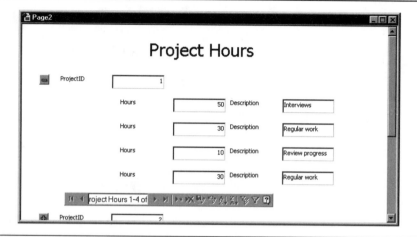

FIGURE 13.11: The page in Figure 13.10 after the Expand button for ProjectID 1 was clicked

Use a PivotTable List on a Page

Earlier in this skill, you saw that when you drag an entire table or query from the Field List to the Page Design view window, you have the option of placing the fields as individual controls or as a *PivotTable list*. A PivotTable list is similar to a Datasheet view in that data are arranged in rows and columns: a row for each record and a column for each field. But a PivotTable list has many unique features for summarizing and analyzing data instantly. You can:

- Filter and sort records the same way you can in Datasheet view

- Calculate summary values like the sum, count, minimum value, or maximum value for a field

- Select fields for row and column headers to summarize data by categories you choose

- Show subtotals

In the next section, you'll see how to add a PivotTable list to a page and then use it to analyze data.

Add a PivotTable List

When you drag a table or query from the Field List onto a page, one of the options offered by the Layout Wizard is a PivotTable list. In this example you'll use this technique to add a PivotTable list for the Project Hours table to a new page.

1. Follow steps 1–5 in the last example.

2. On the Field List under Tables, select Project Hours. Drag it to the unbound section in the middle of the Page Design view window and drop it where you want the upper left corner of the PivotTable list to appear. A Layout Wizard dialog box like this will open:

3. Select PivotTable List and click OK. Access will add a PivotTable list with its own toolbar to the page. It will look like the one shown in Figure 13.12.

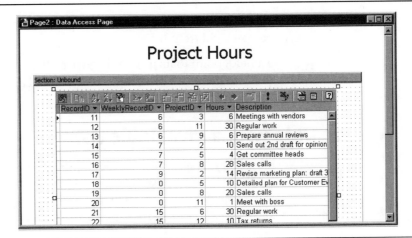

FIGURE 13.12: This page includes a PivotTable list for the Project Hours table.

Resize a PivotTable List

A PivotTable list can be resized just like any other object on a page. First, select the list so it appears in the Page Design view window with handles. Then drag the handles to change the PivotTable list's dimensions.

TIP TIP TIP TIP TIP TIP TIP TIP TIP TIP TIP TIP TIP TIP TIP TIP TIP TIP TIP TIP TIP TIP TIP TIP TIP

If you have problems selecting the PivotTable list, part of it may already be selected. To get around this problem, click the background of the page. Then click the PivotTable list once. You should see handles indicating that it is selected.

Move a PivotTable List

When a PivotTable list is selected, you can drag it to change its position in the Page Design view window. If you prefer to use the keyboard, select the Pivot-Table list and then use the Ctrl and arrow keys to move it a bit at a time.

Change the Fields on a PivotTable List

After you add a PivotTable list to a page, you can change its appearance by adding, deleting, or moving fields:

- To add a field to a PivotTable, click Field List on the toolbar. Then drag the desired field to the table.

- To delete a field from a PivotTable list, right-click the field's header and select Remove Field from the shortcut menu.

- To move a field, point to its header. Then drag the field to its new position and drop it into place. As you drag, a blue bar will appear to mark the place the field will land when it is dropped.

Analyze Data with a PivotTable List

With a PivotTable list, you can analyze data in Design view or Page view. Just drag and drop column and row headers to change the way records are grouped. You can also show calculated values like sums and counts, sort records, and apply filters to change the records that appear on the list.

You can work with a PivotTable list to summarize data from Design view or Page view. Any changes you make in Design view will determine how the PivotTable list appears each time the page is opened. Changes made in Page view only last as long as the page is open.

The PivotTable toolbar has several tools to help you with some of these tasks. To show the PivotTable toolbar, right-click the PivotTable's title bar and click Toolbar on the shortcut menu that appears. (If the title bar isn't visible, right-click the background of the PivotTable and choose Property Toolbox from the shortcut menu. Click the Show/Hide bar, if it's not already expanded, and then select the Title bar. You can also use the Property Box to bring the toolbar into view. Just click the Toolbar icon on the Show/Hide list.) If you show the toolbar in Design view, it will also appear in Page view.

SKILL
13

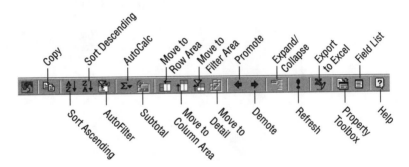

This book does not delve into an extensive discussion of how to use all the features of the PivotTable list toolbar. (Check Microsoft Access Help for detailed information.) But here's a quick illustration of the kind of thing you can do with a PivotTable on a page. Following the example, you'll also find some guidelines on filtering a PivotTable list's records, changing the way records are grouped, and removing fields.

If you'd like to learn more about working with data presented this way, open the Office Assistant, enter "PivotTable," and explore the topics that are shown.

Open the PivotTable shown in Figure 13.12 and follow these steps to summarize project hours by project and week, instead of viewing the individual records:

1. Make sure you are viewing the PivotTable in Page view.

2. Click the header for the Hours field to select it.

3. Click the AutoCalc button to sum the Hours field. A field labeled Sum Of Hours will appear under the last record in the PivotTable.

4. Click the header for the ProjectID field to select it.

5. Click the Move To Row Area button on the toolbar. The PivotTable will now look like this:

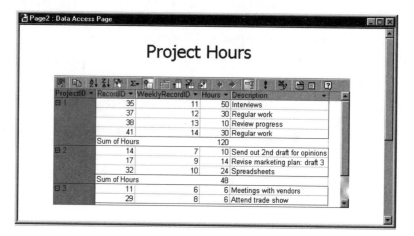

6. To make it easier to see the essential information in the PivotTable, right-click the header for the RecordID field and choose Remove Field from the shortcut menu. Repeat this for the WeeklyRecordID field. Then drag the right border of the Hours column header to make the column wider. The final result is shown in Figure 13.13.

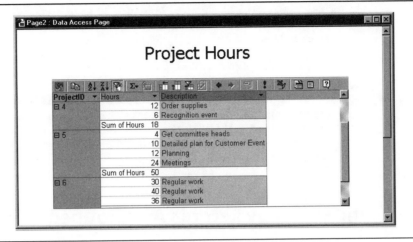

FIGURE 13.13: This PivotTable shows the total hours by ProjectID for records in the Project Hours table.

Filter Records in a PivotTable List

If you look at the column headers in the PivotTable list shown in Figure 13.13, you'll see that there are small drop-down buttons on the right side of each field name. These buttons can be used to quickly filter the records that you see in a PivotTable list. If you click one, you'll see a list of the values for the field the column belongs to. Each value is preceded by a check box. Use the check boxes to filter records as follows:

- To remove the records for a particular value from the PivotTable list, uncheck the box for that value.

- To include the records for a value, check the box for the value. More than one box can be checked at the same time.

- To quickly create a filter that shows records for one value only, uncheck the box for Show All at the top of the list; then check the box for the value you want to see.

After you work with the check boxes on the value list, click the OK button at the bottom of the list. A filter will be applied to the PivotTable list based on the boxes you checked.

When a field has a filter applied to it, its drop-down button will change from black to blue.

If you want to use a field to filter records without showing it as part of the PivotTable list, right-click the field's header and choose Move To Filter Area from the shortcut menu. The field will be moved above the area of the Pivot-Table list where records appear.

Change the Way Records Are Grouped

The best thing about PivotTable lists is probably the ease with which you can change the way records are grouped. By dragging and dropping, you can create or remove groups along the row axis or the column axis. You can also use the Move To Row Area and Move To Column Area buttons on the PivotTable toolbar to create groups.

Add a Group to a PivotTable List

There are two ways to add a group to a PivotTable list. You can do either of the following:

- Select the field you want to use for grouping and click the Move To Column Area or Move To Row Area button on the PivotTable toolbar.

- Drag the header for a field to the left side of the PivotTable list to create a row grouping. To create a column grouping, drag a field header and drop it just above the data area.

When you have multiple groups in the row area, you will see each column on the left side of the PivotTable list. The row area columns will have a gray background so you can distinguish them from the data area.

If you change your mind about a group and you decide to remove it, right-click the group field header and choose Move To Detail from the shortcut menu.

Change the Level of Grouping

You can use the Promote or Demote buttons on the PivotTable toolbar to change the order in which records are grouped. First, select the column for the field you want to move. Then click Promote to move the field up one level of grouping. To move a field down, click the Demote button. If a field is not already part of a group, clicking the Promote and Demote buttons will move the field to the left and the right, respectively.

Remove a Field from a PivotTable List

To remove a field from a PivotTable list, just drag it off the table. If you are working with the PivotTable list in Page view, the field will not be permanently removed from the list; the next time you open the page, the field will again appear as part of the list.

If you do want to permanently remove a field, open the page the PivotTable list is part of in Design view. Then drag the field off the list. When you remove a field this way in Design view, it is no longer part of the PivotTable list. To add it back to the design, you will have to drag it back into the PivotTable list from the Field List.

Save a Page

When you're finished working on a page, close its window, choose Yes to save your work, and enter a page name when Access asks you for one. The page will then appear in the Database window in the Pages section.

Edit an Existing Page

You can use the Page Design view window to work on pages you created with the Page Wizard or on your own.

1. In the Database window, click the Pages button.

2. Right-click the page you want to work on.

3. Choose Design view from the shortcut menu.

If you want to work on a page that was created outside of Access (and therefore does not appear in the Database window), in step 2, double-click Edit Web Page That Already Exists and choose an HTML file in the Locate Web Page window that opens.

Browse a Page

From Access, you can open a data access page and view it right from Access or with Internet Explorer 5:

- To open a page in Access, right-click the page in the Database window and select Open from the shortcut menu.

- To view the page using Internet Explorer without leaving Access first, right-click the page in the Database window and choose Web Page Preview from the shortcut menu.

- To view the page directly from Internet Explorer, enter the location of the HTML file for the page in the Address box.

For example, `C:\My Documents\Project Hours PivotTable.htm` is the name of the page shown in Figure 13.13. The same page is shown open in Internet Explorer 5 in Figure 13.14. In the latter figure, the PivotTable has not yet been used to change the way the data is summarized and presented.

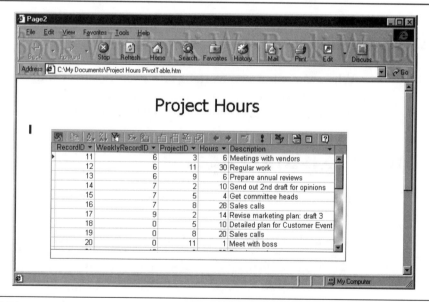

FIGURE 13.14: The same page shown in Figure 13.13 viewed with Internet Explorer 5

Are You Experienced?

Now you can...

☑ **Export a document to HTML**

☑ **Know data access page basics**

☑ **Create a page with the Page Wizard**

☑ **Create a page on your own**

☑ **Choose a theme for a page**

☑ **Group records on a page**

☑ **Use a PivotTable on a page**

☑ **Browse a page**

Bypass Database Drudgery with Command Buttons and Macros

- Learn command button and macro basics
- Use the Command Button Wizard
- Add a command button to a form yourself
- Customize a command button
- Create a macro
- Use conditions in a macro
- Organize macros in groups
- Tie a macro to a command button
- Run a macro when an event occurs

Once you have a database set up and you start working with it, you'll probably notice that you do some of the same tasks over and over. Any repetitive jobs like this are prime candidates for automation. Access 2000 has some great tools you can use to automate and streamline your database work, even if you're not a computer programmer.

Command Button and Macro Basics

In this skill, you'll find out how to use command buttons and macros in a database to get your computer to do the some of the repetitive tasks involved in managing a database. This will free you to spend your time on more creative efforts, such as formulating queries and reports to find out what's really happening with your data. Before getting into some examples, read on to find out more about command buttons and macros and how they work.

Command Buttons

Command buttons are controls like the OK button you find in so many Access dialog boxes. When you click a command button, Access automatically performs a predetermined function. There are various ways to associate one or more actions with a command button:

- Use the Command Button Wizard to create a button, select an action for it, and then choose a label or a graphic for the button's face.

- Create a button without the Wizard and then use the button's properties sheet to say which macro or code should be run when the button is clicked.

Later in this skill, you'll see how to create command buttons using both these techniques.

Macros

Macros are little programs that tell Access to perform one or more actions—for example, open a form, print a report, run a query, or even import data. And you don't have to be a programmer to use macros. In a special window called the Macro Builder, you select the actions you want Access to perform along with parameters, like form or report names, that are needed for the action.

Once you create a macro, you can run it from the Database window any time you need it. You can also tie a macro to a command button on a form. Then, when you want to run it, all you have to do is click the button. Or, you can tell Access to run a macro when an event occurs, such as opening a form or updating a field value.

Most of this skill is devoted to working with macros. You'll see how to:

- Define macros

- Save and run macros

- Set up macros that perform actions conditionally

- Tie a macro to a command button

- Run a macro when an event occurs

- Create macros to perform various kinds of tasks

You may be able to adapt some of the examples included at the end of the skill for your own use.

Add a Command Button to a Form

As mentioned at the beginning of this skill, you can set up command buttons to open forms, print reports, open dialog boxes, and more. Starting with the form shown in Figure 14.1, the following procedures will walk you through adding command buttons to:

- Open the Employees With Photos form for the person whose time records are being viewed

- Print the current form

- Open the Find dialog box

- Switch to Microsoft Word

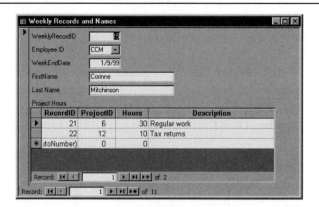

FIGURE 14.1: In the following examples you'll add command buttons to this form to open the Employees With Photos form for a selected employee, print the current form, open the Find dialog box, and switch to Microsoft Word.

Use the Command Button Wizard

You can use the Command Button Wizard to create all the buttons listed for the form in Figure 14.1. Here are the steps for getting the wizard started:

1. In Design view, open the form you want to add buttons to.

2. Make room for the buttons on the form.

3. Click the Toolbox button on the toolbar to open the Toolbox, if it's not already visible.

4. To make sure the Command Button Wizard offers its help, verify that the Control Wizards button in the Toolbox is pressed (dimmed).

5. Click the Command Button tool in the Toolbox.

6. In the Form Design view window, point to where you want the upper-left corner of the new command button to appear. Then drag to create the button. When you release the mouse, the Command Button Wizard will open.

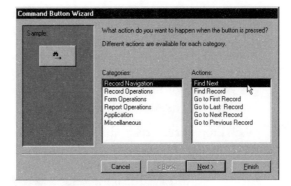

What you see in the remaining steps of the wizard depends on the type of action you chose in the first step. You can review the following sections and create a few different types of command buttons so that you can get familiar with what's available through the wizard.

Add a Button to Open a Form for a Specific Record

This example creates a command button that opens another form called Employees With Photos. When you tell the wizard to open a form, it asks whether you want to show a particular record, as you'll see next.

1. Start the Command Button Wizard as described in the previous section.

2. In the first step of the wizard, under Categories, click Form Operations. The Actions list on the right side of the dialog box changes to show this list:

3. Under Actions, double-click Open Form to go to the next step of the Command Button Wizard.

4. Double-click the form you want the button to open. This example uses Employees With Photos.

5. In the next step, select Open The Form And Find Specific Data To Display, and click Next. (You're changing the setting here to make sure the Employees With Photos form opens for the same person being viewed in the Weekly Records And Names form.)

6. Click EmployeeID on both field lists in the next dialog box. Then click the <-> button so that the window looks like this before you click Next:

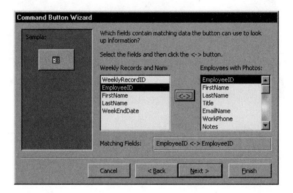

7. Select Text in the next step and enter **Employee Info** in the box that follows. Then click Next.

8. Enter a name for the button (this is for reference only; it does not show on the form) and click Finish.

When you return to the Form Design View window, you'll see a button with the text or label you chose in the next to the last step. Figure 14.2 shows the Weekly Records And Names form in Design view with the finished command button.

To test the button, simply switch to Form view and click it. Figure 14.3 shows the Access window after the button was clicked to show additional information for the person with the EmployeeID CCM. (The Employees With Photos form was moved to the right so you can see that it matches the record that's open in the Weekly Records With Names form.)

Command button that
opens another form

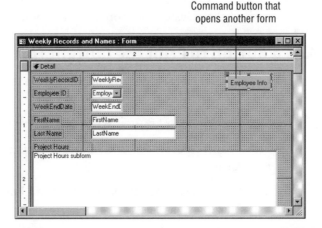

FIGURE 14.2: The command button added to this form opens a form called Employees With Photos when it's clicked.

FIGURE 14.3: The active form in this window, Employees With Photos, was opened by clicking the command button added to the Weekly Records With Names form. Notice that the form shows information for the same person whose record was being viewed when the button was clicked.

To return to work in the Design view window, close the Employees With Photos form and click Design View on the Form toolbar.

Add a Button to Print the Current Form

This next series of steps adds a command button that prints the form being viewed:

1. Start the Command Button Wizard as described earlier.

2. Select Form Operations on the Categories list, and double-click Print Current Form under Actions.

3. Select Text and change the label from Print Form to **Print This Form**. Then click Next.

4. Change the button's name to Print This Form and click Finish.

TIP TIP TIP TIP TIP TIP TIP TIP TIP TIP TIP TIP TIP TIP TIP TIP TIP TIP TIP TIP TIP TIP TIP TIP

Don't worry if the buttons on the form aren't the same size. You can adjust them all later. To make them the same height and width, simply select all the buttons together and use Format ➢ Size. Then select To Tallest, To Widest, or whatever choice will work best to make your buttons the same size.

Add a Button to Open the Find And Replace Dialog Box

If you're creating a database for someone who's not familiar with Access, it can be helpful to add a command button that opens the Find And Replace dialog box. This way, the person using the database can click the command button instead of searching for the right button on the toolbar. Follow these steps to create a command button that opens the Find And Replace dialog box:

1. Start the Command Button Wizard as described earlier.

2. Leave Record Navigation selected under Categories.

3. Select Find Record and click Next.

4. Select Text, leave Find Record as the label for the button, and click Next.

5. Enter **Find Record** for the button's name and click Finish.

Figure 14.4 shows the result of clicking this button after switching to Form view.

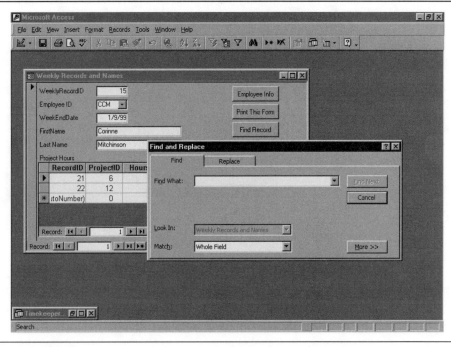

FIGURE 14.4: The Find And Replace dialog box in this window was opened by clicking the Find Record command button.

Add a Button to Switch to Microsoft Word

The following steps show how to set up a command button that opens a window in Microsoft Word without closing the active database:

1. Start the Command Button Wizard as described earlier.

2. In the first step of the wizard, select Application on the Categories list.

3. Under Actions, double-click Run MS Word.

4. Select Text, change the label for the button to **Switch to Word**, and click Next.

5. Enter **Switch to Word** again (for the button's behind-the-scene name) and click Finish.

If you've followed along through the last four exercises, you'll now have a form with four command buttons:

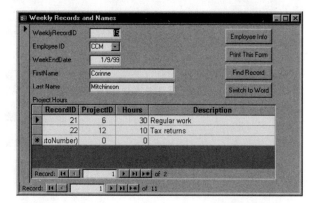

If you click the Switch To Word button, a Microsoft Word window like the one in Figure 14.5 opens. Once Word is open, you can open an existing Word document or create a new one. When you're finished with Word, simply close its window to return to Access. If you want to leave Word active, minimize the Word window instead, or use the Taskbar to switch back to Access.

Create a Command Button Yourself

A situation may come up in which you want to create a command button that will have a macro or Visual Basic code attached to it that's not ready yet. In this case, you can place a command button on a form without associating an action with it. To do this, perform one of the following:

- Follow the steps to start the Command Button Wizard and click Cancel in the first step.

- Be sure the Control Wizards button in the Toolbox is not pressed (it should not be dimmed) before you use the Command Button tool to place a button on the form.

Once you place a button on a form using one of these methods, it will have a label such as *Command11*. To make the button do something when it's clicked, you'll have to add a macro or a Visual Basic event procedure (some code) to the button's On Click property using its properties sheet. See "Tie a Macro to a Command Button" later in this skill for detailed instructions on doing this.

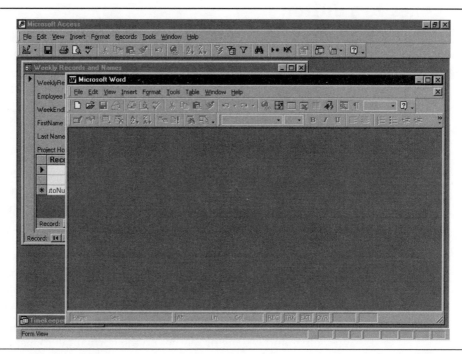

FIGURE 14.5: This Word window was opened by clicking a command button on an Access form.

Customize a Command Button

After you place a command button on a form, you may want to change its label or other properties. Using the command button's properties sheet or the Formatting (Form/Report) toolbar, you can do things like:

- Change the font size and style for a button's label
- Add a picture to the button's background
- Change the macro or code that's attached to a button

Resize a Button

A command button can be resized like any other object on a form. Click the button to select it. Then point with your mouse to any one of the handles that appears around the button and drag to change the button's size. If you change your mind about the changes you make, use Edit ➢ Undo to return the button to its former size.

Edit a Button's Label

A button's label can be edited easily. If the button you want to edit is not already selected, click it twice, and an insertion bar will appear. You can drag over all or part of the label to select it. Make your changes and click anywhere off the button to save them.

Change the Style of a Button's Label

To change the style of the text on a button, click the button to select it. Then use the buttons on the Formatting (Form/Report) toolbar to change the font size, style, color, and other characteristics. Or, click the Properties button on the Form Design toolbar and use the properties on the Format tab to make your changes.

Change the Action for a Button

Every command button has an On Click property that lists the name of the macro or Visual Basic procedure that runs when the button is clicked. Or, if the button was created with the Command Button Wizard and has code attached, *[Event Procedure]* will be listed for the On Click property. To change the macro or procedure for this property, click the Event tab on the button's properties sheet. Then edit the On Click property setting directly. Alternatively, click the line you want to change and use the drop-down menu for the property to select a new macro.

NOTE NOTE NOTE NOTE NOTE NOTE NOTE NOTE NOTE NOTE NOTE NOTE NOTE NOTE NOTE

For examples of working with the On Click property for a command button, see "Tie a Macro to a Command Button" later in this skill.

TIP TIP TIP TIP TIP TIP TIP TIP TIP TIP TIP TIP TIP TIP TIP TIP TIP TIP TIP TIP TIP TIP TIP TIP

To view the code or macro that's attached to a button, right-click the button and choose Build Event from the shortcut menu.

Create a Macro

Macros are different from command buttons in a couple of ways:

- A macro is an object that can be run from the Database window, or it can be attached to an event such as clicking a command button or opening a form.

- A macro consists of one action or a group of actions that can be set up to execute conditionally.

In this section, you'll see how to use the Macro Builder to create macros and include conditions in them.

NOTE NOTE NOTE NOTE NOTE NOTE NOTE NOTE NOTE NOTE NOTE NOTE NOTE NOTE NOTE

The last section of this skill includes some examples of macros you may be able to adapt for use with your own database.

Start the Macro Builder

When you create a macro, the basic process involves choosing actions and supplying any parameters the action needs. For example, if you want a macro to open a form, you open the Macro Builder, select the Open Form action, and then enter a parameter that tells Access the name of the form to open. Because you can enter multiple actions, macros are perfect for accomplishing multi-step tasks such as printing a report and then running an update query to flag the records that were printed.

To create a macro, start from the Database window and follow these steps:

1. Click the Macros button in the Database window.

2. Click New to open a Macro window:

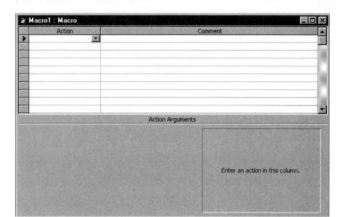

3. To add an action, click the drop-down arrow for the first line under Action and select an action. Table 14.1 shows a list of the actions you can use in a macro along with brief descriptions of what they do.

4. For each action, fill out the list of Action Arguments in the bottom half of the Macro dialog box. Figure 14.6 shows the Macro window as it appears for the Open Form action.

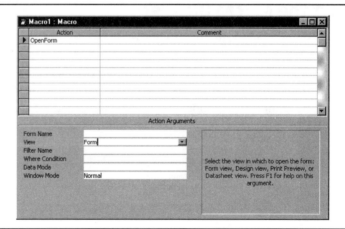

FIGURE 14.6: The Macro window showing Action Arguments for an Open Form action

TIP TIP TIP TIP TIP TIP TIP TIP TIP TIP TIP TIP TIP TIP TIP TIP TIP TIP TIP TIP TIP TIP TIP

When you enter actions for a macro, you can bypass the drop-down list by typing the first unique characters of the action's name. Access will fill in the rest of the name for you.

TABLE 14.1: Macro Actions and What They Do

Choose This Action...	To...
AddMenu	Create custom menus (à la earlier versions of Access)
ApplyFilter	Apply a saved filter to the open object
Beep	Have the computer beep
CancelEvent	Cancel the event that made the macro run
Close	Close the active window or a specified window
CopyObject	Copy a database object
DeleteObject	Delete a database object
Echo	Hide or show what happens while a macro runs
FindNext	Find the next record that matches the last find
FindRecord	Find a record and specify search conditions
GoToControl	Move to a certain field or control
GoToPage	Go to a different page on a multipage form
GoToRecord	Move to a different record
Hourglass	Show an hourglass while the macro runs
Maximize	Fill the Access window with the active window
Minimize	Minimize the active window
MoveSize	Move or resize the active window
MsgBox	Show a message
OpenDataAccessPage	Open a data access page in Access
OpenDiagram	Open a diagram for an Access project (.adp)
OpenForm	Open a form
OpenModule	Open a code module
OpenQuery	Open a query
OpenReport	Open a report

TABLE 14.1: Macro Actions and What They Do *(continued)*

Choose This Action...	To...
OpenStoredProcedure	Open a stored report for an Access project (.adp)
OpenTable	Open a table
OpenView	Open a view for an Access project (.adp)
OutputTo	Export Access data to another file format
PrintOut	Print the active object
Quit	Leave Access
Rename	Rename a database object
RepaintObject	Update the screen for a specified object
Requery	Update the data for a control or database object
Restore	Restore a window to its previous size
RunApp	Run another program such as Excel or Word
RunCode	Call a Visual Basic function procedure
RunCommand	Execute an Access menu or toolbar command
RunMacro	Run a macro
RunSQL	Run a query using an SQL statement
Save	Save a database object
SelectObject	Select a specified database object
SendKeys	Send keystrokes to Access or another active Windows program
SendObject	Send a database object via e-mail or fax
SetMenuItem	Set the state of an item on a custom menu
SetValue	Set a field, control, or property to a specified value
SetWarnings	Turn system messages on or off
ShowAllRecords	Show all records in the active object
ShowToolbar	Show or hide a toolbar
StopAllMacros	Stop any macros that are running
StopMacro	Stop the current macro
TransferDatabase	Import, export, or link data
TransferSpreadsheet	Import, export, or link a spreadsheet
TransferText	Import, export, or link a text or HTML file

NOTE NOTE NOTE NOTE NOTE NOTE NOTE NOTE NOTE NOTE NOTE NOTE NOTE NOTE NOTE

For more details on macro actions, use the Office Assistant to find help on the specific action you want to use. For example, for details on the SetValue action, enter "setvalue" in the Office Assistant text box. Then click the topic for *SetValue Action*.

Insert and Delete Rows

Once you've added actions to a macro, you can go back and insert rows or delete them:

 Insert a row: Click the row selector for the action that will appear under the new action. Then click Insert Rows on the Macro Design toolbar, or press Insert.

 Delete a row: Click the row selector for the action you want to delete, and then click Delete Rows on the Macro Design toolbar or press Delete.

Undo a Delete

If you delete an action too quickly, you can get it back by clicking Undo on the Macro Design toolbar or by choosing Edit ➤ Undo Delete from the menu.

Delete a Group of Actions

To delete a group of contiguous actions, hold down Shift while you click their row selectors, and then press Delete or click Delete Rows.

NOTE NOTE NOTE NOTE NOTE NOTE NOTE NOTE NOTE NOTE NOTE NOTE NOTE NOTE NOTE

The row selector for each action is the gray box to the left of the action column.

Copy a Macro Line

After you create a line for an action in a macro, it can be copied to another line. This technique is especially helpful when you're creating a macro to do similar actions like run multiple reports. All you have to do is edit the arguments for the copied line. For example, if you are creating a macro to print four reports, enter the first OpenReport action. Then copy this line three times and edit the Report Name argument for each line.

**SKILL
14**

To copy a line in a macro:

1. Click the record selector for the action you want to copy. (The record selector is the box just to the left of the box for the action name.)

2. Click Copy on the toolbar, or press Ctrl+C.

3. Click an empty line. Then click Paste on the toolbar (or press Ctrl+V) to paste the copied line to the blank spot. Or, to paste the line between two lines, click the line below the place you want the new line to appear and then press Ctrl+V or click Paste.

 TIP TIP TIP TIP TIP TIP TIP TIP TIP TIP TIP TIP TIP TIP TIP TIP TIP TIP TIP TIP TIP TIP TIP TIP TIP TIP TIP

You can copy multiple lines in the Macro window. Just hold down Shift and click the first and last lines in the group you want to copy.

Move a Macro Line

To move a macro line, click the line's record selector. Then point to the record selector and hold down the mouse key. When a small cross-hatched box appears under the pointer, drag the line to its new position.

To move a group of lines, drag over their record selectors to select them as a group. Alternatively, hold down Shift while you click the first and last lines in the group. Then drag them as a group to their new place in the macro.

Save a Macro

Once you're finished formulating a macro, you have to save it with a name so it can be run from the Database window or attached to other database objects:

1. Close the Macro window.

2. Choose Yes when asked if you want to save your changes.

3. Enter a name for the macro and select OK.

Once a macro is saved, it appears in the Database window on the Macros page like this:

In this particular Database window, three macros appear: Autoexec, Beep, and Bonus Letters.

Run a Macro

You can run a macro in several ways:

- Select the macro in the Database window and click Run.

- In the Macro window, click Run on the Macro Design toolbar.

- In the Database window, right-click the macro and select Run from the shortcut menu.

- Associate the macro with an event such as the On Open property for a form. Then, when the event occurs, the macro will run automatically.

Later in this skill, you'll find out more about how to tie a macro to a command button or run it when an event occurs.

Use Conditions in a Macro

Macros are quite flexible because you can optionally include *conditions* in them. When a condition is associated with a macro action, Access executes the action only if the condition is true. If the condition is false, the action is skipped.

SKILL
14

The next example defines a macro with conditions that tell Access to print one report if the Date Of Hire field has a value in the last year and to print a different report if the Date Of Hire value is over a year past. The reports are called New Employee Bonus Letter and Established Employee Bonus Letter. Later, another example will tie this macro to a command button on the Employees With Photos form to print different letters for "new" employees and for those who were hired more than a year ago.

1. In the Database window, click the Macros button and click New.

2. Click the Conditions button on the Macro Design toolbar to add a Condition column to the left side of the Macro window:

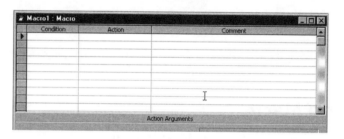

3. In the first row of the Condition column, enter **[Date Of Hire] > Date() - 365**.

4. In the Action column of the same row, enter **OpenReport**, or select this action from the column's drop-down menu.

5. Fill in the Action Arguments section so the Macro window looks like this except for the last line:

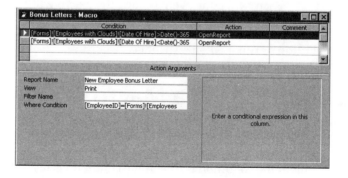

The argument for Where Condition should read
[EmployeeID]=[Forms]![Employees with Photos]![EmployeeID].

This argument tells Access to print a report only for the employee currently being viewed in the form called Employees With Photos.

6. In the second row of the Condition column, enter **[Forms]![Employees With Photos]![Date Of Hire] < Date() - 365**.

7. In the Action column of the same row, enter **OpenReport**.

8. Fill in the Action Arguments section as for the first line, but change the Report Name to **Established Employee Bonus Letter**.

9. When you close the Macro window, save the macro with a name like Bonus Letters.

To test this macro, open the Employees With Photos form. Then run the macro from the Database window or from the Macro window as described in the last section. The value in the Date Of Hire field determines which report the macro prints.

SKILL
14

NOTE NOTE NOTE NOTE NOTE NOTE NOTE NOTE NOTE NOTE NOTE NOTE NOTE NOTE

While running the macro from the Database window or the Macro window as just described works, it is an awkward way to get a bonus letter printed. In "Tie a Macro to a Command Button" later in this skill, you'll see how to create a command button for this macro on the Employees With Photos form so it can be run with one click from that form.

TIP TIP TIP TIP TIP TIP TIP TIP TIP TIP TIP TIP TIP TIP TIP TIP TIP TIP TIP TIP TIP TIP

To print letters for all employees at once instead of one at a time from the Employees With Photos form, base the bonus letter reports on queries for the new and established employees. Then create a macro with two OpenReport actions to print both reports, one after the other.

Create a Macro Group

If you need to set up many macros in a database, you might want to store a group of related macros under one name in the Database window. This makes it easier to find macros and keep them organized. To do this:

1. Open a Macro window.

2. Click the Macro Names button on the Macro Design toolbar to add a Macro Name column to the Macro window.

3. Enter a name for the first line of a macro in the Macro Name column, and add the rest of the actions for the macro on the following lines. You do not have to repeat the macro name in the Macro Name column for each macro line. Repeat this step for each macro to be stored in the group.

4. When you're finished entering all the macros in the group, close the macro window. Click Yes to save your changes and enter a name in the Save As dialog box. This name, although it is entered as a macro name, is actually the name of the macro group.

When you choose a macro stored in a group from a drop-down list (say in a properties sheet), it will appear like this:

```
MacroGroupName.MacroName
```

For example, if you have a macro called Beep stored in a macro group called UtilityMacros (the name that will appear in the Database window), the macro will show up on macro lists as `UtilityMacros.Beep`.

Tie a Macro to a Command Button

When you set up a command button with the Command Button Wizard, you can choose to have a macro run when the button is clicked. However, sometimes you might not have the macro completed when you create the button. Or you might want to change what happens when a button is clicked. In either case, follow these steps to tie a macro to a command button that already exists:

1. Open the form the button appears on in Design view.

2. Right-click the button and choose Properties.

3. Click the Event tab.

4. Click the line for the On Click property.

5. Use the drop-down menu for On Click to select the macro you want to run when the command button is clicked.

6. If you need to change the button's label, click the Format tab and change the Caption property.

Figure 14.7 shows the Employees With Photos form with a button added that runs the Bonus Letter macro when it's clicked. The same form is shown in Form Design view in Figure 14.8. In that figure, the Bonus Letter button is selected and the properties sheet is open so you can see how the On Click property is set.

FIGURE 14.7: The command button labeled Bonus Letter on this form runs a macro called Bonus Letter when it is clicked. The macro prints a certain letter depending on when the employee was hired.

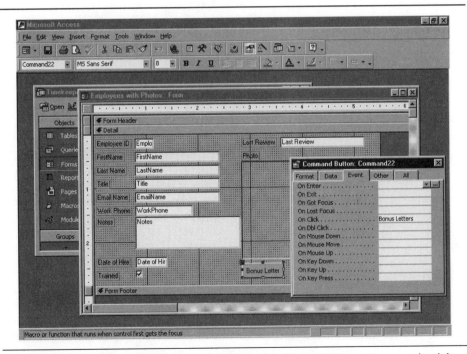

FIGURE 14.8: The Bonus Letter button is selected here so you can check its On Click property on the properties sheet.

Run a Macro when an Event Occurs

Running a macro can be triggered by events other than clicking a command button. For example, you can have Access run a macro when a form opens. To do this:

1. Open the form or other database object to which the event belongs.

2. Open the properties sheet for the object and click the Event tab.

3. Click the line for the event that will trigger the macro.

4. Select the desired macro from the drop-down menu for the event.

This properties sheet is for a form that runs a macro called Beep when it opens:

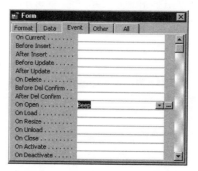

TIP TIP TIP TIP TIP TIP TIP TIP TIP TIP TIP TIP TIP TIP TIP TIP TIP TIP TIP TIP TIP TIP TIP TIP

To run a macro when a database is opened, name the macro Autoexec. Any actions included in the Autoexec macro are executed after any options specified in the Startup dialog box take effect. To bypass the Autoexec macro, hold down Shift while the database opens.

Macro Examples

Access macros are so powerful and versatile that you can use them to perform all kinds of database tasks. The examples that follow show some of the things you can do to automate database work without doing any programming. You'll see macros that can be attached to command buttons to perform these jobs with one mouse click:

- Empty a table, import new information, format the new data, and export the result to Excel.

- Open a form, add a new record, and fill in fields with values shown on another open form.

- Print letters and make a record that the letters were printed.

- Print the results of an ad hoc filter.

Before getting into the examples, here's a list of the basic steps needed to automate a multi-step process with a macro:

1. Make a list of the actions the macro should perform.

2. Create any forms, reports, queries, or data access pages that the macro will work with. For example, if you are writing a macro to print three reports, design and save all the reports.

3. Create the macro that will perform the necessary tasks.

4. Decide whether you want to run the macro from the Database window, or when an event occurs, by clicking a button on a form.

5. If you opt to use a command button to run the macro, add the command button to whatever form you want to run the macro from.

It's impossible to show all the actions in a macro with their arguments at the same time in one figure. So, in the examples below, the macro actions, arguments, and any necessary explanations are listed in tables rather than shown in figures. Also, the tables, forms, queries, and reports for all the macro actions are not shown. The focus is on the macro actions instead. These examples are meant to show how various actions can be used together to automate complex tasks.

Import New Information, Format It, and Export It to Excel

This example lists the actions and arguments for a macro that empties a table called Sales Figures with a Delete query, imports a text file into the same table, runs an Update query to do some formatting of the new data, and exports the resulting records to an Excel spreadsheet. This type of macro would probably be run from the Database window instead of with a command button.

Macro Action	Action Arguments	Value for Argument	Comments
OpenQuery	Query Name	EmptySalesFigs	Runs a Delete query called EmptySales-Figs that removes all records from the table called Sales Figures.
	View	Datasheet	Leave this argument unchanged.
	Data Mode	Edit	Leave this argument unchanged.
TransferText	Transfer Type	Import Delimited	Imports a delimited text file.
	Specification Name	ImpSales	The import specifica-tion called ImpSales has to be saved ahead of time.
	Table Name	Sales Figures	Provides the name of the table to receive the new records.
	File Name	Salesfig.txt	The name of the text file being imported.
	Has Field Names	No	Leave this setting unchanged, unless the first row of the file holds field names.
	HTML Table Name		Leave this setting blank.
	Code Page		Leave this setting blank.
OpenQuery	Query Name	FormatNewData	Runs an Update query called Format-NewData that adds formatting characters like dashes and slashes to the new data.
	View	Datasheet	Leave this argument unchanged.

Macro Action	Action Arguments	Value for Argument	Comments
	Data Mode	Edit	Leave this argument unchanged.
TransferSpread-sheet	Transfer Type	Export	Exports records to an Excel file.
	Spreadsheet Type	Microsoft Excel 8-9	
	Table Name	Sales Figures	Provides the name of the table with the records being exported.
	File Name	`Salesfig.xls`	The name of the new Excel file.
	Has Field Names	No	Leave this setting unchanged.
	Range		Leave this setting blank.

Open a Form, Add a Record, and Fill in Fields from Another Form

This macro is designed to speed up data entry when you want to add a new record to a table in Form view using values from a record shown on another open form. The macro is run by clicking a button on a form for a table called Employees. It opens a form for another table called Phonebook, adds a new record to the Phonebook table, and copies some values into the new record from fields shown on the other form for the Employees table.

Macro Action	Action Arguments	Value for Argument	Comments
OpenForm	Form Name	Phonebook	Opens a form called Phonebook that shows records from the Phonebook table.
	View	Form	Leave this argument unchanged.
	Filter Name		Leave this argument blank.

Macro Action	Action Arguments	Value for Argument	Comments
	Where Condition		Leave this argument blank.
	Data Mode		Leave this argument blank.
	Window Mode	Normal	Leave this argument unchanged.
GoToRecord	Object Type		Leave this argument blank to work on the open form.
	Object Name		Leave this argument blank.
	Record	New	Creates a new record.
	Offset		Leave this setting blank.
SetValue	Item	[Forms]![Phonebook]![FirstName]	Refers to FirstName field on Phonebook form.
	Expression	[Forms]![Employees1]![Firstname]	Refers to FirstName field on Employees1 form.
SetValue	Item	[Forms]![Phonebook]![LastName]	Refers to LastName field on Phonebook form.
	Expression	[Forms]![Employees1]![Lastname]	Refers to LastName field on Employees1 form.

Print Letters and Flag the Action

When you have to send letters to customers, perhaps regarding a special discount offer, you might want to make note of the action in your Customer table. This macro assumes that the open database has a table named Customers with a date type field called Letter Sent. The macro prints letters using a report called Discount Letter. This report is based on a query that selects Customer records where the Letter Sent field is blank. Then an Update query is run that marks the Letter Sent field with today's date for all Customer records where that field is currently blank.

The dates in the Letter Sent field can be erased using an Update query. Enter Null for the Update To value along with any criteria needed to select the records to be changed. See Skill 8 for details.

SKILL
14

Macro Action	Action Arguments	Value for Argument	Comments
OpenReport	Report Name	Discount Letters	Opens a report called Discount Letters.
	View	Print	Leave this argument unchanged.
	Filter Name		Leave this argument blank. Assumes that the report is based on a query that selects desired records.
	Where Condition		Leave this argument blank.
OpenQuery	Query Name	MarkDateSent	Runs an Update query that looks for all records where the Letter Sent field is blank and fills that field with today's date using the Date() function.
	View	Datasheet	Leave this argument unchanged.
	Data Mode	Edit	Leave this argument unchanged.

Print the Results of an Ad Hoc Filter

This macro lets you print the records selected by an ad hoc filter with a custom report design. The trick to making this work is to use the macro to perform these actions:

- Save the current filter to a query called Query1.

- Open a report that's based on the query called Query1.

For this to work, you have to already have a report designed that looks for a query called Query1 that has the same fields as the table being filtered. The best way to do this is to create a filter for the table in question and save it as Query1. Then go ahead and design the report using this query. In this example, the report used to print the filtered records is called FoundRecords. The macro can be run by clicking a button on the form being viewed, or by choosing Macro ➤ Run Macro from the Tools menu while viewing the form.

Macro Action	Action Arguments	Value for Argument	Comments
RunCommand	Command	AdvancedFilterSort	Opens the Advanced Filter/Sort window for the form being viewed. It assumes that the user has already formulated the desired filter, has returned to the Form View window, and is viewing the filtered records.
SendKeys	Keystrokes	Query1{Enter}y	Sends these key-strokes to Access.
RunCommand	Command	SaveAsQuery	Performs this action and uses the key-strokes sent in the last action to save the filter as a query called Query1.
Close	Object Type		Closes the filter win-dow. Leave this argu-ment blank.
	Object Name		Leave this argument blank.

Macro Action	Action Arguments	Value for Argument	Comments
	Save		Leave this argument blank.
OpenReport	Report Name	Found Records	Opens a report called Found Records. This report is based on a query called Query1, so it reports on the records found by the filter saved by the last RunCommand action.
	View	Print	Sends report to printer.
	Filter Name		Leave this argument blank.
	Where Condition		Leave this setting blank.

SKILL
14

Are You Experienced?

Now you can...

☑ **Understand command button and macro basics**

☑ **Use the Command Button Wizard**

☑ **Add a command button to a form yourself**

☑ **Customize a command button**

☑ **Create a macro**

☑ **Use conditions in a macro**

☑ **Organize macros in groups**

☑ **Tie a macro to a command button**

☑ **Run a macro when an event occurs**

Create an Application

- → Analyze your work flow
- → Create custom switchboards
- → Provide paths through your database
- → Make a database friendly with startup options
- → Use an Autoexec macro

This skill shows you how to take a database and turn it into an *application*. There are two big differences between a basic database and an application:

- Tasks that you do on your own using a basic database (such as running a query and printing the results) are automated as much as possible in an application.

- An application has a custom interface that makes it easier for someone to use a database.

It used to be that only programmers could create bona fide database applications. This is no longer true. Access tools make it possible for a person to create a fairly complex application without doing any programming at all.

NOTE NOTE NOTE NOTE NOTE NOTE NOTE NOTE NOTE NOTE NOTE NOTE NOTE NOTE NOTE

If your project involves complex tasks that need to be automated, you may need to use Visual Basic to create part or all of the application. See the *Access 2000 Developer's Handbook* or the *Access 2000 VBA Handbook*, both from Sybex (summer 1999), to learn about Access programming.

Analyze Your Work Flow

Analyzing the way you work in a database is a good place to begin when you're creating an application. You should think about:

- How your tasks are related

- Which jobs you do repetitively

The next sections look at each of these in a little more detail before moving on to the work of creating an interface and automating tasks.

List Your Tasks

The easiest way to get started is to jot down a list of the main tasks for your application. Looking at the Timekeeper database you've worked with for most of the examples in this book, you can make a list with these jobs:

- Each person enters their weekly time records.

- The manager reviews the records weekly.

- The manager prints reports, including a weekly summary of hours worked by project, and monthly charts of the hours worked by each employee by week.

- The department coordinator occasionally updates the employee list and prints contact information for departmental use.

Decide on Your Main Switchboard Items

After you have a list of the basic database jobs, decide on categories for them. The purpose of this is to help you decide which command buttons you need on the main switchboard for your application. (Switchboards were introduced in Skill 1. You might want to quickly review that topic if you don't remember what switchboards do.) For the Timekeeper application, you can use these categories:

- Weekly Records

- Print Reports

- Update Employees

You can always add other categories to the list later as you go through the planning process.

See How Tasks Are Related

The next job is to review each task on the main list to see if it depends on other tasks. For example, the Timekeeper database has lookup tables for Employees and Projects. These tables need to have current information before weekly time records can be entered. Because of this, we should add a command button for updating projects to the main switchboard.

Also, consider how you work:

- Do you want to print reports from a switchboard, or does it make more sense to generate reports right from forms?

- Do you prefer to finish one task at a time, or do you need to jump freely between various database objects, other programs, and even the Web while you are working?

SKILL 15

- Will other people using the database be familiar with Access? If not, you might want to include command buttons for tasks such as adding records, finding records, and closing windows for form views.

After you consider these questions, make a list of the hyperlinks or command buttons you will need for each form in your database.

A flow chart works nicely to document database tasks, but you can also use simple lists if that's more comfortable for you. Table 15.1 shows the main tasks for the Timekeeper database (the ones that will appear on the main switchboard) along with a list of the hyperlinks and command buttons for each form opened from the switchboard.

TABLE 15.1: Switchboards, Command Buttons, and Hyperlinks for the Timekeeper Application

Main Switch-board Item	Click to...	Form Includes Command Buttons to...	And Hyperlinks to Jump to...
Weekly Records	Open Weekly Records form (for entering, editing, and reviewing data)	Print form being viewed; Find a record; Switch to Word; Switch to specific employee record	Employees form Projects form
Reports	Open Reports switchboard	Open individual reports	
Update Employees	Open Employees form	Print bonus letter; Print phone list	Projects table
Update Projects	Open Projects form		Employees form
Exit	Close database		

TIP TIP TIP TIP TIP TIP TIP TIP TIP TIP TIP TIP TIP TIP TIP TIP TIP TIP TIP TIP TIP TIP TIP

If you are creating an application for other people to use, be sure to ask them questions about how they work before you begin. Organizing switchboards with the work flow in mind makes the difference between an application that's a boondoggle and one that's a time-saver.

List the Jobs You Do Over and Over

List any repetitive tasks for your database to see where you can set up hyperlinks, command buttons, or macros to save time. Obvious candidates for automation are jobs such as printing reports that need to be generated regularly. With a little thought, you'll probably find other jobs that could be speeded up with a command button, a hyperlink, or a macro. Perhaps you switch to Word or Excel frequently while you are working in Access. Or you may print a group of reports and record when this was done. Add each of these repetitive jobs to the plan for your database switchboards and forms.

Create Custom Switchboards

With your application planned, you are ready to start creating *switchboards*. A switchboard is simply a form with command buttons that open other switchboards or do tasks such as open forms or print reports. The great thing is that you don't have to create switchboards on your own. You can use the Switchboard Manager to set them up and change them as your application evolves.

Start the Switchboard Manager

To start the Switchboard Manager:

1. Choose Tools ➤ Database Utilities ➤ Switchboard Manager.

2. If you see a dialog box that asks if you want to create a switchboard, choose Yes. You'll see this dialog box:

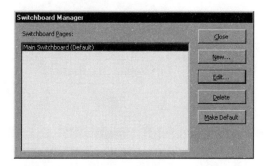

Switchboard Pages

Each separate switchboard in an application is called a *switchboard page*. When you choose Yes to create a switchboard in step 2 of the previous example, the Switchboard Manager adds a page called Main Switchboard (Default) to its window. If you want to look at this switchboard before adding any command buttons to it, follow these steps:

1. Close the Switchboard Manager, if it's open.

2. In the Database window, click the Forms tab.

3. Select the form called Switchboard and click Open, or simply double-click the form.

Figure 15.1 shows the empty Main Switchboard created by the Switchboard Manager for the Timekeeper database. When you're finished looking at the switchboard, close it and start the Switchboard Manager again to add items to it.

FIGURE 15.1: A form called Switchboard created by the Switchboard Manager for the Timekeeper database

NOTE NOTE NOTE NOTE NOTE NOTE NOTE NOTE NOTE NOTE NOTE NOTE NOTE NOTE NOTE

The background you see on a switchboard depends on the Form Template you specified in the Options dialog box. If there is no form template, you'll see a plain background like the one in Figure 15.1. You can add a graphic to a switchboard as described later in this skill.

Add Items to the Main Switchboard

Add some items to the Main Switchboard for the Timekeeper database by following these steps:

1. In the Switchboard Manager window, select Main Switchboard, if you have more than one switchboard page defined.

2. Click Edit to open this dialog box:

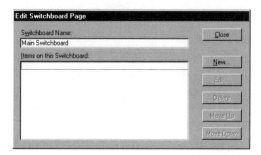

3. To add an item, click New. You'll see this Edit Switchboard Item dialog box:

4. Type **Weekly Records** as the name for the new item in the Text box.

5. Change the setting for Command to Open Form In Edit Mode.

6. Choose the Weekly Records form (or whatever form you created that shows information from the Weekly Records table and related records from Project Hours).

7. Click OK to return to the previous dialog box.

8. Repeat steps 3 through 7 for the switchboard items listed in Table 15.2, except the Reports item, using the commands and arguments noted in the table. (You have to create a Reports switchboard before you can add its item. The next section describes how to do this.)

9. In the Edit Switchboard Page dialog box, click Close.

**SKILL
15**

TABLE 15.2: Main Switchboard Items and Commands for the Timekeeper Database

Switchboard Item	Command	Type of Argument	Argument
Weekly Records	Open Form in Edit Mode	Form	Weekly Records
Reports*	Go to Switchboard	Switchboard	Reports
Update Employees	Open Form in Edit Mode	Form	Employees
Update Projects	Open Form in Edit Mode	Form	Projects
Exit	Exit Application		

*Add this item after the Reports switchboard page is created.

Add a New Switchboard Page

For the Timekeeper switchboard, you need to add another page called Reports.
To do this:

1. In the Switchboard Manager window, click New:

2. In the Create New dialog box, enter **Reports** for the Switchboard Page
    Name.

3. Click OK.

To add items to the new switchboard:

1. In the Switchboard Manager window, click the name of the new switch-
    board and choose Edit.

2. To add an item, click New.

3. Type the name for the new item in the Text box.

4. Use the drop-down list for Command to select the action for the item.

5. Select any arguments that may be needed for the command you chose in the
    last step.

6. Click OK to return to the previous dialog box.

7. Repeat steps 3 through 7 for each item you want to include on the new switchboard.

8. In the Edit Switchboard Page dialog box, click Close.

Rearrange Switchboard Items

You can move the items on a switchboard around after they are created. First, select the switchboard page you want to change in the Switchboard Manager window and click Edit. Then:

- To move an item up on the Items On This Switchboard list, select the item and click Move Up until it is in the desired position.

- To move an item down, select the item and click Move Down as needed.

When you're finished moving items, click Close to return to the main Switchboard Manager window.

Leave the Switchboard Manager

To leave the Switchboard Manager, click Close in its window.

Add a Graphic to a Main Switchboard

When you create a switchboard, it will have the same background behind the items as your default Form Template. (See Skill 6 for details on changing the form template that Access uses when you create new forms.) The left side of the Main Switchboard has an empty Image object that you can display a graphic in by following these steps:

1. In the Database window, click the Forms button.

2. Highlight the Switchboard form and click Design.

3. Click the left side of the window to select the Image object as shown in Figure 15.2. You'll see Picture displayed in the Object drop-down list on the Formatting (Form/Report) toolbar.

4. Click Properties on the Form Design toolbar.

5. Click the Format tab.

SKILL 15

6. On the Picture line, enter the name of a graphic file or click the ellipse (…) to open the Insert Picture dialog box.

7. If you need to resize the image object, drag its handles to do so. You may also want to resize the gray box that runs along the right side of the image object.

When you switch to Form View, you'll see the picture on the left side of the Main Switchboard as shown in Figure 15.3. The picture in the figure was taken from the file `C:\Program Files\Microsoft Office\Office\bitmaps\dbwiz\timebill.gif`. In Form Design view, you can drag the borders of the Image object or change its properties to alter the way the picture is displayed.

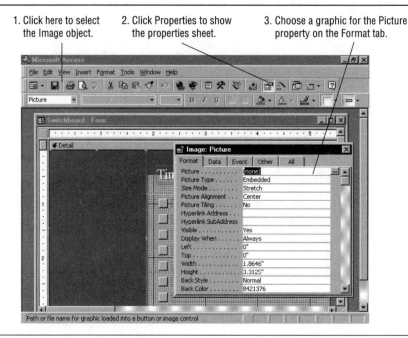

FIGURE 15.2: You can add a picture to an empty Image object in the Main Switchboard.

TIP TIP TIP TIP TIP TIP TIP TIP TIP TIP TIP TIP TIP TIP TIP TIP TIP TIP TIP TIP TIP TIP TIP TIP

You might find a picture you like in `C:\ProgramFiles\Microsoft Office\Office\Tutorial` **or** `C:\Program Files\Microsoft Office\Office\bitmaps\dbwiz`**. The latter folder has the graphics used for the switchboards created by the Database Wizard.**

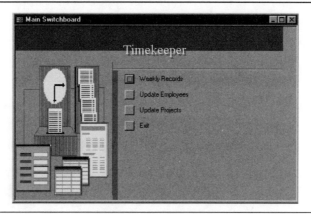

FIGURE 15.3: A picture called `timebill.gif` from `C:\Program Files\Microsoft Office\Office\bitmaps\dbwiz` has been added to this Main Switchboard.

Provide Paths through Your Database

As you just saw, switchboards are a nice way to put a "front end" on a database to make it easier to navigate from one object to another. However, there's another level of navigation to think about: how you want to move around when you're already in Form view. You can use hyperlinks and command buttons to switch tasks without returning to the Database window first.

Add a Hyperlink to a Form

In Skill 4, you saw how to use hyperlinks in Datasheet view. You can also include hyperlinks on a form to jump to other database objects, programs, network files, or Web sites. To add a hyperlink to a form:

1. Open the form in Design view.

2. Click the Insert Hyperlink button on the Form Design toolbar.

3. Enter a hyperlink address in the Insert Hyperlink dialog box as described in Skill 4 and click OK. (To jump to an object in the open database, click the button for Object In This Database on the left side of the Insert Hyperlink dialog box. Then use the expand buttons to select the object you want to jump to.)

4. Drag the hyperlink that appears in the upper-left corner of the Form Design view window to the place it should be.

Switch to Form view if you want to test the new hyperlink. Figure 15.4 shows the Employees form with a hyperlink in the upper-right corner that jumps to a Datasheet view for the Projects table.

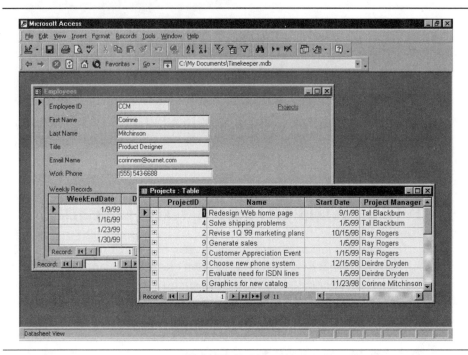

FIGURE 15.4: The hyperlink in the upper-right corner of the Employees form jumps to a Datasheet view for the Projects table.

NOTE NOTE NOTE NOTE NOTE NOTE NOTE NOTE NOTE NOTE NOTE NOTE NOTE NOTE NOTE
Command buttons are covered in Skill 14. Please refer to that skill for detailed instructions on adding command buttons to forms.

Make a Database Friendly with Startup Options

Access has a Startup dialog box you can use to change what happens when a database opens. Choose Tools ➤ Startup to open this dialog box:

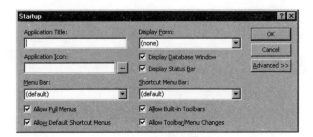

Show an Opening Form or Switchboard

If you want Access to automatically show a form when a database opens, choose that form from the drop-down menu for Display Form. To open a switchboard you've created, simply select the form called Switchboard.

Hide the Database Window

Uncheck Display Database Window to hide the Database window automatically when a database opens. You can always choose Window ➤ Unhide to show the Database window if you need it.

NOTE NOTE NOTE NOTE NOTE NOTE NOTE NOTE NOTE NOTE NOTE NOTE NOTE NOTE NOTE

For information on other options in the Startup dialog box, click the Question Mark button in the upper-right corner of the window and point to whatever option you have a question about.

Use an Autoexec Macro

Using a macro called *Autoexec* is another way to change what happens when a database opens. Simply follow the instructions for creating a macro outlined in Skill 14 and name the macro Autoexec when you're done. Figure 15.5 shows an Autoexec macro that minimizes the Database window and then opens the Switchboard form.

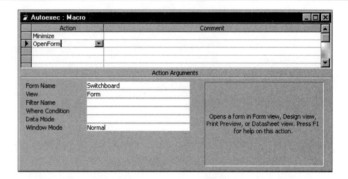

FIGURE 15.5: This Autoexec macro minimizes the Database window and opens the Switchboard form when the database it belongs to opens.

WARNING WARNING WARNING WARNING WARNING WARNING WARNING WARNING

If there is an Autoexec macro in a database, Access runs the macro after it applies any options set in the Startup dialog box. Be careful not to include commands in an Autoexec macro that conflict with Startup options.

Are You Experienced?

Now you can...

- ☑ **Analyze your work flow**
- ☑ **Create custom switchboards**
- ☑ **Provide paths through your database**
- ☑ **Customize a database's startup options**
- ☑ **Use an Autoexec macro**

Customize Access

- → **Change general database properties**
- → **Change the default table design properties**
- → **Personalize Datasheet views**
- → **Change the default Find/Replace behavior**
- → **Turn confirmation messages on/off**
- → **Customize menus and toolbars**

Earlier in this book, you saw how to create custom forms and reports to present data in a unique way. Access also lets you customize Datasheet views, menus, and toolbars, as well as the way Access works in some situations. This skill shows you how to do all these things so that you end up with a work environment that suits your own preferences.

NOTE NOTE NOTE NOTE NOTE NOTE NOTE NOTE NOTE NOTE NOTE NOTE NOTE NOTE NOTE

When you can create a new form or report with Design view, Access uses the Normal form or report templates. You can use your own templates, instead, to change the background and other characteristics of new forms and reports. To find out how to create a template and put it to use, see Skill 6.

The Options Dialog Box

You can change many of the default characteristics of how Access works in the Options dialog box. To do so:

1. Choose Tools ➤ Options from the menu to open the Options dialog box:

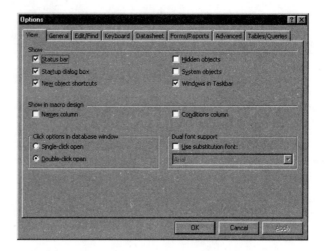

2. Click the tab for the type of option you want to change.

Because many settings in the Options dialog box are self-explanatory, this chapter won't discuss each tab in detail. Instead, only some of the options you may be likely to change will be described.

Change General Database Properties

You use the General tab of the Options dialog box to set your preferences for:

- Print margins

- Name AutoCorrect options

- A database's sort order

- The folder where Access looks for databases and saves them by default

- The size of the Recently Used File list that appears at the bottom of the File menu

- Whether sound should be used

- Whether Access should compact a database when it is closed

The Default Database Folder

To change the default database folder:

1. Click the General tab in the Options dialog box:

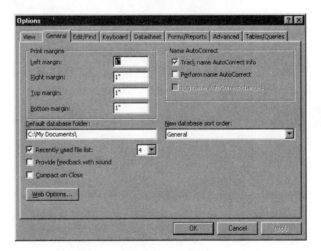

2. Enter the name of the folder you want to use in the text box under Default Database Folder.

3. Click OK to close the Options dialog box if you don't need to make any other changes.

The Default Open Mode

When Access opens a database on a shared drive, by default it lets other people open the same file. You can change this so that only one person at a time can open a database. To do so:

1. Click the Advanced tab in the Options dialog box:

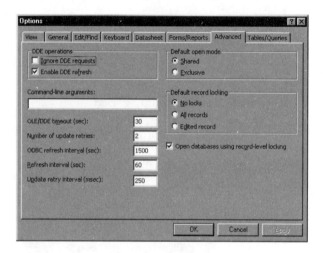

2. Change the Default Open Mode to Exclusive.

3. Click OK if you don't need to change any other options.

Change Table Design Properties

When you're working with a table in Design view, you may find yourself frequently changing the default field size for Text fields to a smaller value. Or you may need to use a field type other than Text as the default. To change the defaults that Access uses in the Table Design view window:

1. Click the Tables/Queries tab in the Options dialog box, as shown on the next page.

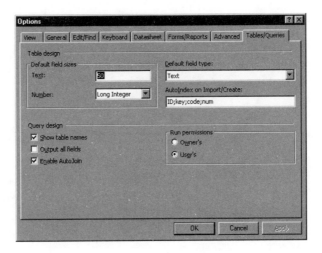

2. Change the settings under Default Field Sizes for Text and Number and for the Default Field Type, if you need to.

3. Click OK if you're done changing Options.

Personalize Datasheet Views

When you open a table in Datasheet view, Access usually displays the table with properties like the ones in Figure 16.1.

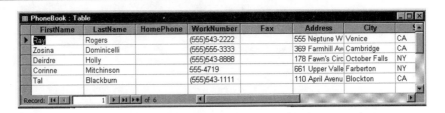

FIGURE 16.1: A table with the default properties for a Datasheet view

You can change the colors, font type and style, gridlines, column width, and cell effects in the Options dialog box. To do so:

1. Click the Datasheet tab in the Options dialog box, as shown on the following page.

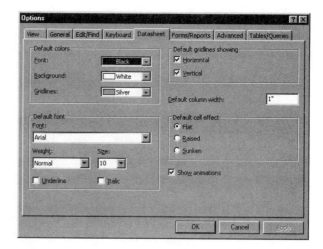

2. Change the settings for Default Colors, Default Font, Default Gridlines Showing, Default Column Width, and Default Cell Effect however you like.

3. Click OK if you're done changing Options.

Figure 16.2 shows a table opened in Datasheet view after the default Datasheet properties were changed.

FIGURE 16.2: This table was opened in Datasheet view after the default Datasheet properties were changed in the Options dialog box.

Change the Find/Replace Behavior

The Find And Replace dialog box has settings that say whether Access should search all the fields in a table or only the current field. Another setting tells Access to look for matches of entire or partial field values. You can change these default settings in the Options dialog box:

1. Click the Edit/Find tab in the Options dialog box:

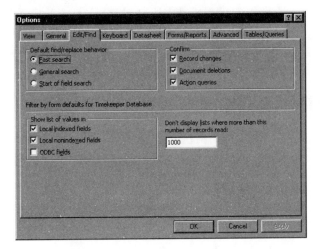

2. Under Default Find/Replace Behavior, select one of the search options. These options are described in Table 16.1.

3. Click OK if you're done changing Options.

TABLE 16.1: How the Default Search Options Work

This Option...	Searches...	And Matches...
Fast Search	The current field only	The entire field value
General Search	All fields in the table	Any part of the field value
Start of Field Search	The current field only	The beginning of the field value

Turn Confirmation Messages On/Off

Access usually asks you to confirm whether you really want to delete records or database objects, or whether you want to run action queries that delete, append, or update records. You can turn these messages off in the Options dialog box:

1. Click the Edit/Find tab in the Options dialog box.

2. Uncheck the boxes for Record Changes (deleting records), Document Deletions (deleting database objects), and Action Queries (Append, Delete, and Update queries) under Confirm as you need to.

3. Click OK if you're done changing Options.

Customize Menus and Toolbars

Access comes with built-in menus and toolbars that change depending on the task you are doing. You are free to customize these menus and toolbars and even create your own. Each menu and toolbar also has its own properties that determine whether it can be moved, resized, customized, docked, or hidden.

The Customize dialog box is the place you work with menus and toolbars. There are two different ways to open this tool:

-   Right-click any toolbar and choose Customize.

-   Choose View ➤ Toolbars ➤ Customize from the menu.

You'll see a Customize dialog box that looks like this:

In the Customize dialog box and the instructions that follow, "toolbars" refers to both toolbars and menus, unless otherwise noted.

Change a Toolbar

With the Customize dialog box open, you can drag tools from the Commands tab to any visible toolbar, or you can drag tools off a toolbar. Follow these steps to change a toolbar or a menu:

1. Open the Customize dialog box as described earlier.

2. Drag the dialog box down a bit if you want to work with more than one toolbar at the same time, or drag the toolbars so that they aren't obscured by the dialog box.

3. On the Toolbars tab, click (check) the check boxes for any toolbars you want to customize. You'll find choices for Menu and Shortcut Menus at the end of the Toolbars list.

Add a Tool to a Toolbar

Once a toolbar is visible and the Customize dialog box is open, you are free to add tools to it. Here's how to do this:

1. Click the Commands tab in the Customize dialog box:

2. On the Categories list, click the type of command you want to add.

3. Scroll through the Commands list on the same tab until the tool you want to add is in view.

4. Drag the tool from the Customize dialog box to the desired toolbar.

5. When you're finished making changes to the toolbars, click Close.

Remove a Tool from a Toolbar

To delete a tool from a toolbar, simply drag it off the toolbar when the Customize dialog box is open. Be careful not to drop it onto another menu or toolbar, though. If you do, the tool will be added to the toolbar it lands on.

Reset a Toolbar

After you alter a toolbar, you can return it to its original state. To do so:

1. Open the Customize dialog box.

2. On the Toolbars list in the Toolbars tab, click the toolbar you want to reset to highlight it.

3. Click Reset and choose OK when asked whether you really want to reset your changes.

Create a Toolbar

If you want to create your own toolbar or menu:

1. Open the Customize dialog box.

2. Click the Toolbars tab.

3. Click New. You will see this dialog box:

4. In the New Toolbar dialog box, enter a name for the new toolbar and choose OK.

The new toolbar is added to the Access window, usually next to the Customize dialog box. You may have to look hard for it. It will be small since there are no tools on it yet. Figure 16.3 shows a new toolbar called My Buttons. You can only see part of its title, My…, because the toolbar is so small.

TIP TIP TIP TIP TIP TIP TIP TIP TIP TIP TIP TIP TIP TIP TIP TIP TIP TIP TIP TIP TIP TIP TIP TIP

If for some reason a new toolbar isn't visible, click it on the Toolbars list in the Customize dialog box to uncheck it. Then check it again. It should come into view near the Customize dialog box. You can drag a toolbar to a new place where it can't be obscured by the Customize dialog box, or you can dock it like any built-in toolbar.

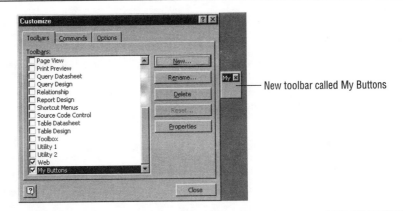

New toolbar called My Buttons

FIGURE 16.3: A new toolbar called My Buttons shown next to the Customize dialog box

Add Tools to a New Toolbar

To add tools to a custom toolbar, see the instructions in "Add a Tool to a Toolbar" earlier in this skill. The custom toolbar, My Buttons, is shown here with tools added for Save, Print, Print Preview, Save As, and Export:

NOTE NOTE NOTE NOTE NOTE NOTE NOTE NOTE NOTE NOTE NOTE NOTE NOTE NOTE
The last two tools on the My Buttons toolbar are shown as text rather than as icons. See "Change a Tool's Properties" later in this skill to see how you can change how a tool appears. You can choose a different picture for a button, edit the picture already on it, or switch text to an image and vice-versa.

Delete or Rename a Toolbar

You can delete or rename any of the toolbars you create yourself. (These options are dimmed in the Customize dialog box when one of the built-in toolbars is selected.) To delete or rename a toolbar:

1. Open the Customize dialog box.

2. On the Toolbars list in the Toolbars tab, click the toolbar you want to delete or rename.

3. Click Delete or Rename, depending on what you want to do.

4. If you are renaming a toolbar, enter the new name and click OK. If you chose delete, just click OK.

Change a Toolbar's Properties

Each menu and toolbar has its own properties that determine whether it can be moved, resized, customized, docked, or hidden. To change these properties:

1. Open the Customize dialog box.

2. Click the Toolbars tab.

3. Select the toolbar you want to change.

4. Click Properties. The following dialog box will open:

5. Change the properties as you like.

6. Click Close when you are finished with your changes.

Some of the properties for built-in toolbars can't be changed. The Toolbar Name, Type, and Show On Toolbars Menu options fall into this category, so they are dimmed in the Toolbar Properties dialog box for all built-in toolbars.

Create a Shortcut Menu

You can create your own shortcut menus and attach them to forms, reports, or controls. (Use the Office Assistant to search for help on "shortcut menus." Then click the topic called *Attach a shortcut menu to a form, form control, or report*.)

To create a shortcut menu, first create a new toolbar. Then:

1. Open the Toolbar Properties dialog box for the new toolbar as described in the last section.

2. Change the setting for Type to Popup.

3. Click OK after you read the instructions.

4. Select Close.

5. Back in the Customize dialog box, select (check) Shortcut Menus on the Toolbars list. Access displays a Shortcut Menus toolbar with a choice called Custom:

6. Click Custom to show a list of custom shortcut menus.

7. Select the shortcut menu you want to work with.

8. Add tools to the shortcut menu as described earlier.

9. Close the Shortcut Menus toolbar.

10. Click Close in the Customize dialog box if you are finished working with toolbars and menus.

Change a Tool's Properties

Each tool has its own properties you can use to change how it appears on a tool-bar or menu. To customize a tool:

1. Open the Customize dialog box.

2. Click the Toolbars tab and check the toolbar the tool appears on, if it's not already visible.

3. Right-click the tool you want to change to open a shortcut menu like this:

Use this shortcut menu like any other shortcut menu in Access. When you click a choice followed by an ellipse (…), another dialog box opens. For other options, just click them to select them. You'll have to right-click to open the shortcut menu again for each change you want to make to a tool.

Change the Image on a Button

If you want to change the image that appears on a button, right-click the button and choose Change Button Image from the shortcut menu. You'll see a palette of pictures like this:

Just click the picture you want to show on the button.

Edit the Image on a Button

You can also edit the image that's shown on a button using the Button Editor:

1. Right-click the button whose picture you want to change.

2. Choose Edit Button Image from the shortcut button to open the Button Editor:

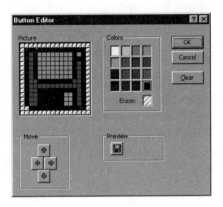

3. You edit a picture by changing the colors of the various squares. To change part of the image, click a shade under Color. Then click the square you want to recolor.

4. Repeat step 3 until you have changed the colors of all squares necessary to end up with the picture you want.

5. Click OK to save your changes.

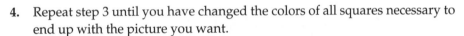

If you want to undo your changes to a button's image, choose Reset Button Image from the button's shortcut menu.

Show an Image Instead of Text on a Button

Some buttons, like the Save As and Export tools added to the custom toolbar shown in the section "Add Tools to a New Toolbar," appear as text instead of pictures. To change a button like this so it displays a picture instead of text:

1. With the Customize dialog box open, right-click the button you want to change.

2. Click Default Style. The button will appear as a blank image.

3. Right-click the tool again and select Change Button Image.

4. Click an image on the palette.

   In Figure 16.4, the Export button was changed to appear as a diskette with an arrow instead of as text.

Export button shown as an image

FIGURE 16.4: The Export button on this custom toolbar was customized to show an image of a diskette instead of text.

Close the Customize Dialog Box

When you're finished working with the Customize dialog box, click Close. Any toolbars shown in the Access window will return to their normal mode of operation. If you need to make further changes to them, open the Customize dialog box again.

Are You Experienced?

Now you can...

- ☑ **Change general database properties**
- ☑ **Change the default table design properties**
- ☑ **Personalize Datasheet views**
- ☑ **Change the Find/Replace behavior**
- ☑ **Turn confirmation messages on/off**
- ☑ **Customize menus and toolbars**

APPENDIX A

More Features for Power Users

This book is meant to familiarize you with all the basics you need to know to create a fully functioning Access 2000 database. It doesn't cover every option in every dialog box, or all the tools in the program. Because Access is a database for people with a wide range of experience, from beginners to programmers, it has a broad base of features that would be impossible to describe in a book this size.

As you become more expert with Access, you may want to experiment with some of the additional features listed in Table A.1 to see if they can help you with your work. For instructions on how to use them, check the Microsoft Access Help system.

Projects are another feature of Access 2000 that are not covered in detail in this book. Projects are special purpose databases that are designed to work with data that's stored on a SQL server. Project basics and how to create projects are briefly explained in the early skills of this book, as well as in Appendix B. If you want to learn more about working with projects, see *Mastering Access 2000*, published by Sybex (1999). Or, check one of the books on Microsoft SQL Server that are available from Sybex for more information on creating SQL Server databases.

TABLE A.1: Access 2000 Features Not Covered in This Book

This Feature...	Found on This Menu...	Helps You...
Security	Tools ➤ Security	Protect database objects with passwords, set up user and group accounts, assign rights to users and groups, and encrypt or decrypt a database.
Table Analyzer	Tools ➤ Analyze ➤ Table	Check the structure of a table to see if it duplicates data. If so, it can help you split the table into related tables.
Database Splitter	Tools ➤ Database Utilities ➤ Database Splitter	Separate a database into two databases: one with tables and one with other database objects.
Linked Table Manager	Tools ➤ Database Utilities ➤ Linked Table Manager	View or refresh the paths to linked objects.
Add-Ins Manager	Tools ➤ Add-Ins ➤ Add-In Manager	Install or uninstall add-ins. Add-ins are Visual Basic programs like the Microsoft Access wizards.
Replication	Tools ➤ Replication	Create replicas of a database, synchronize a database and its replicas, and resolve replication conflicts.

APPENDIX B

Working with Projects

*P*rojects are a new feature of Access 2000 that let you use Access as a front-end for a SQL Server database. With older versions of Access, you could link tables on a SQL server to an Access database and work with them like any other Access table. Projects are different from Access databases, because they connect directly to SQL Server data and include tools for creating client/server applications. Creating client/server applications is beyond the scope of this book, but this appendix offers some introductory information about projects and how they work.

An Access project can work with data on these SQL servers:

- The integrated store that's part of Access 2000

- SQL Server 6.5

- SQL Server 7

NOTE NOTE NOTE NOTE NOTE NOTE NOTE NOTE NOTE NOTE NOTE NOTE NOTE NOTE NOTE

If the data you'll be working with resides on a SQL server, you may still want to use an Access database (.mdb file) instead of an Access project (.adp file) for your application. A project has special tools for people who are familiar with working with client/server applications. If you prefer to use the tools that are available for Access databases, use a database instead and link the SQL Server data to it.

Elements of an Access Project

Many of the elements of an Access project are the same as those for an Access database. For example, a project can have forms, reports, pages, macros, and modules. However, a project has no queries. Instead it has *views*, *stored procedures*, and *database diagrams*. If you look at the database window for the Access 2000 sample NorthwindCS project (discussed in the following section) shown in Figure B.1, you'll see these buttons on the Objects bar:

Tables   Use this button to show the SQL Server tables the project is connected to.

Views   Click this button to list any views that are part of the project. Like queries, views can show records from related tables, find selected information, and perform calculations.

B

Database Diagrams   Use this button to shows the project's database diagrams. Database diagrams show the relationships between SQL Server tables.

Stored Procedures   Click this button to list the stored procedures in a project. Stored procedures are similar to views in that you can use them to show related data, find data, and do calculations.

Forms   Use this button to show the forms in a project. Forms are for viewing and editing information, just as with databases.

Reports   Click this button to see the reports that are part of a project. Reports in projects work like those for databases; they let you preview or print data.

Pages   Click the Pages button to display any Web pages that are included in a project. Pages are HTML files that let you view project data with Internet Explorer 5.

Macros   Use this button to show a list of the macros in a project. Macros perform one or more database actions automatically.

Modules   Click the Modules button to see the modules that have been added to a project. Modules hold Visual Basic code used to automate or otherwise customize a project .

NOTE NOTE NOTE NOTE NOTE NOTE NOTE NOTE NOTE NOTE NOTE NOTE NOTE NOTE NOTE

Access includes special design tools for working with views, stored procedures, and database diagrams. If you want to learn more about working with these tools, open the Office Assistant while the sample Northwind project is open. Then search for help on "views," "stored procedures," or "database diagrams" and explore the topics that appear.

Using the Sample Northwind Project

Access 2000 includes a project version of its sample database, Northwind, that you can use to see how projects work. You don't need to have access to a SQL server to be able to experiment with this project. The tables for the project are created and accessed using the Microsoft Data Engine (MSDE). This program is part of Office 2000, and you can install it on your computer to work with SQL Server tables.

Before you can use the Northwind project (which is stored in a file called NorthwindCS.adp), you'll have to install the project and MSDE as outlined next.

Installing the Sample Northwind Project

If you want to install the Northwind project on your computer, follow these steps:

1. Insert your Office 2000 CD in your CD-ROM drive.

2. When the Setup program starts, click the button for Add Or Remove Features.

3. In the Update Features dialog box, click the expand button (+) for Microsoft Access For Windows.

4. Click the expand button for Sample Databases.

5. Under Sample Databases, change the setting for Northwind SQL Project File to Run From My Computer. (By default, the setting for this database is Not Available.)

6. Click the Update Now button.

7. Click OK when the Setup program finishes adding the database to your computer.

Installing the Microsoft Data Engine

The NorthwindCS project works with SQL Server tables that are available through Microsoft Data Engine (MSDE). If you try to open the project without MSDE running, you will not see any tables in the database window. First you need to install MSDE and start it as outlined here:

1. Close any programs you have running on your computer.

2. Insert your Office 2000 CD into your CD-ROM drive.

3. Double-click My Computer on your Windows Desktop.

4. Navigate to `D:\Sql\X86\Setup`.

5. Double-click the icon for `Setupsql.exe`.

6. Follow the prompts to complete the installation. You can accept the default settings in all the dialog boxes.

Starting the Microsoft Data Engine

You need to have the MSDE Service Manager running before you can open the Northwind project. Otherwise, the tables that are part of the project will not be available. To start the Service Manager:

1. Click the Start button and choose Programs Msde Service Manager. You'll see a dialog box like this:

2. Click the Start/Continue button to start the Service Manager.

3. At this point, you can minimize the SQL Server Service Manager window.

Opening the Northwind Project

Once the Northwind project is installed and the SQL Server Service Manager is running, you can open it like any other database:

1. Start Access and click Open on the toolbar.

2. In the Open dialog box, change the setting for the Look In box to C:\Program Files\Microsoft Office\Office\Samples.

3. After you switch to the Samples folder, a file called NorthwindCS.adp should appear in the Open dialog box. Select this file and click Open. You'll see a database window like the one shown in Figure B.1.

Creating the Project Tables

The first time you open the Northwind project (NorthwindCS.adp), you will have to create the SQL Server tables the project is connected to. To do this:

1. Under Objects in the NorthwindCS database window, click the Tables button.

FIGURE B.1: The database window for the sample `NorthwindCS.adp` project

2. You'll see an Install Database dialog box that asks if you would like to install the sample database. Click Yes to create the tables for the Northwind project.

3. When the Installation Successful dialog box opens, click OK.

The Northwind project includes tables for Categories, Customers, Employees, Order Details, Orders, Products, Shippers, and Suppliers.

NOTE NOTE NOTE NOTE NOTE NOTE NOTE NOTE NOTE NOTE NOTE NOTE NOTE NOTE NOTE
As noted earlier, you can find information on working with projects in Access Help. Use the Office Assistant to look for "projects" and explore the topics that appear.

This glossary contains common terms that you're likely to run into when you work with Access. Here you'll find short definitions, along with references to chapters where you can learn more about the topic.

Also remember that any time you see a word underlined with dots, in any Help screen, clicking that word will take you to a definition (or to a screen where you can make a more specific selection).

action

The basic building block of a macro. An action is a task the macro performs, such as opening a table or sounding a beep. You can assign actions to a macro by dragging and dropping an object from the database window to the macro window's Action column. Or you can click in the Action column and choose an action from the drop-down list (Skill 14).

action query

A type of query that takes an action on your data. This category includes Append, Delete, Make Table, and Update queries. Delete and Update queries change existing data; Append and Make Table queries copy existing data. See Skill 8; see also *select query*.

append

To add records from one table to the bottom of another table (Skill 8).

application

A program designed to do a specific job. Microsoft Access, Microsoft Word, and Microsoft Excel are all examples of Windows applications. An Access application is a database that's designed to do a specific job, such as manage orders, juggle names and addresses, manage accounts receivable—whatever. You can design switchboards, dialog boxes, and data entry forms to help people who know little about Access to use your application (Skill 15).

argument

The part of an action or expression that defines what to operate on. For example, in Sqr(81), Sqr() is a function (square root), and 81 is the argument (the value that Sqr() will operate upon) (Skills 14).

attach

See *link*, which is the new name for the Access 2.*x* Attach feature.

AutoNumber field

A field in a table that automatically numbers each new record entered into a table. Auto-Number fields can be incremental or random (Skill 3).

bitmap

A graphic image stored in bitmap (.bmp) format (Skills 4 and 6).

bound control

A control on an Access form or report that displays data from the underlying table (Skill 6).

Gloss

bound object frame

A control on an Access form or report that displays an OLE object stored within the underlying table (Skill 6).

bound OLE object

An OLE object that's stored in an Access table (Skills 4 and 6).

calculated control

A control on a form or report that gets its value by performing some calculation on data in the underlying table (Skill 9).

calculated field

A field in a query that computes a value based on data in the table. Access will refresh the value in a calculated field automatically, whenever you change values of fields used in the calculated field. You could, for example, define a query field with the expression [Quantity]*[UnitPrice] to calculate the extended price of an item (Skill 8).

case-sensitive

In a case-sensitive search, text must match uppercase and lowercase letters exactly. A non–case-sensitive search, by contrast, matches any combination of uppercase and lowercase text. When you ask Access to find or replace text values in a table, you can search with case-sensitive matching on or off (Skill 4).

cell

The intersection of a row and column in a datasheet or grid. Each cell in the datasheet stores a single piece of data (Skills 1, 2, and 4).

chart

A graphical representation of data in a form or report. Charts can summarize large amounts of data graphically and make the data easier to understand (Skill 10).

check box

A control that shows whether you've selected or cleared an option. A check mark (✓) appears in the box when you've selected it. Check boxes on forms enable you to assign a Yes or No value to Yes/No fields in a table (Skill 6). Some Windows dialog boxes also use check boxes to let you turn an option on or off.

Clipboard

A general storage area used by all Windows programs, mainly for copying and moving things from one place to another. For example, selecting an item and then pressing Ctrl+C copies that item to the Clipboard.

code

Instructions for the computer to follow, expressed in a written language such as Visual Basic. The act of creating programs is sometimes called "writing code" or "coding" (by people who do that sort of thing).

column

The visual presentation of a field in a Datasheet, Query, or filter window. A relational database stores data in tables that you can display in horizontal rows (records) and vertical columns (fields) (Skills 1 and 2).

combo box

A control that works like a combined text box and list box. Combo boxes on forms or data-sheets allow you to enter values into fields either by typing in the value or by selecting the value from a drop-down list. Some Windows dialog boxes also use combo boxes to let you choose options (Skill 6).

command bar

Another name for a toolbar, which can include toolbar buttons, menus, and shortcut menus.

command button

A control that opens a linked form, runs a macro, or calls a Visual Basic function. You simply click a command button on a form to open the linked form or start the macro or function. Command buttons work like the push buttons in many Windows dialog boxes and programs (Skill 14).

comparison operator

An operator that compares two values, such as > (greater than) and < (less than) (Skill 7).

control

An item on a form, data access page, report, or dialog box. Controls typically display data, provide decoration, or let the user make choices. For instance, a command button in a dialog box is a control (Skills 6, 9, and 14).

control menu

Activated by the tiny icon in the upper-left corner of a window, this standard Windows component lets you close, restore, and otherwise manipulate the window it controls. (For these jobs, however, many people prefer to use the Minimize, Maximize/Restore, and Close controls at the upper-right corner of a window, instead of the Control menu.)

Crosstab query

A query that computes summary totals based on values for each row and column. Crosstab queries answer questions such as what are my monthly sales by region, who has ordered each of my products, and how many items of each product did they order? (Skill 8).

current record

The record that currently holds the focus (see also *focus*).

data access page

An object that's used to browse data from Access or Internet Explorer 5. Data access pages, also referred to as pages, are stored in their own HTML files instead of in the database (.mdb file) or project (.adp file) they belong to (Skill 13).

data type

The kind of information that will be stored in a field, such as Text, Number, or Date/Time. You define data types in Table Design view (Skill 3).

database

A collection of all the objects—tables, queries, forms, data access pages, reports, macros, and modules—related to a particular topic or subject (Skill 1).

Database window

The container window that shows all database objects. This window often appears first when you open a database. Usually, you can display the Database window by pressing the F11 key (Skill 1).

Datasheet view (or datasheet)

The view that lets you see several records in a table or query result at a time, as opposed to Form view, which generally shows only one record (Skill 4).

DBMS

An abbreviation for *database management system*. Popular database management systems include dBASE, Paradox, and of course, Microsoft Access.

default

A setting that is assumed, and used, unless you change it. For example, the default margin on a report might be 1 inch.

Delete query

An action query that deletes whatever rows match criteria that you specify. Delete queries provide a fast, automatic way to delete a certain set of records from a table without disturbing other records that don't match the criteria (Skill 8).

delimited text file

A text file that contains values separated by commas, tabs, semicolons, or other characters. You can import delimited text files into new or existing Access tables (Skill 11).

Design view

The view that lets you create an object or change its appearance. Clicking an object name in the Database window and then clicking the Design button takes you to the Design view of that object (Skills 1, 6, 9, and 13).

detail section

The part of a form or report that displays records from your table or query. Also called the *detail band* (Skills 6 and 9).

developer (application developer)

A person who uses Access to create specialized, user-friendly applications for less-sophisticated computer users to work with (Skill 15).

dialog box

A window that lets you select options or provide more information so that Access can carry out a command. Many dialog boxes include an OK button (that continues the command) and a Cancel button (that cancels the command).

drop-down list

A control that allows you to choose a value from a list on a data access page.

duplicate key

A value that already exists in a table's primary key field or in an index field that does not allow duplicates. Access won't allow you to enter duplicate key values into a table (Skills 2 and 3).

dynaset

The result of running a query or filter, which shows only the set of records requested (Skill 7).

embed

What you do when you insert an object into a form or report. You can embed objects in these ways:

- Use drag-and-drop techniques (Skill 6).
- Use the Insert ➤ Object command (Skill 6).
- Use Copy and Paste options on the Edit menu (Skill 6).
- Use Insert ➤ Chart or the Chart Wizard toolbox button to embed a chart in a form or report (Skill 10).
- Use the PivotTable Wizard to embed a Microsoft Excel PivotTable into a Microsoft Access form.
- Add a PivotTable to a data access page (Skill 13).

equi-join

See *inner join*.

event

An action, taken by the user, that Access can recognize. For example, a mouse click is an event (Skill 14).

expression

A calculation that results in a single value. An expression can contain any combination of Access operators, object names (identifiers), literal values, and constants. You can use expressions to set properties and action arguments; to set criteria or define calculated fields in queries, forms, and reports; and to set conditions in macros. You also can use expressions in Visual Basic (Skills 6 and 9).

field

One column, representing a category of information, in a table. Also refers to a fill-in blank on a form (Skills 1, 2, and 3).

field list

A small window or drop-down list that shows all the fields in an underlying table or query. You can display field lists in tables, filters, forms, reports, data access pages, and queries (Skills 6, 7, 8, 9, and 13).

field name

The name that you assign to a field. A field name can have up to 64 characters (including letters, numbers, spaces, and some punctuation characters) and must be unique within the table (Skills 2 and 3).

field properties

Characteristics of a field in a table, as defined in the Table Design view (Skill 3).

filter

A "mini query" that isolates specific records by filtering out unwanted records (Skill 7).

focus

A general term for the insertion point, cursor, highlight, or whatever is indicating where your next action will take place. For example, if you click a person's name and the cursor jumps there, we say that the person's name "has the focus."

foreign key

When a one-to-many relationship exists between tables, the field that uniquely identifies each record on the "one side" of the relationship is called the *primary key*. The corresponding field in the table on the "many side" of the relationship is called the *foreign key* (Skill 2).

form properties

Properties assigned to an entire form, as opposed to a section or control on a form. To change form properties, you open the form in Design view, open the property sheet, choose Edit ➢ Select Form, and then choose your properties (Skill 6).

Form view

A way of viewing data in a table one record at a time, similar to a printed fill-in-the-blank form (Skills 5 and 6).

function

A procedure that returns a value. For example, in Sqr(81), Sqr() is the square-root function. (The expression returns 9, or the square root of 81.) For a list of built-in Access functions, search the Help Index for "References, Functions" (Skills 7 and 8).

group

In a secure network system, you can use groups to identify a collection of user accounts, each with its own group name and personal identification number (PID). Permissions assigned to a group apply to all users in that group.

In a report, you can sort records and organize them into groups based on field values or ranges of values. You also can display introductory and summary data for each group (Skill 9).

In a query, you can use groups to categorize data and perform summary calculations (Skill 8).

In a data access page, data can be shown as groups of records that can be expanded and collapsed (Chapter 13).

HTML

Hypertext Markup Language is used to tag files for publication on the World Wide Web. HTML has codes for referencing graphics and formatting text (Skill 11 and 13).

hyperlink

Text or a graphic associated with a hyperlink address which, when clicked, jumps to information in the same database, another database, another location on your computer or network, or on the Internet (Skills 3, 4, 15, and 16).

hyperlink address

The path to a database object, document, Web page, or other file. A hyperlink address may consist of the name of an object in the open database, a specific address in a file like a spreadsheet, a URL pointing to an Internet or intranet location, or a UNC network path pointing to a file on a local area network.

hyperlink base

A path name added to the beginning of all relative hyperlink addresses.

I-beam

Another name for *mouse pointer*. The I-beam appears when the mouse pointer is on some text. To position the cursor with your mouse, move the I-beam to where you want the cursor to appear and then click the left mouse button.

index

A feature that speeds up sorting and searching for data in a table. Access maintains each index in sorted order and keeps it in memory for quick retrieval. Primary key fields and certain other fields are indexed automatically. You can define additional index fields in Table Design view (Skills 2 and 3).

inner join

A join that combines records from two tables that have matching values in a common field. Suppose two tables—Customers and Orders— each have a CustomerID field. An inner join of these tables would match customers and the orders they placed. No information would appear about customers who haven't placed orders (Skill 3).

insertion point

The blinking vertical bar on the screen that indicates where any characters you type will appear. More generally referred to as the *cursor* or the *focus*.

join

A query operation that combines some or all records from multiple tables. Access supports three types of joins: *inner join, outer join,* and *self-join* (Skill 3).

key field

The field in a table that uniquely identifies each record in that table, such as a product code or SKU in a products list (Skills 2 and 3).

label

A control on a form or report that displays descriptive text, such as a title, caption, or instructions (Skills 6 and 9).

link (object)

A connection between a source document and destination document. A link inserts a copy of the object from the source document into the destination document, and the two documents remain connected. Thus changes to the linked object in the source document are also reflected in the destination document. Links provide a powerful and convenient way to share objects among Windows programs (Skill 4). You also can link main forms or reports with subforms and subreports so that the data on the subform/subreport is in sync with the corresponding data on the main form/main report (Skills 6 and 9).

link (table)

You can link tables from other database programs (Paradox, dBASE, FoxPro, and ODBC), from text files and spreadsheets, or from closed Access databases. The linked tables will appear in your open Database window. Depending on the file format, after linking tables, you can add, delete, and change their records, just as if you were using "native" Access tables (Skill 11).

list box

A control that displays a list of values to choose from. List boxes on forms or datasheets allow you to enter values into fields. Some Windows dialog boxes also use list boxes to allow you to choose options (Skill 6).

lookup field

A field that displays and stores values looked up from a field in another table or another part of a form. You can display a lookup field as a *combo box* or *list box* (Skills 3 and 6).

macro

A series of actions that can be played back with a single action (Skill 14).

Make-Table query

A query that creates a new table from the results (the dynaset) of a previous query. Make-Table queries are a handy way to create copies of tables that you want to edit, print, chart, or cross-tabulate. They're also helpful when you need to export data to a nonrelational program, such as a spreadsheet (Skill 8).

many-to-many relationship

A relationship in which many records in one table might refer to many records in another, and vice versa. A classic example is an Orders and Products relationship in which an order can include many products and each product can appear on many orders. Often we set up a third table as a go-between so that we end up with two one-to-many relationships. For

instance, if we use an Order Details table as the go-between, Orders would have a one-to-many relationship with Order Details and Order Details would have a one-to-many relationship with Products.

Memo field

A field that can store a large amount of text (Skill 4).

modal

Describes a form that keeps the focus until you explicitly close the form. Most dialog boxes are really modal forms.

module

An Access object that contains one or more custom procedures, each written in Visual Basic. A global module is one you create. A form or report module is one that Access creates automatically.

move handle

A square that appears at the top-left edge of a control when you draw or select it in form design or report design view. You can drag a move handle to move the control (Skill 6; see also *sizing handle*).

null

An object that has no value. An empty field (Skill 7).

null propagation

The tendency for a blank (as opposed to zero) numeric value to cause any calculations that rely on the calculation to be null (blank) as well.

object

Any element of a database system. Access recognizes these types of objects:

- Controls and database components, including tables, queries, forms, data access pages, reports, macros, and modules
- Special system objects used in Visual Basic programming
- Linked or embedded objects, such as a chart, drawing, spreadsheet cell, Pivot-Table, and table

ODBC

An acronym for *open database connectivity*, a standard created by Microsoft for allowing a single user to access many different databases (Skill 11).

Office Assistant

A Help tool opened by clicking the Office Assistant button on the toolbar. With this dialog box, you can type in a few words about whatever you want help with and get a list of related topics to view.

OLE

An acronym for *Object Linking and Embedding* (pronounced "olay"). A technique that allows multiple Windows programs (for example, Access, Excel, or Word) to share objects such as pictures, sounds, or charts (Skills 2 and 4).

OLE client

A program that can hold an object that was initially created by some other program (the *OLE server*) (Skill 4).

OLE server

A program that can "serve up" an object to an *OLE client*. For example, Paint can serve up pictures to put in your Access database. Sound Recorder can serve up sounds to put in your database (Skill 4).

one-to-many relationship

Describes a natural relationship between two types of information where for every single item on one side of the relationship, there may be many items on the other side. For example, any *one* customer might place *many* orders with a particular business (Skill 3).

one-to-one relationship

Describes a relationship between two tables in which each record in the first table can be associated with exactly one record in the second table. A one-to-one relationship usually suggests a poor database design (Skill 3).

operator

A character (or characters) used to perform an operation or comparison. For example, + is the operator used for addition (Skills 7 and 9).

option group

A control on a form that frames a set of check boxes, option buttons, or toggle buttons. You can use option groups to provide a limited set of alternative values to choose from (for example, Cash, Check, or Credit Card). The selected option will store a number in the underlying table field. Therefore, if you select the first button in an option group, Access will store the number 1 in the field; if you select the second button, Access stores 2; and so forth. You can use the stored number to make decisions in a macro or Visual Basic program (Skill 6).

page

Page can refer to several different things:

- The portion of the database (.mdb file) in which Access stores record data. Each page may contain more than one record, depending on the size of the records.

- A screen of data in a form or a page in a report (Skills 5, 6, and 9).

- A shorter way of referring to a data access page (Skill 13).

parameter query

A query that asks for specific information before doing its job (Skill 8).

PivotTable

A special type of Microsoft Excel worksheet that's embedded within an Access form or a data access page. Like Crosstab queries, Pivot-Tables let you quickly summarize large amounts of data in a tabular format. They're more flexible than Crosstab queries, though, because they let you rearrange rows and columns interactively and filter out unwanted data on the fly (Skill 13).

primary key

The field in a table that contains information unique to each record in that table. Your social security number is the primary key on the IRS's database; nobody else has the same social security number as you (Skills 2 and 3).

project

A collection of Access objects similar to a database (.mdb file) that is used to work with data stored on a SQL server. Projects are stored in .adp files. They don't include queries, but can include database diagrams, stored procedures, and views (Skill 1 and Appendix B).

property

A characteristic of an item. Typical properties include size, color, screen location, whether you can update a control, and whether a control is visible (Skills 6 and 16).

property sheet

A window that lets you define the properties (characteristics) of a database, a database object, or its individual controls. To display the property sheet for objects other than the database, choose View ➤ Properties from any menu in which it's available. To display database properties, choose File ➤ Database Properties (Skill 6).

query

An Access tool that lets you ask questions about your data, such as, How many customers live in New York? You use filters and/or queries (Skill 7) to structure such questions.

query by example (QBE)

The query technique used by Access and many other modern database management systems. With QBE, you create an *example* of the fields to show, calculations to perform, and sort order to use (Skills 7 and 8).

QBE grid

The part of the query design window in which you enter the field names and other example elements to construct the query (Skills 7 and 8).

read-only

A property of a field, record, or database that allows you to view data but not change it.

record

A collection of related data (fields) that describes a single item (row) in an Access table (Skill 2).

Referential Integrity

A set of rules that prevents you from inadvertently deleting, adding, or changing data in one table if that change would cause problems in another table (Skill 3).

report

A formatted display of Access data that you can print or preview on the screen (Skill 9).

report properties

Properties assigned to an entire report, as opposed to a section or control on a report. To change report properties, you open the report in design view, open the property sheet, choose Edit ➣ Select Report, and then choose your properties (Skill 9).

row

The visual presentation of a record in a Datasheet, Query, or filter window. A relational database stores data in tables, which you can display in horizontal rows (records) and vertical columns (fields) (Skills 1, 2, and 4).

row selector

A small box or bar that you can click to select an entire row when you edit a table, design a table, or create a macro (also called a *field selector*) (Skills 3, 4, and 14).

ScreenTip

A short description that appears beneath a toolbar or toolbox button if you rest the mouse pointer on the button for a couple of seconds without clicking. To turn ScreenTips on and off, choose View ➣ Toolbars ➣ Customize, click the Options tab, and then either select (check) or deselect (clear) Show Screen-Tips on Toolbars.

section

Part of a form, data access page, or report, such as the header, footer, or detail section (Skills 6, 9, and 13).

select query

A query that asks a question about your data and returns a dynaset (result) without changing the data. See Skill 7; see also *dynaset* and *action query*.

self-join

A table that's joined to itself in a query. For example, if a part consists of other parts, you could identify the "parts of a part" using a self-join on a Parts table.

sizing handle

A tiny square that appears around a control when you draw or select it in form design or report design view. To resize the control, drag one of its sizing handles vertically, horizontally, or diagonally (depending on which handle you choose) (Skill 6; see also *move handle*).

sort

To put data into some meaningful order, such as alphabetical (A–Z) or numeric (smallest to largest) (Skill 4).

SQL

An acronym for *structured query language*—a standardized language for asking questions about data in a database. In Access you set up questions by designing queries. Access converts your query to an SQL statement before it answers your question (Skill 7).

status bar

The bar along the bottom of the screen that displays the current status of things. To hide or display the Access status bar for a specific database, choose Tools ➤ Startup and then either select (check) or deselect (clear) Display Status Bar. To control the default status bar setting for all Access databases, choose Tools ➤ Options ➤ View and then either select or deselect Status Bar.

string

A computer buzzword for "a chunk of text." For example, "Hello there" is a string (as opposed to 123.45, which is a number).

subform

A form that's inside another form or report. You can use subforms to combine (or *link*) data from multiple related tables onto a form (Skills 5 and 6).

subreport

A report that's inside another report. You can use subreports to combine (or *link*) data from multiple related tables onto a report (Skill 9).

tab control

A control on a form that has multiple tabbed pages, like the ones seen in Access dialog boxes (Skill 6).

table

The Access object that holds the data you want to manage (Skills 1, 2 and 3).

text box

A control in a form or report that lets you view or enter text (Skill 6).

title bar

The bar across the top of a window that describes what's in the window.

toggle

A menu command or setting that can have only one of two possible values: On or Off (or Yes or No).

toolbar

A bar or box that offers buttons as shortcuts to specific features. To turn the default Access toolbars on or off, choose Tools ➤ Startup and then select (check) or deselect (clear) Allow Built-In Toolbars. You also can turn individual toolbars on and off by right-clicking on any visible toolbar or by choosing View ➤ Toolbars and selecting or deselecting the toolbars you want to show or hide (Skill 16).

Toolbox

A toolbar in the form design and report design windows that lets you place controls on your design. You can hide or display the Toolbox in those windows by choosing View ➤ Toolbox (Skills 6, 9, and 13).

unbound control

A control on a form or report that isn't tied to the underlying table (Skill 6).

unbound object frame

The container for an object that's displayed on a form or report, but isn't tied to the underlying table (Skills 6 and 10).

Update query

An action query that lets you change data in all or selected records in a table (Skill 8).

UNC

A standard format, also called *Uniform Naming Convention*, for referring to path locations on a local area network file server.

URL

An address called a *Uniform Resource Locator* that refers to an object, document, page, or even a newsgroup on the Internet or on an intranet. It may also refer to an e-mail address.

user

The person who uses an application.

validation rule

A rule that defines whether data will be accepted into a table or form. You can define validation rules in the table design window's field properties (Skill 2) or in the form design property sheet (Skill 6). Forms automatically inherit rules defined in the table design. Validation rules defined in a form are active only when using the form to enter and edit data. Those validation rules are used in addition to any validation rules defined in the table structure.

value

The contents of a field or control. For example, if you type *Smith* into the Last Name field in a table, "Smith" is the value of Last Name in that particular record. If you say "X=10," then X has a value of 10.

view

View can have two meanings:

- A way of looking at an object. In Access, you often can pick a view from the Database window, the View menu, or a toolbar button. When the focus is on an expression, you can zoom in by pressing Shift+F2.

- A selected group of records from an SQL server.

Visual Basic (VB)

The programming language that comes with Microsoft Access to give knowledgeable programmers more control over the custom applications they develop.

WHERE clause

An SQL statement that isolates specific records in a table. WHERE clauses are created automatically when you design a query. Not to be confused with bear claws or Santa Claus.

wizard

A tool that asks you questions and creates an object according to your answers. For example, you can use wizards to create databases, tables, queries, forms, and reports with just a few mouse clicks. Wizards are available throughout Microsoft Access, Microsoft Office, and Windows 95/98 (Skills 1, 2, 3, 5, 8, 9, 10, 11, and 13).

zoom

An expanded text box that lets you enter expressions or text more conveniently. You can press Shift+F2 to open a zoom box in property sheets and in the grid in various Access windows (Skill 4).

You can zoom in Print Preview to change the magnification of the report page, ranging from a close-up view to a full-page view (Skill 9).

Finally, OLE and picture objects have a Size Mode (or Picture Size Mode) property called Zoom that grows or shrinks the object to fit its frame but keeps the proportions the same (Skill 6).

Index

Note to the Reader: Throughout this index **boldfaced** page numbers indicate primary discussions of a topic. *Italicized* page numbers indicate illustrations.

G

N

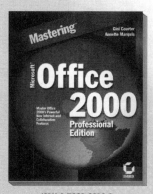

ESSENTIAL SKILLS

for the
ESSENTIAL TOPICS

WINDOWS 98

ISBN 0-7821-2128-4
$24.99; 544 pages

OFFICE 2000

ISBN 0-7821-2293-0
$24.99; 704 pages

THE INTERNET

ISBN: 0-7821-2385-6
$19.99; 496 pages

LOTUS NOTES 5

ISBN: 0-7821-2184-5
$24.99; 560 pages

WORD 2000

ISBN 0-7821-2400-3
$19.99; 452 pages

OUTLOOK 2000

ISBN 0-7821-2483-6
$19.99; 400 pages

ACCESS 2000

ISBN 0-7821-2485-2
$24.99; 608 pages

EXCEL 2000

ISBN 0-7821-2374-0
$19.99; 432 pages

FRONTPAGE 2000

ISBN 0-7821-2482-8
$19.99; 400 pages

SYBEX

www.sybex.com